The Practice of Humanitarian Intervention

This book examines the practices in Western and local spheres of humanitarian intervention, and shows how the divide between these spheres helps to perpetuate Western involvement.

   Using the Democratic Republic of the Congo as a case study – an object of Western intervention since colonial times – this book scrutinizes the contemporary practice of humanitarian intervention from the inside. It seeks to expose how humanitarian aid and peacekeeping works, what obstacles they encounter and how they manage to retain their legitimacy. By examining the relationship between the West and the DR Congo, this volume asks why intervention continues to be so central for the relationship between Western and local spheres. Why is it normal and self-evident? The main answer developed here is that the separation of these two spheres allows intervention to enjoy sufficient degrees of legitimacy to be sustained. Owing to the contradictions that surface when juxtaposing the Western and Congolese spheres, this book highlights how keeping them separate is key to sustaining intervention. Bridging the divide between the liberal peace debate in International Relations and anthropologies of humanitarianism, this volume thus presents an important contribution to taking both the legitimizing proclamations and 'local' realities of intervention seriously.

   The book will be of much interest to students of statebuilding, peacebuilding, peacekeeping, anthropology, research methods and IR in general.

Kai Koddenbrock is lecturer at the Institute of Political Science at the RWTH Aachen University, Germany, and a fellow of the Global Public Policy Institute, Berlin. He holds a PhD in Political Science from the University of Bremen.

Routledge Studies in Intervention and Statebuilding
Series Editor: David Chandler

This meticulous study of international engagement in the Congo draws out the two worlds of humanitarian intervention: the self-referential and self-legitimising world of Western actors, engaged in projects of assistance and protection, and the other, less studied, world of Congolese social and political interaction. These two worlds coexist and interact in a multitude of ways which challenge Western self-understandings and help to clarify the contradictions and limits of international practices on the ground. Conceptually informed and empirically rich, this book is a major contribution to the field.

David Chandler, *University of Westminster, UK*

From the heart of darkness under the colonial rule to the heart of goodness epito-mized by humanitarian interventions, Kai Koddenbrock traces the fate of Congo in its tragic encounters with the various avatars of the Western world's engage-ment on the African continent. Focusing on the actual practices of peacekeepers and aid workers, this short and dense book is an important contribution to the understanding from below of contemporary international relations.

Didier Fassin, *Institute for Advanced Study, USA*

The Practice of Humanitarian Intervention is a fine supplement to the emerging literature that looks beyond and beneath policy statements and headquarter levels and aims for a grounded ethnographic approach to external interventions. Through a detailed case study of DR Congo, Dr. Koddenbruck adds to our under-standing of the multitude of external interventions in this country, but also con-tributes strongly to opening up a new and promising terrain for theorising and conceptual elaborations in-between IR and ethnographic-inspired work.

Morten Boas, *Norwegian Institute of International Affairs, Norway*

This book is a showcase how empirical depth and up-to-date theoretical reflec-tion can reveal the ambiguity – if not at times the absurdity – of those instances of internationalized rule that we call 'interventions'. In a world in which more and more layers of authority overlap, these might well be insights into our common future.

Klaus Schlichte, *University of Bremen, Germany*

The Practice of Humanitarian Intervention is an original analysis full of fascinat-ing insights and grappling stories about international aid in Congo. It is an excel-lent resource for all those interested in better understanding the peculiar world that interventional interveners inhabit.

Séverine Autesserre, *Columbia University, USA*

Social transformation takes deep social penetration. As Koddenbrock demon-strates in minute detail, half a century of Western intervention amounts to little more than a road trip. Predictably, superficial engagement spells superficial transformation.

Iver Neumann, *LSE, UK*

The Practice of Humanitarian Intervention

Aid workers, agencies and institutions in the Democratic Republic of the Congo

Kai Koddenbrock

Routledge
Taylor & Francis Group

LONDON AND NEW YORK

First published 2016
by Routledge
4 Park Square, Milton Park, Abingdon, Oxon OX14 4RN

and by Routledge
605 Third Avenue, New York, NY 10017

First issued in paperback 2017

Routledge is an imprint of the Taylor & Francis Group, an informa business

British Library Cataloguing-in-Publication Data
A catalogue record for this book is available from the British Library

Library of Congress Cataloging-in-Publication Data
Koddenbrock, Kai.
The practice of humanitarian intervention: aid workers, agencies and institutions in the Democratic Republic of the Congo / Kai Koddenbrock.
  pages cm. – (Routledge studies in intervention and statebuilding)
  Includes bibliographical references and index.
  1. Humanitarian intervention–Congo (Democratic Republic)
  2. Humanitarian assistance–Congo (Democratic Republic)
  3. Non-governmental organizations–Congo (Democratic Republic)
  I. Title.
  JZ6369.K64 2016
  361.2'6096751–dc23   2015012295

Typeset in Times New Roman
by Wearset Ltd, Boldon, Tyne and Wear

ISBN 13: 978-0-8153-4765-1 (pbk)
ISBN 13: 978-1-138-89018-3 (hbk)

Contents

Acknowledgements

Many kind people helped me along the way of preparing this book. My engagement with humanitarian aid and peacekeeping in the Democratic Republic of the Congo began during my time at UN Headquarters in New York in late 2006. I am grateful to Manuel Bessler, Christina Bennett, Hansjoerg Strohmeier and Jim Freedman. At the Global Public Policy Institute in Berlin, I thank Thorsten Benner, Andrea Binder and Julia Steets for stimulating debates and support during the early stages of this research.

I want to thank all the humanitarians and peacekeepers who so generously shared their time and thoughts with me during my stays in Goma in 2008 and 2009. A special and heartfelt thank you goes out to Harriet Cochrane and Hugues van Brabandt who were important door-openers. I am also grateful to Désirée Lwambo and Christiane Kayser for linking me to the Heal Africa residence which provided a unique entry point into life in Goma. I also thank Jonny Polonski and Naomi Woods for inviting me over to stay for a few weeks in their residence in the heart of Goma. I am indebted to Tatiana Kourline who recommended anthropological literature that proved crucial. During my first research stay in Goma, Sylvia Sergiou helped me generously to find a place to stay in the city. Dominic Johnson was crucial for putting me in touch with experts among the Congo scene. For inspiring talks on the bigger picture of Congolese politics, I wish to thank Michel Kassa and Onesphore Sematumba at Pole Institute. For great nights out and discussions on life in Goma, I am grateful to Wazir, Léon and Silke Oldenburg.

Klaus Schlichte and David Chandler have been inspiring and engaging supervisors of the PhD stage of this book. Their critique, suggestions and encouragement have been essential. Colloquia at the Frankfurt Research Center of Postcolonial Studies, at the Max Planck Institute for Ethnology in Halle at the Magdeburg Research School helped to sharpen the arguments. I am grateful to colleagues in Europe and the US who have taken the time to discuss my research with them or who have read and commented on parts of the manuscript: Mahmood Mamdani, Gayatri Spivak, Miriam Ticktin, Didier Fassin, Susan Woodward, Samuel Moyn, Timothy Mitchell, Amadou Diouf, Richard Rottenburg, Séverine Autesserre, Judith Renner, Stefan Engelkamp, Daniel Bendix, Jörg Husar, Berit Bliesemann de Guevara, Alex Veit, Peer Schouten, Philipp

Baumgartner, Stefanie Wodrig, Markus-Michael Müller, Nikolas Kosmatopoulos, and last but not at all least Lars Ostermeier.

I am deeply grateful to Sanja Boehler, Martin Ebeling and Sebastian Jacob for commenting on earlier versions of the entire manuscript and the two anonymous reviewers and the series editor at Routledge for their criticism and valuable suggestions. Thanks to Andrew Humphrys and Hannah Ferguson at Routledge for their support of the project. Stefan Wilhelm performed a helpful language check and Tanja Rother, Laurette Kitumani, Ulika Bornkamm and Alija Catic did a fantastic job at transcribing the interviews.

Without the four-year scholarship by the generous Heinrich-Böll-Foundation and the postdoc fellowship at the Käte Hamburger Kolleg/Center for Global Cooperation in Duisburg this book would not exist. Thank you!

Abbreviations

AFDL	Alliance des Forces Démocratiques pour la Libération du Congo-Zaire
ANC	Armée Nationale Congolaise
CNDP	Conseil National pour la Défense du Peuple
FAR	Forces Armées Rwandaises
FARDC	Forces Armées de la République Démocratique du Congo
FDLR	Forces de Libération du Rwanda
ICRC	International Committee of the Red Cross
IDP	internally displaced person
IR	International Relations
LRA	Lord Resistance Army
M23	Mouvement du 23 Mars
MLC	Mouvement de Libération du Congo
MSF	Médecins Sans Frontières
MONUC	Mission de l'Organisation des Nations Unies en République démocratique du Congo
MONUSCO	Mission de l'Organisation des Nations Unies de stabilisation en République démocratique du Congo
MaxQDA	MaxQualitativeDataAnalysis
PALU	Partie Lumumbiste
RCD	Rassemblement Congolais pour la Démocratie
RPA	Rwandan Patriotic Army
RPF	Rwandan Patriotic Front
SOMINKI	Société Minière et Industrielle du Kivu
UDPF	Uganda People's Defence Force
UDPS	Union pour la Démocratie et le Progrès Social
UN	United Nations
UN DPKO	United Nations Department of Peacekeeping Operations
UN ECOSOC	United Nations Economic and Social Council
UN OCHA	United Nations Office for the Coordination of Humanitarian Affairs
UNDP	United Nations Development Programme
UNHCR	United Nations High Commissioner for Refugees
UNICEF	United Nations Children's Fund
WFP	World Food Programme

Democratic Republic of Congo, main cities (source: http://d-maps.com/carte.php?num_
car= 25932&lang=en).

Introduction

'We engage, then we see what happens', the former Under-Secretary General for UN peacekeeping explained. Sitting in his salon on Park Avenue in New York, for him, intervention was essentially a game of chess during which the next steps and the ultimate result remain unknown.[1] This tentative approach to intervention is however reserved for the private realm. In public, intervention actors like the United Nations or humanitarian NGOs convey the impression that they are urgently needed and that there are objective criteria calling for their help. High numbers of internally displaced persons, entrepreneurs of ethnic violence and a weak and malevolent national government call for a sustained international presence. In places like the Democratic Republic of the Congo, intervention actors assume they hardly have to justify and substantiate their case for intervention.[2] Intervention in the Congo appears as normal and needed. This book questions and investigates this normality and shows how it comes about.

In Europe and the United States, the Congo has served as a rallying call for global solidarity since the atrocities of Belgian colonialism. In fact, the Western human rights movement dealing with King Leopold's rubber mania often features as one of the cradles of contemporary human rights advocacy (Barnett, 2011: 29; Hochschild, 1998: 185–194; Dunn, 2003: 51). In today's international advocacy, the Congo has it all: sexual and ethnic violence, blood minerals, state failure and corruption. This plethora of identified problems explains why most of the instruments of Western intervention have already been tried in the Congo: election support, 16 years of peacekeeping, massive budget aid and a longstanding multi-billion dollar humanitarian aid industry in the east of the country.

Despite this wealth of measures, most Western scholars and activists argue that the West does not care enough (Stearns, 2011a: 334).[3] They claim the West does not show enough solidarity towards the Congo. The interventions undertaken in the name of global solidarity should be improved and better funded (Stearns, 2011a: 336; Autesserre, 2010: 272). Hence, Western scholars, policy analysts and interveners working in and on the Congo generally agree with the wealth of measures taken by the West and wish for more of it. They consider these interventions as the right and most useful expressions of solidarity the West has to offer.

The present study interrogates the production and maintenance of this normality, from the ground up. To be considered normal, intervention needs to appear legitimate and as the right thing to do. Thus intervention actors, i.e. the field of researchers and practitioners of peacebuilding, development aid and humanitarian aid, constantly have to reiterate their legitimacy despite existing doubts. This production of legitimacy happens through various conduits like think tank publications catering to the knowledge needs of these actors, and through strategy papers and reports. As the book sets out to show, these public practices are quite distinct to operational practice on the ground. Furthermore, the people engaging in intervention negotiate their legitimacy and impact on a daily basis. How they think about their own work reveals why people chose and remain in this line of work.

In line with the growing debate on the 'everyday dimensions' and 'on-the-ground' realities of intervention (Autesserre, 2014), this book is an inside look at the practice of humanitarian intervention, understood here in the Congolese case as the amalgamated field of humanitarian aid and UN peacekeeping. It takes part in the debate on intervention, and the subjectivities and practices or agencies, institutions and aid workers on the ground which sustain and reproduce it.

Building on recent practice theoretical work in International Relations (IR), the book 'follows the actors' (Latour 2005: 12) and their practices to allow for a better understanding of how intervention works and what may be problematic about it. The book thus takes what intervention actors say and do at face value and shows how this serves to legitimize and perpetuate intervention. The analysis of contemporary intervention practice mirrors the often self-contained and self-referential approach intervention adopts. Because of this focus, the book hardly discusses global structures of inequality and domination which are intervention's enabling conditions. However, to allow for a fuller understanding the book engages with the limits of a pure practice theoretical analysis of intervention and situates contemporary humanitarian aid and peacekeeping in the colonial and postcolonial history of the Congo and the strategies of rule employed by the Belgian colonialists and by its main postcolonial rulers Joseph Désiré Mobutu and Joseph Kabila.

The practice of humanitarian intervention

The practice perspective on intervention connects to number of recent works in social anthropology and International Relations (IR). The 'turn to the local' in intervention research (Chandler, 2013; Koddenbrock, 2013b, MacGinty and Richmond, 2013), the focus on the 'everyday' (Autesserre, 2014) and the broader trend to adopt interpretive methodologies like grounded theory, ethnography (Vrasti, 2008) or discourse analysis (Hansen, 2006; Milliken, 1999) in the discipline of International Relations has paved the way for a study such as this. This book implements the classic ethnographic mode of 'opening the black box' of intervention to make use of an analysis of 'the local' based on observation of intervention practice in and around Goma and more than 60 in-depth interviews conducted with UN and NGO staff in Goma and New York between 2009 and 2011.[4]

Critiques of intervention building on research from within intervention have had a long and prolific history in social anthropology. Following the dominant resources of critical theorizing, these critiques have broadly evolved from a more structuralist Foucauldian perspective to a thoroughly relational and non-structuralist perspective over the past decades (Koddenbrock, 2015). Building on Foucault's early work on discourse and the advent of postcolonial studies (Sylvester, 1999; Baaz, 2005; Ziai, 2006a; Kapoor, 2008; Sabaratnam, 2013; Rutazibwa, 2013),[5] intervention scholars criticized development intervention as subordinating the Global South (Escobar, 1995) or as acting as a managerial smokescreen making invisible the actual politics going on under the radar of development discourse (Ferguson, 2007. The emerging focus on governmentality and biopolitics was picked up avidly by both anthropology and IR in recent years. Anthropologists produced meticulous ethnographies of humanitarian aid both at home and abroad (Fassin, 2012; Agier, 2008; Ticktin, 2011; Li, 2007) while IR used Foucault's analysis of biopolitics to name the ruling rationality of global governing visible in intervention (Duffield, 2008 Dillon and Reid, 2009; Chandler, 2010; Koddenbrock, 2012a).

The recent interest in Bruno Latour's work, in Science and Technology Studies and their relational ontology has further strengthened the anthropological inclination in intervention research (Rottenburg, 2009a; Mitchell, 2002; Lewis and Mosse, 2006b; Bachmann, Bell and Holmqvist, 2014; Koddenbrock and Schouten, 2014) and in IR more broadly (Mayer, 2012; Aradau and Huysmans, 2013; Salter and Mutlu, 2013; Schouten, 2013; Acuto and Curtis, 2014). The meticulous tracing of associations and controversies and the analysis of practices and assemblages has now come in focus.[6]

This book builds on these advances in practice theory. Programmatically initiated in the discipline by Iver Neumann (2002), both trained in IR and social anthropology, the field of practice theory has been growing in recent years (Adler and Pouliot, 2011; Büger and Gadinger, 2014). Next to its general allure as an empirical research approach willing to investigate the world of international politics through mundane practices like drinking beer (Büger and Gadinger, 2014: 5) or the practice of diplomatic speech writing (Neumann, 2007), it also comes with inevitable debates about ontology, epistemology and methodology, that is about what there is and whether and how it can be known. While Adler and Pouliot, for example, propose an ontology of practice theory as place of dialogue and as 'via media' which all kinds of actor- and structure-oriented research should be allowed to subscribe to (2011a, 2011b), Büger and Gadinger come from a more relational and post-structuralist angle and defend a core of practice theory that should be preserved: 'a performative understanding of the world' (2014: 13).

A performative understanding of the world means that the world is constantly recreated through practice. The world is done, 'performed' at each moment in time. Performativity, with its roots in speech act theory (Austin, 1962; Derrida, 1976) and its important role in feminist theory (Butler 1990; Weber, 1998), has been taken further in sociological and anthropological quarters which specialize in meticulous ethnographic research: actor-network theory and Science and Technology Studies. Here, a relational and pragmatist ontology is taken seriously to posit a reality 'multiple' (Mol, 2002) in which what is always depends on the practices it consists of. As Annemarie Mol, one of the leading thinkers of this emerging field, puts it: 'To be is to be related. The new talk about what is, does not bracket the practicalities involved in enacting reality. It keeps them present' (Mol, 2002: 53–54).

My analysis of the practice of humanitarian intervention follows in these footsteps. While intervention does take place in a structure of global inequality and power differentials, the practice of intervention itself constantly recreates itself, it performs its continuation. Emerging from my field research, including interviews and participant observation in Goma, eastern Congo, and New York, I realized that intervention constantly brings about a world it is able to operate in. This performative practice entails knowledge practices by the UN and NGOs itself, by connected think tanks which inadvertently and strategically cater to these operational actors' needs. This practice is also carried and strengthened by individual reflections, gratifications and doubts of those individuals performing intervention because without them, these practices would crumble.

This book focuses on the Congo as a single case study for two reasons. Immersion into several fields of operations is not possible in a rather short period of time of three two- to three-month field research trips. Moreover, this book is not only about how intervention tries to legitimize itself and about how it works on the ground, but also about how it deals with the Congo. The Congo with its longstanding history of intervention warrants a closer look at its history and current politics alongside the study of contemporary peacekeeping and humanitarian intervention. Without this analysis of history and political economy, this study would be as self-referential as much contemporary humanitarian aid and peacekeeping currently are.

Congolese history of intervention

The Congo has gone through several rounds of 'international' intervention: a personal property of the Belgian King Leopold II between 1884 and 1908, the Congo remained under Belgian colonial rule until 1960. When it became independent, the first Prime Minister Patrice Lumumba was killed by eastern Congolese separatists with the help of the United States and the Belgians. Ruled with iron fist by dictator Joseph Désirée Mobuto between 1965 and 1997, the Congo evolved from a Western donor darling and stalwart against communism in the Sub-Saharan proxy wars of the 1970s and 1980s, to a so-called fragile and failed state to be supported by European military missions, the biggest UN peacekeeping mission of all times and longstanding humanitarian aid of unprecedented total amounts since the late 1990s.

In postcolonial times, the Congo has witnessed the full arsenal of foreign policy instruments at the disposal of Western powers. In the post-independence turmoil, the Congo hosted the first-ever robust peacekeeping mission (ONUC) from 1960 to 1964 under then Secretary General Dag Hammarskjöld, who died in a dubious plane crash in 1961 during this mission. Western-supported president Mobutu could rely on substantial financial and military aid during occasional rebellions that originated mostly in the east. When Mobutu's rule entered into its first economic crisis after the Oil crisis in 1973, the World Bank and IMF stepped up their activities, and at one point even ran the Congolese central bank (see Chapter 1).

But Mobutu was not a Western puppet. He shifted from Western ally to Afrocentrism and back again depending on the political and economic needs of his regime. Crippled by structural adjustment policy and his highly kleptocratic ruling elite in the 1980s and 1990s, the Congo was economically broke when the Rwandan civil war spilled over into eastern Congo and set the stage for a regional war playing out on Congolese soil that was only to stop in 2002. After this war, sometimes called 'Africa's World War' (Prunier, 2009), infrastructure was terminally dilapidated and state-owned mining companies in shambles. When Joseph Kabila came to power in 2001 after his father Laurent Kabila had been killed by one of his guards, which ended his father's short-lived succession of Mobutu, the Congo slowly re-emerged from years of conflict.

Heading a Western-brokered government of national unity at first, Joseph Kabila was elected in the first free, fair and transparent election in the Congo since independence in 2006. The UN and Western donors paid for much of these elections and helped with logistics. President Kabila embarked on an ambitious political and economic programme that has borne fruit in some economic sectors (World Bank, 2012). However, the east has continued to be volatile and it remains a challenge for most of the involved to disentangle the international, regional, national and local components of this longstanding imbroglio.[7] One thing is obvious: Joseph Kabila is not very hard-pressed to pacify and rule the area once and for all. The complex alliance politics between his government and various armed actors, as well as the Rwandan and Ugandan roles in the conflict, warrant for continued simmering conflict in the years to come.

North Kivu, an eastern Congolese province with its capital Goma, has been the main location of simmering conflict throughout the last decades and the key field research site for this book. It is also one of the regions where the impact of colonialism is palpable. Life in North Kivu has been in turmoil since at least 1920 when the Belgian colonialists intensified their indirect colonial administration including the manipulation of ethnicity as a technology of rule. The Belgians expropriated large swathes of land for plantation economies and increased the population of the area massively to make both indirect administration and the plantation economy viable.

This colonial legacy has played a major role in shaping the social institutions at work in North Kivu in the postcolonial period. Fights over land distribution and the manipulation of ethnicity have been central in sustaining the political economy of conflict in the region next to national and regional politics and accumulation strategies. Reasons of conflict are thus entrenched and for *Kivutiens* cyclical outbursts of violence have become habitual although they continue to place a heavy burden on everyday life in Goma, regional hubs and rural areas.

The self-empowering nature of Western intervention

The response of the Western 'Congo community' to renewed large-scale fighting is always swift. UN and NGO staff members post their analysis on Facebook or on their personal blogs,[8] correspondents of those rare news agencies and journals taking pride in detailed Congo reporting send around their articles on mailing lists. Shortly after, UN and NGO press releases warn about the dangers faced by displaced populations and the need to act fast to prevent mass atrocities.

This global network of Congo analysts and activists genuinely cares about the Congolese and their difficult situation. Yet, whenever conflict flares up again, the irony involved in the call for more and effective intervention remains unnoticed: despite the billions spent on aid and the presence of thousands of peacekeepers in the Congo, the cycle of rebellions has not been broken. What makes people so certain that more of it would suddenly change this fact? Where does this narcissistic belief come from? Maybe intervention is not that crucial for a change of this situation after all?

When substantial fighting takes place in North Kivu, instead of engaging in soul-searching, the reporting and advocacy machine bolsters the self-empowering claim for more intervention. A couple of days into the fighting press releases and policy reports from the International Crisis Group,[9] Human Rights Watch or, with some delay, the UN Group of Experts (2012a, 2012b) will scandalize the atrocities committed by all of the armed forces involved and point to the horrible plight of the concerned populations with their sparse belongings transported in a simple plastic bag on old women's backs. This has happened in the late 1990s, in 2004, in 2008 and more recently in 2012. Analysis and recommendations remain: more of the same.

The crucial feature of these cyclical calls for more and better intervention is their self-referential nature. Reality out there is not much different but the new intervention, contrary to what was tried before, will certainly be more effective. This becomes understandable when taking into account that these advocacy practices address the public face of intervention. They hardly communicate with the Congo but with Western audiences and funders. From this perspective, these practices are no longer surprising but functional. They are needed to keep humanitarian aid and peacekeeping legitimate and funded.

A short history of peacekeeping and humanitarian aid

Studying peacekeeping and humanitarian aid jointly might seem counter-intuitive. Specialist think tanks and analysts treat them as separate forms of intervention and organizational realms. Think tanks usually work either on peacekeeping or on humanitarian aid not both. This book studies them jointly for three important reasons. First, from a practice theory perspective, humanitarian aid and peacekeeping are simply the two sets of intervention practices that you encounter when studying the practice of humanitarian intervention in the Congo with special emphasis on North Kivu and Goma. Humanitarians and peacekeepers populate the streets and the lakeside of Goma and they operate in its surroundings.

Second, humanitarian aid and peacekeeping share an important number of practical traits. Among the practical traits are that they cater to the public face of intervention by engaging in constant normative-conceptual debate, they tend to hide their comparably anarchic operational practice or they manage what and how evidence from operations becomes public.[10] Moreover, contrary to popular belief, humanitarian aid and peacekeeping constantly negotiate with local, regional and national government structures or with rebel leaders to be able to do their operational work. Chapter 3 will provide details on this. On the ground in Goma, humanitarians and peacekeepers also drive in similar cars, live in the same houses, go to the same parties, read the same policy papers and operate much of their time in bureaucratic 'cubicle land' (Schlichte, 2012b), i.e. they sit at their desk most of the time, write reports and share offices.

The third core trait uniting both humanitarian aid and peacekeeping next to their local proximity and similarities of practice is their common morality. With their non-transformative focus on survival and protection, both inhabit a primarily moral universe, as Didier Fassin argues in his recent book on *Humanitarian Reason* (2012):

> Whereas volunteers eager to come to the aid of victims of conflict and oppression would previously have done so through political and sometimes military struggle, like Lord Byron in Greece, George Orwell in Spain, or Jean Genet in Palestine, today they do it via humanitarian assistance and advocacy, symbolized by Bob Geldof organizing a concert for Ethiopia, Bernard Kouchner carrying a sack of rice on the Somalian shore, or George Clooney pleading for the persecuted people of Darfur.
>
> (Fassin, 2012: 7)

The rise of these conceptions of politics is intertwined with the growth of UN activities and the increasing number of NGOs working on a global scale.

Historically, humanitarian aid and peacekeeping have intersected, collaborated and worked in parallel in interesting ways. The foundation of the first humanitarian organization, the Red Cross, by Henri Dunant[11] in 1863 and the subsequent establishment of the Geneva Conventions had a moral base: all victims of war had to be allowed treatment notwithstanding their political allegiances. This was the birth of the humanitarian principles of neutrality, impartiality and independence which continue to be central points of reference today.

UN peacekeeping came into being to ensure the moral aspiration of the UN Charter of a world with less armed conflict after 1945. While peacekeeping was not explicitly mentioned in the Charter, it slowly developed as one of the instruments of the UN Secretary General to deal 'impartially' (Orford, 2011: 65) with a 'threat to the peace' and to 'maintain or restore international peace and security' (UN Charter, Chapter VII, Article 39). Despite humanitarian aid's civilian and peacekeeping's military approaches respectively, the claim of being impartial and disinterested united peacekeeping and humanitarian aid from the start. They claimed primarily to appeal to an abstract humanity.

During the Cold War, humanitarian aid and peacekeeping parted ways. While peacekeeping was rarely used because of the Cold War stalemate in the UN Security Council, humanitarian aid witnessed a fundamental change and expansion thanks to the founding of Médecins Sans Frontières (MSF) and the increasing role played by UNHCR beyond the European continent (Barnett and Finnemore, 2004: 88–100; Barnett, 2011, Redfield, 2013). Starting with the Biafra crisis in Nigeria in 1967, MSF openly challenged the neutrality of the International Committee of the Red Cross (ICRC) and called for a more political approach to humanitarian aid. According to the founders of MSF at the time, in cases of excessive violence and obstructive government behaviour, speaking-out against these acts was a moral imperative and more important than remaining neutral and silent, something the ICRC deemed essential to maintain a working relationship with national authorities.

After 1989, the number of humanitarian and peacekeeping missions exploded. UN missions were sent to all kinds of places that had hosted US–Soviet proxy wars and other violent conflict, and a wave of new humanitarian organizations from the West flooded the African continent in particular. In line with the liberal hubris of the day both humanitarian aid and peacekeeping started to face increasing pressure to abandon their neutrality and impartiality for more transformative approaches. Peacekeeping was forced to reconsider its operating principles because of their apparent incapacity to separate the warring parties in Somalia, Bosnia and Rwanda. Calls for peace enforcement and robust and 'multi-dimensional' mandates were more often made.

For humanitarian aid, the Rwandan genocide and its aftermath was a serious challenge. Their impartial assistance in the Congolese refugee camps in 1994 which were hosting numerous ex-combatants and leading *génocidaires* of the Rwandan civil war came under heavy fire and it is well established that the camps were indeed used to continue conflict (Waal, 1997; Terry, 2002). Pundits and experts began to ask whether mass-murderers should really receive equal treatment because of the principle of impartiality. This was the birth of 'new humanitarianism' which was much more prepared to be transformative and openly political. This implied a greater willingness of humanitarians to adopt development and human rights thinking to counteract criticism of their insistence on short-termism despite long-term presence (Chandler, 2002: 21–22; Koddenbrock, 2009a).

While humanitarians were forced to reconsider their apolitical stance because their political effects had come to the attention of the international public, peacekeeping was pushed into a more assertive role after the NATO bombing campaign of Kosovo and peacekeeping failures in Somalia, Bosnia and Rwanda in the early 1990s. During the height of the Cold War, the UN's activities had mostly consisted of non-military activities mandated by the UN's Economic and Social Council (ECOSOC). The Security Council was in deadlock because of United States and Soviet Union confrontation (Koskenniemi, 1995: 340ff.). But after Rwanda and Srebrenica and the unwillingness to sanction the Kosovo campaign, the UN thought it had to change and improve to survive. Frantic peacekeeping activities were seen as the answer to prove the UN's continued relevance (Benner *et al.*, 2012). After 1999, dozens of peacekeeping missions, including the second Congo mission were mandated. In line with the transformative desires of the liberal peace paradigm of the day, their mandates became increasingly broad, including election support, institution building, and monitoring of child soldier deployments among others.

The wars in Afghanistan and Iraq, however, started a process – still ongoing – in which nothing about intervention is certain any longer. David Chandler has called this lack of certainty 'post-liberal' (2010). Yet, the exact contours between liberal intervention and post-liberal disengagement are still being worked out. Nothing is certain because lines of activities are blurred. The military has been engaging in humanitarian aid and provincial reconstruction and humanitarians lost their unique selling proposition. On the other hand, the apparent difficulties in imposing political order from outside overshadowed all ambitious attempts at social engineering from without. All shades of politicization and apolitism have been tested. Large-scale military interventions and large-scale multi-sectorial peacekeeping missions have lost their liberal hubris but continue to operate nonetheless. The normative and political terrain is confusingly complex. It is here that public positioning becomes particularly essential as part of the practice of intervention.

The argument and structure of the book

The following pages scrutinize the practice of humanitarian intervention from the inside and situate it in the Congolese historical and political context. This look from inside elucidates how humanitarian aid and peacekeeping in the Congo work, what obstacles they encounter and how they manage to stay legitimate and funded nonetheless. Intervention produces a particular Congo ripe for intervention, it carefully manages the tensions between public proclamations made for the project market and operations on the ground, and it is carried out by individuals who have more doubts than we expect and often grow tired of the job and return to less controversial and stressful pursuits after a few years.

Expanding on the short history of the Congo in this introduction, Chapter 1 provides a reading of Congolese history focusing on the interplay between political economy and strategies of rule. Zooming in on the two main postcolonial regimes of Joseph-Désiré Mobutu between 1965 and 1997 and Joseph Kabila between 2001 and 2015, I show that dealing with international and regional actors as part of governmental calculus has always been an important component of ruling the Congo. International intervention has for more than a hundred years been an important factor in shaping the political economy of the Congo and the current moment is no exception to this.

Chapters 2, 3 and 4 focus on the contemporary practice of humanitarian intervention in the Congo. Chapter 2 discusses how a Congo that is ripe for intervention is produced by recent think tank and advocacy reports and among intervention personnel in the Congo. Chapter 3 zeroes in on the ways in which humanitarian NGOs and UN peacekeeping deal with the project market, i.e. how they distinguish themselves from competing agencies by making particular kinds of public proclamations that relate only loosely to what these organizations and their staff do on the ground in and around Goma. Chapter 4 offers a unique look at the individuals carrying out intervention practice. It gives texture to the non-initiated reader and shows how intervention feels and how it is experienced by those implementing it. The qualms and problems they have and the ways they legitimize their own work indicate that even among individual intervention personnel, Congo intervention is not a self-evident practice but in constant need of legitimation.

Notes

1 Jean-Marie Guéhenno, New York, 11 November 2011.
2 For reasons of brevity, I will use the short form 'Congo' throughout the text because the term 'DRC' is technocratic and because Congolese citizens like to call their country 'Congo', despite its colonial overtones.
3 Some interveners interviewed for this book bemoaned that the Congo is neglected and strategically not important enough for the West to really care (NGO Goma 19, 18 September 2009; Donor Goma 1; 5 October 2009).
4 This book is the based on a grounded theory analysis of four months of participant observation in Goma, 66 interviews conducted between 2009 and 2011 in Goma and New York (see appendix), 60 policy papers mostly from 2008 to 2012, 32 strategy and discussion papers issued by the UN, MSF, Oxfam and the ICRC, and a review of recent and less recent intervention and Congo scholarship. Initiated by the American sociologists Barney Glaser and Anselm Strauss (2009 [1967]), grounded theory has become one of the prime methodologies of qualitative research both in sociology and anthropology (Breuer, 2009; Strauss and Corbin, 1998; Strübing, 2008). Calling for the researcher's immersion into the practice under study, grounded theory is essentially a set of tools designed to help build explanations about social phenomena through an iterative process of gathering data, reflecting on them, triangulating them, and finally, narrowing them down by condensing the wealth of data initially gathered.
5 IR has only started to seriously engage with postcolonial theory in the last years but has grown into a considerable constituency (Grovogui, 2002; Inayatullah and Blaney, 2004; Agathangelou and Ling, 2009; Sabaratnam, 2013; Hobson, 2012; Anievas *et al.,* 2014).
6 The growing genre of the humanitarian (auto-)biography also speaks to this analysis. After about 25 years of growth of the peacekeeping and humanitarian enterprise, aid worker biographies have multiplied in number. *Emergency sex* (Cain *et al.,* 2006), *Chasing misery* (Hoppe, 2014) and *Chasing chaos* (Alexander, 2013) are fitting titles for a genre dealing with the lived experiences of aid workers between war zones, their estrangement from home and the adventures they live through during their months- or years-long stints (Smirl, 2012).
7 Séverine Autesserre's influential recommendation to focus more on local conflict causes in the Congo risks being taken up in as one-sided a manner as the previous focus on national elections was (Autesserre, 2010; 2014). The most important challenge consist in making sense of the different layers of local, national, regional and international political economy together. See the 2014 forum on 'Future direction for peacekeeping research' in *International Peacekeeping*.

8 The most widely read blogs in English are 'Congo Siasa' run by Jason Stearns, 'Texas in Africa' by Laura Seay and 'Christophvogel.net'. The well-informed Belgian journalist Colette Braeckman runs a blog called 'Le carnet de Colette Braeckman' in French.

9 See ICG 'alert' 20 November 2012 at www.crisisgroup.org/en/publication-type/alerts/2012/dr-congo-s-goma-avoiding-a-new-regional-war.aspx, last accessed 23 February 2015.

10 See also Fassin (2010: 288) on the similarities between humanitarians and the military.

11 As is little known, Henri Dunant was also one of the founding fathers of the Young Men's Christian Association (YMCA). See Warner (2013) for a fascinating analysis of the role of Dunant's politico-religious influences.

1 Ruling the Congo

Colonial legacies and strategies of rule today

The history of the Congo is often written as a history of questionable personalities: wrecked by Belgian King Leopold, the ruthless megalomaniac; led into postcolonial turmoil by Patrice Lumumba, the overly impulsive revolutionary; ruled with an iron fist by Mobutu, the slick dictator. The short-term president Laurent Kabila is seen as mediocre and crazy and the current ruler Joseph Kabila is an enigma, spending too much time on his ranch, roaming Kinshasa on his motorbike but neglecting his country in the meantime.[1] Yet, making sense of the role of personalities in ruling the Congo can only take place with solid knowledge about its history and political economy.

The Congo has witnessed three main governmental regimes since the early twentieth century: Belgian colonial rule, Mobutu's decade-long dictatorship and Joseph Kabila's now 14-year rule since 2001. The Congo has inherited structural challenges from colonialism such as its archipelago economy created for resource and wealth extraction, business elite networks requiring smart patronage politics and the dependence on regional and international support structures. These have been a challenge in most postcolonial African societies. The Congo is no exception to this rule.

In essence, all postcolonial African governments have struggled with their fragmented and problematic political economy, internal elite competition, persistent regional conflicts and international interference until today. Congolese rulers have had to negotiate and calculate with international interventions as part of their international operating environment. More recently these interventions have come to be dominated by humanitarian aid and peacekeeping forces.[2] International support or interference has been an object of bargaining and an object of strategic reflection by all postcolonial governments to this day. This chapter serves to situate the practice of humanitarian intervention among these long-standing challenges of ruling the Congo. Intervention is part of the bigger struggle to rule the Congo but is often unable to reflect on this and to assess its own strategic importance.

Governmental strategies in the Congo have since colonial times been about national, regional and international alliance politics and about control over hubs of economic profit generation. Because of its size, geography, regional political vulnerability and insertion into the conduits of global capitalism, governmental room for manoeuvre has been limited. While the Belgians were left alone by European colonial competitors because of a mutually guaranteed colonial state system in Africa since the Berlin Conference in 1884, Congolese leaders since independence have had to tackle sizeable challenges to their rule both from within as well as outside the country.

Roughly 74 million people live in the Congo today.[3] It is the fourth most populous African country after Nigeria, Ethiopia and Egypt. The Congo has, since colonial times, been an archipelago economy with subsistence agriculture at its heart[4] and widely spread economic centres. These were dominated by economic activities such as rubber collection, plantation agriculture or both industrial and alluvial mining. Colonial urban centres have remained important today. The capital Kinshasa has been the political centre since 1926.[5] Its population has risen since its colonial foundation as Léopoldville from a few hundred to about ten million today. While Katanga has been the industrial heart of the country with its important copper industry, Kasai has been the centre of diamond collection. The east, including North and South Kivu, was at the centre of the Belgian plantation economy. The Kivu provinces have remained important for agricultural production and have assumed a more central role in mining in recent decades.

Early kingdoms and the slave trade

The area now known as the Congo was populated by several kingdoms long before Portuguese imperialism and Belgian colonialism. The question of statehood and political order did not arise with colonialism. The Kongo kingdom, the Luba or the Lunda 'Empire', as Isidore Ndaywel è Nziem calls it, were only some of the then existing political orders (Ndaywel è Nziem, 2012: 127–147; 1998a). The Kongo Kingdom extended from the fifteenth to the eighteenth century across Western Congo, Congo Brazzaville and present day Northern Angola (Ndaywel è Nziem, 1998a: 80–103). Its history was intertwined with that of Portuguese imperialism from the fifteenth century onwards. The Luba and Lunda kingdoms, by contrast, dominated the South and a highly centralized mode of organization had prevailed in the Great Lakes region around Lakes Kivu and Edward (Ndaywel è Nziem, 1998a: 212): 'modal forms of political organization, centralized administration and small-scale autonomy, were thus present well before the colonial era' (Schatzberg, 1988: 136).

The internationalization of rule intensified with the growing slave trade between the sixteenth and nineteenth century (Exenberger and Hartmann, 2011: 23). Most Congolese kingdoms had participated in the slave trade and changed their modes of rule considerably once they engaged in the violent practice of slave-hunts with their immense profitability. The internationalized nature of Congolese political-economy thus did not begin with colonialism (Depelchin, 1981: 35). Yet, according to Georges Nzongola-Ntalaja most of these precolonial political orders had passed the peak of their coherence and power and were easily co-opted by the Belgian colonialists when these arrived (2002: 42).

Belgian royal property and colonization

Any analysis of international interventions that takes account of the legacy of colonialism inevitably comes up against the question of how decisive Western interference is to be made in the narrative. The slave trade in itself was already highly disruptive and it was driven mostly by European and later American ascendance to global hegemony (Beckert, 2014). The debate among historical sociologists on the colonial legacies enshrined in contemporary social order in Africa and the Congo (Mamdani, 1996; Mbembe, 2001; Bayart and Bertrand, 2006; Ferguson, 2007) negotiates how disruptive colonialism was for previously existing modes of social organization or for the colonized individual (Fanon, 1981, 2008).

It is safe to say that colonialism in the Congo was highly intrusive and destructive. A few years into the colonization the state came to be called 'bula matari', the smasher of rocks, by the Congolese. This metaphor not only referred to the infrastructure projects the Belgian King Leopold II pursued from the start, breaking rocks across the country to drive roads and railroads forward. Colonialism in the Congo was special. It was late, more lethal than others and the transition to postcolonial rule was sabotaged in a particularly malevolent way by Belgium, its Western allies and the UN.

Nominally and legally, the Congo became a 'state' once King Leopold II of Belgium managed to secure legal title to the Congo Free State as his personal property during the Berlin conference 1884–1885. The borders he drew with the help of the explorer Henry Morton Stanley (Dunn, 2003: 37) first existed on a conference map and were subsequently 'enacted' by fighting or co-opting the inhabitants of the areas concerned (Nzongola-Ntayala, 2002: 43ff.). The Congo Free State (80 times the size of Belgium) served as a source of *grandeur* for the Belgian people and enabled Leopold II to invest in lavish infrastructure and arts projects in Brussels (ibid.: 29).[6]

Leopold II generated profits from taxes and exports. Taxes like the *impôt indigène* (indigenous tax), were initially paid in kind and were used to finance colonial administration including the military police, the notorious *force publique*. Increasing demand for rubber in Europe and the United States led to a focus on wild rubber as chief export commodity. A draconic system of forced labour made sure that labour supply was steady. This approach ultimately overused the workforce and led to depopulation of important extractive areas (Coates, 1987: 101). The resulting lack of labour and the opening of rubber plantations in Asia destroyed the Congolese rubber market over time. Prices fell and by 1910 rubber export from the Congo had subsided (Exenberger and Hartmann, 2011: 10).

In 1908, the Belgian Parliament was forced to turn the Congo from royal possession to a colony proper because humanitarian advocacy movements had created outrage among the European public over the practices employed by Leopold's underlings to extract as much profit as possible from the territory (Hochschild, 1998; Fairhead, 1992: 18). According to Hochschild's controversial figures,[7] millions died because of the working conditions during the rubber frenzy and in the course of building Congolese streets and railways. When workers did not harvest sufficient amounts of rubber from the trees they had climbed they where whipped by the *chicotte* (a whip) or one of their hands was cut off. When public pressure in Europe mounted, turning the colony into a possession of a democratic government was believed to ease some of these practices that had started to embarrass the Belgians.

Once in the driver's seat, the Belgian government took its mission seriously and intensified governmental technologies and administration. It started to pursue a highly motivated policy of both creating unified *natives* and a system of total control whose implications are still highly visible in North Kivu and South Kivu today (Mararo, 2005: 192–193). According to Schatzberg, the Belgians came closer to this aim of total control 'than either the French or the British' (Schatzberg, 1988: 137; see also Young, 1965). The state now came to be called *Bula Matari*, the smasher of rocks (Nzongola-Ntajala, 2002: 16). It was impossible for anyone living on Congolese territory not to feel governed by the Belgians (Nzongola-Ntajala, 2002: 43; Devisch, 1998: 222). According to Congolese scholar N'Kanza Lusibu Zala: 'for all Bakongo the name of Bula Mata(r)i signified terror' (quoted in Young, 1985: 251).

Administration in the colony operated increasingly through incentivizing Congolese intermediaries and by turning so-called customary chiefs into their collaborators (Depelchin, 1981: 24; Mamdani, 1996; Veit, 2010: 72–75). The Belgians overhauled their entire administrative structure, created new provinces, districts, territories, *chefferies* and *secteurs* in order to rule more effectively (Veit, 2010: 72–75). The 'invention of tradition' (Hobsbawm and Ranger, 1983) implied by installing 'customary' chiefs was a strategic technology of government. There was nothing archaic or 'traditional' to it. As Jacques Depelchin's highlights:

> [B]y the end of colonial rule, customary law had become an academic discipline studied at the University of Kinshasa not because it was academic, but because it served an important function in the resolution of conflicts in those areas which had remained, purposely or not, unaffected by capitalist relations of production.
>
> (Depelchin, 1981: 24)

In the run-up to World War I, European demand for minerals exploded and the Belgian colonialists seized the opportunities found in Congolese soil. They switched their preferred form of economic exploitation from 'one to the other strictly extractive business' (Exenberger and Hartmann, 2011: 11). The east of the country turned into the new economic epicentre. Copper came from Katanga and gold from Ituri (Veit, 2010: 68). This geographic and economic shift required ways to govern these new centres of accumulation.[8]

Belgium now generated growing profits from its colony through agricultural and mining exports. As it 'moved beyond primitive extraction to develop a permanent base of accumulation' (Young, 1994: 252), it had to transform the Congolese labour supply to achieve this purpose. It needed manpower for these pursuits and for the building of further infrastructure and the military. As Craw-ford Young put it, the now more sophisticated 'territorial administration had turned into a veritable man-hunting machine' (ibid.: 253).

The extraction of profit from the Congo went smoothly through both World Wars because state administration from Brussels to Kinshasa and the local chiefs was well organized, the *force publique* engaged in discouraging shows of force whenever strikes or other expressions of discontent occurred. When riots broke out in Kinshasa in summer 1959, the Belgian government was surprised. While it had introduced a number of reforms inspired by the French and British after World War II, they considered their colony secured. As a reaction, Belgians now allowed for some degree of formal education of the Congolese – focusing on vocational training (Veit, 2010: 83) – and even introduced a certain degree of labour rights in mines and plantations.

Secondary education, however, was still restricted to the select few who had managed to forge good relations with the colonizers or had the wherewithal to pay for it. These Congolese came to be considered *évolués* and started voicing modest demands.[9] According to Nzongola-Ntalaja, peasants and workers' revolts and politico-religious movements had been constant since 1900 but had failed to derail colonial power. Only in the mid-1950s, did the *évolués* begin to take the masses more seriously and consider them as veritable political actors in their own right. The mobilization organized by later president Kasavubu and prime minister Lumumba among others since 1956 (Nzongola-Ntajala, 2002: 85) cul-minated in the riots in Kinshasa in January 1959 which led to a swift and surpris-ing end of Belgian colonialism in the Congo.

In spite of these revolutionary events, the *longue durée* of the Congolese political economy remains. Rule and capital accumulation had until 1959 been conducted in a highly violent manner and extraction of rubber, minerals or plan-tation agriculture had formed the backbone of the Congolese economy. Penetra-tion of the countryside was patchy at best. The Belgians did not need to rule the whole country, just the promising parts of it. As Peer Schouten puts it:

> the colonial state was an apparatus geographically concentrated around those spheres of activities of 'rational' interest to the regime, […] a trans-national extractive assemblage that forcibly translated Congolese natural products into economic commodities through complex machinations com-posed of Congolese labor, machines, colonial law, shipping, and so forth.
>
> (Schouten, 2013: 11)

At independence, the Congolese state was highly internationalized, primarily linked to Belgium but, because of its export dependency, intertwined with global capitalism. While industrialization of the copper mines in Katanga was advanced, most of the country still lived on subsistence agriculture or on meagre wages given to them by Belgian entrepreneurs. The following 50 years had to deal with these structures of rule and accumulation. They have proven to be durable. Ruling the Congo has remained challenging to this day.

Postcolonial rule between internal challenges and regional and international allies

The increasing strength of decolonization movements and the realization in the West that economic profits could just as well be extracted from formally independent states through trade had resulted in a wave of independence across Africa (Anghie, 2004: 269). The Congo became independent in 1960 and held its first democratic elections. Belgium, however, actively boycotted the elected government led by Prime Minister Patrice Lumumba and, in concert with the CIA, contributed actively to his assassination in late 1960 (Witte, 2002). Right after independence, the 'Congo crisis' ensued – 'a mixture of a civil, a secessionist, and a proxy war (Exenberger and Hartmann, 2011: 3), – which, from a Belgian perspective, conveniently plunged the country into turmoil from 1960 to 1965.

The increasing demands for economic reform and redistribution voiced during the 'Congo crisis' put Belgian long-term economic interests and the United States' Cold War strategy at risk. As a consequence, both the US and Belgium adopted a strategy of weakening the Lumumba government and of eventually removing him. To sideline Lumumba, the Belgians first engaged in a 'humanitarian intervention' in Katanga, the most mineral-rich Congolese province in the south-east and started supporting a secessionist movement there. They claimed to pursue the sole purpose 'of ensuring the safety of European and other members of the population and of protecting human lives in general' (UN Security Council, quoted in Orford, 2011: 72). This intervention took place one day after the Lumumba government had asked for UN – not Belgian – support in training and restructuring its national army to deal with the secessionists. But the UN let Belgium go first and thus gave them carte blanche.

The first ever UN peace enforcement mission ONUC played a critical role in Lumumba's demise because it pretended to be neutral between an elected government and the Katangan rebels supported by Belgium and the US (Orford, 2011: 69–90). Although there was an elected government and parliament, UN Secretary General Dag Hammarskjöld was not shy to proclaim that the situation 'had revealed the special possibilities and responsibilities of the Organization in situations of *vacuum*' (quoted in Orford, 2011: 84, emphasis added).[10] The notion of vacuum is obviously not just a contemporary legitimation for Western intervention. It is now widely acknowledged that ONUC acted in line with US and Belgian interests at the time. Most of the senior UN bureaucrats dealing with ONUC were Americans who were highly suspicious of Lumumba and not shy to pursue American interests from within the UN (Nzongola-Ntajala, 2002: 107).

Joseph-Désiré Mobutu: from the West's best friend to liability

Having participated in the assassination of Patrice Lumumba, Joseph-Désiré Mobutu seized power in 1965 and stayed in power for 32 years. Mobutu was one of the very few *évolués* – Congolese that had been allowed to receive higher education in Belgium. The *évolués* were to fill the lack in Belgian manpower and staff in the colonial administration and army. Like in many other African former colonies, the *évolués* transformed into the ruling economic and political class after independence and often displayed a passionate attachment to ideas, practices and the political interests of their former colonialists (Schlichte, 2005a: 119). Moreover, as the new ruling class and important carriers of the decolonization movement, they were faced with internal struggles and challenges that often come with class and state formation.

The consolidation of the ruling class and its eternal frictions and power struggles played themselves out on a domestic and international level. Different factions aligned with international actors or domestic ones whenever it suited their strategy. Over time, Mobutu increasingly used international support to stabilize his rule, i.e. the US, Belgium, France and mining companies investing in the country (Depelchin, 1981: 37). Mobutu was extremely well versed in mustering international support until just before his fall in 1997 (Newbury, 2012: 135). Ruling the Congo continued to take place in a highly internationalized manner.

Belgium and the United States regarded Mobutu as a reliable and cooperating force of stability in the region and thus supported him actively. Initially, Zaire, as he renamed the Congo in 1971, 'was being held up as an example of rapid modernisation' fuelled by state-led development plans as 'economic reforms in 1967 and fiscal austerity convinced foreign investors that Mobutu was serious about promoting economic growth.' (Reno, 2006: 47). Brought to power with Western support, Mobutu never challenged openly the role of foreign companies in the Congolese mining industry. Even during his nationalization campaign between 1971 and 1973, which he called 'Zairinization', he proceeded in a way that gave foreign companies enough time and space to secure their most profitable assets (Depelchin, 1981: 35). Belgian middle class companies, however, suffered. 'Distributorships, small enterprises, plantations, farms, fisheries etc. which were predominantly under the control of Belgians, were given to Zairians' (Lumumba-Kasongo, 1992: 41) without compensation.

Yet Mobutu was not a Western puppet.[11] His dealings with his sponsors and his approaches to improving the well-being of the Congolese rather indicate his way of dealing with the dilemma of elite inclusion (Schlichte, 2005a: 267). Handing over big businesses to some of his key allies responded to this dilemma. Mobutu needed to make some of them happy at the risk of creating dangerous competitors were they to be economically successful.[12] He also had to have the big companies at his side but could dispense with small-scale former colonists. Creating a middle class by expropriating some of the small and medium enterprises was a move towards modernizing the economy that could potentially increase tax returns.

While engaging in these political moves Mobutu always took great care not to alienate his international supporters too much. Belgium was of course unhappy about some of the nationalizations but was relieved that he did not harm their more important businesses and economic interests. Mobutu thus also responded to the 'dilemma of communication' by positing as a newborn Afrocentric nationalist on the national and African stage and by reassuring his Western supporters that they did not have to fear much from him (Schlichte, 2005a: 268–270).

Despite Mobutu's able strategies of rule, challenges to his authority were recurrent. The two Shaba rebellions in 1977 and 1978 were emblematic in this regard.[13] Throughout the decades until today, dealing with competitors has taken place in a particular way in postcolonial Congo and the region. Counterinsurgency tactics mostly amount to 'out-governing' rebels (Day and Reno, 2014). In a postcolonial context with heavy international presence, this 'out-governing' entails co-opting, coercing and fighting competitors and outsmarting Western diplomats in case interests do not converge. It becomes understandable from this perspective that rulers from Mobutu to Kabila have always chosen to react with a mix of co-optation, cooperation and annihilation when former allies or newly emerging competitors have entered the political arena.

Mobutu's patronage system was in constant evolution but the key lifeline was his ability to muster international support. When international copper prices fell and oil-prices rose in the mid-1970s, the International Monetary Fund (IMF) started to exert massive oversight over the Congolese budget and economy. Creditors started to worry about Congolese capacity to pay back its debts. Thus, in 1976, the IMF advanced its first of four stabilization plans. In 1978 it even took over the Congolese Central Bank and put other financial institutions under its tutelage (van Reybrouck, 2012: 444–445). In the 1980s, the Congo became one of the important test labs of massive structural adjustment programmes (Zacharie, 2009: 106). Education, infrastructure and other formerly scarcely funded public goods became even more depleted. Again, the interests of investors and Mobutu were in sync because 'Mobutu believed that investments in economic infrastructure, including those as simple as maintaining the network of roads left by the Belgian colonials, would pose a threat to his hold on political power' (Dunning, 2005: 465).

Increasingly investing meagre tax and export revenues into presidential largesse, the building of his home town Gbadolite into a model African city including a Concorde airstrip, and property in the wealthiest parts of Brussels, Paris and by the shores of the Mediterranean Sea (van Reybrouck, 2012: 450), Mobutu's ability to accommodate interest groups and antagonistic power brokers decreased. Given the vast territory of the country, the deterioration of infrastructure and the wide economic opportunities for local businessmen and administrators to profit from trade, taxation or natural resource extraction, it came as no surprise that by the early 1990s they had started to build their own local or regional power bases. Mobutu was left with only one option to stay in power: destabilize opponents that might threaten his rule and give allied players that were still part of his weakened patronage network 'a free economic rein on the condition that they did not cross the threshold of outright political opposition to his rule.' (Nest, 2006: 20).

The Congo wars

But Mobutu's time had run out. In 1997, he was brought down by an alliance of disgruntled elites supported by the Ugandan and Rwandan governments shortly after the genocide in neighbouring Rwanda. Between 1994 and 1997 more than one million refugees from Rwanda populated the refugee camps built by the UN and NGOs in eastern Congo. This exacerbated political tension and increased economic competition. These challenges remain until today.

It is hotly debated whether the incursion of Ugandan and Rwandan government troops into the Kivu in 1996 leading to the so-called 'first Congo war' was planned and orchestrated or an honest reaction to the threat Rwanda faced by the ex-Forces Armées Rwandaises (FAR) and Interahamwe in the refugee camps in the Kivus (Lemarchand, 1997; Nest, 2006; Reyntjens, 2009: 45–46). Yet, both countries were interested in the removal of Mobutu from power: Rwanda wanted to get rid of him because he was harbouring former *génocidaires* and Uganda wanted him gone because he allowed the Lord Resistance Army (LRA) to operate from Congolese territory against Uganda. Joined by numerous Banyarwanda and Banyamulenge and other eastern Congolese communities as their victory appeared imminent, the Rwandan Patriotic Army (RPA)[14] and the Uganda People's Defence Force (UDPF) organized a coalition under the old Katangan rebel leader Laurent Désiré Kabila to topple Mobutu (Turner, 2007: 5). They chose the name Alliance des Forces Démocratiques pour la Libération du Congo-Zaire (AFDL) and used Kabila to disguise the predominantly foreign character of the rebellion to give the movement Congolese credibility. After an eight month campaign they reached Kinshasa in 1997. Mobutu had fled shortly before the rebel's arrival (Stearns, 2011a: 161).

Mobutu fell because for the first time in his now 32-year reign, his Western backers let him down when he had to deal with a locally and regionally grounded rebellion during the first Congo war. As the various episodes of Western support have shown, Mobutu's rule was not as stable as it seemed. His army was beaten in both Shaba rebellions in the 1970s and he could have been deposed then. His rule did not collapse before because one ally or the other deemed it more useful to keep him in power than to allow for an alternative. The human rights fervour of the mid-1990s in the wake of Western inability to stop the Rwandan genocide demanded a popular victim. Getting rid of Mobutu was a useful practice of fulfilling this urge.

His successor, Laurent Kabila, did not establish a more permanent grip on the ever volatile east than Mobutu. Brought to power through massive support by Rwanda and Uganda, the 'foreigners' of Kivu and opportunistic businesspeople, he would only stay in power and alive for another four years. His coalition would prove too heterogeneous to sustain.

Three steps Laurent Kabila took in 1997 led to the 'second Congo war', a large-scale war witnessing more regional armies involved than any previous war on the African continent. The Zimbabwean and Angolan army fought for Kabila, the Rwandans and Ugandans against him. Numerous other neighbouring and regional governments also played their part (Prunier, 2009; Reyntjens, 2009).[15] Kabila's quick demise depended on how he responded to the challenge of ruling the Congo.

First, his regional alliance politics: appearing like a Rwandan puppet would be the last thing to gain him support among the *Kinois* in Kinshasa and the 'indigenous' Kivutians. Thus, once in power, Laurent Kabila quickly sought to distance himself from his foreign backers Rwanda and Uganda. This obviously displeased them. Second, his strategy of elite inclusion: trying to install a new network of inclusion and strengthening government control by handing out profitable concessions to his business partners and allies[16] infuriated the now sidelined Mobutist elites and influential businessmen in the Kivus who had grown accustomed to striking their deals unimpeded by government oversight. Third, his international alliance politics: Kabila alienated his Western backers because his first overseas trips as president were to China, Libya and Cuba. Kabila planned to create people's councils, a social democracy and wanted to pursue a pan-African foreign policy (Zacharie, 2009: 107). For this 'unreformed communist' (Prunier, 2009: 335), this required the prevention of multi-party democracy (Stearns, 2011a). While initially considered an improvement for Western interests after Mobutu, Kabila no longer appeared as a good choice to the West.

Laurent Kabila's rule was short-lived and took place in tumultuous times. Writing a balanced history of Laurent Kabila's rule still remains to be done. Until today, he only features as an erratic and incomprehensible leader who made irrational decisions. The importance of managing internal constituencies, regional and international alliances to consolidate one's rule in the Congo was obviously known to Kabila. But he was not good enough at it. His move towards China, Libya and Cuba was a provocation in his time. Interestingly, his son and successor has continued the strategy of diversifying international support structures beyond Western support only and has been quite successful at it.

In January 2001, Laurent Kabila was killed by one of his personal guards, a former child soldier from the Kivus. It is unclear who masterminded this plot or whether it was masterminded at all (Stearns, 2011a: 277–284; Prunier, 2009: 249–255).[17] It is obvious, however, that he had not managed to consolidate his power base because his way of dealing with the challenges of the political-economic structure of the Congo and its regional and international links had not been balanced and smart enough.

Joseph Kabila: the virtues of being underestimated

Joseph Kabila, Laurent Kabila's son, has been in power for 14 years now. After Mobutu's several decades long rule, Kabila junior has shaped Congolese politics decisively. His attempts to build infrastructure and his active mining and agricultural policy might even shift the parameters of Congolese political economy. Instated after his father's death, he and his allies have ably navigated the pitfalls of ruling the Congo. In a mixture of slick regional and international alliance politics as well as able strategy of elite inclusion and rotation, Kabila has managed to keep recurrent conflict in the east at a manageable level – without really tackling their longstanding causes – while working steadily towards macro-economic growth.

Joseph Kabila grew up in Katanga, received military training in Rwanda and spoke neither French nor Lingala, the lingua franca of Kinshasa, when he became president. Rumours about him being Rwandese or allied with Paul Kagame's Rwandan government have been voiced since the beginning of his presidency. Despite these doubts and recurring conflict in the east of the country, his rule has been surprisingly steady and durable.

During his tenure, Congolese gross domestic product rose from US$7.4 billion in 2001 to US$32.7 billion in 2013 according to the World Bank.[18] In macro-economic terms, Kabila's governments were very successful. Living conditions for the majority of the population, however, have not improved as much. Similarly to Germany's current boom, GDP growth has not translated into a decline in inequality or a substantial reduction in poverty.

Kabila came to power without elections in 2001 and presided over the Congo during the peace process leading to his internationally and regionally supported government of national unity since 2003. Joseph Kabila was subsequently elected in democratic elections of varying quality in 2006 and 2011. His first election in 2006 took place with the help of the largest and most complex UN electoral assistance mission of all times.[19] To support this effort, the European Union even deployed a military observer mission in and around Kinshasa and in the Kivus.

After the 2006 elections Joseph Kabila embarked on an ambitious programme of the *cinq chantiers* (the five construction sites) which was to boost the Congolese

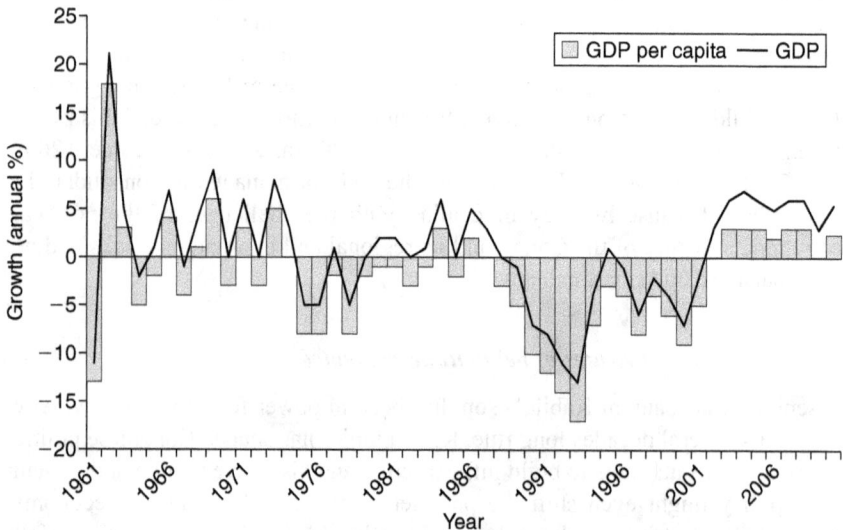

Figure 1.1 Growth rates in the Congo from independence until 2010 (source: World Bank (2012: 25)).

economy. Despite difficult renegotiations of mining deals struck during the Congo wars and continuing troubles in North Kivu, the Congo prospered. The Chinese and South Koreans invested billions in infrastructure projects in the country (Bräutigam, 2009: 146–147, Global Witness, 2011b: 4, World Bank, 2012: 6)[20] and World Bank and European donors tried to maintain their say in the Congo by trying to keep up with what the Chinese were doing. South Africa under President Jacob Zuma also intensified its collaboration with the Congolese government. Not only did Zuma agree to participate in the African intervention brigade in the east under the leadership of MONUSCO starting in 2011, Zuma and Kabila also struck a deal on the electricity generated by the forthcoming Inga dam. Promising to deliver large amounts of electricity to South Africa in the near future, completing the Inga dam would be a major and visible success of Kabila's infrastructure policy.

Contrary to the 2006 elections, Kabila won the 2011 election amid credible allegations of fraud, killings of human rights activists and media crack-downs. In Western policy circles and the media, Joseph Kabila was increasingly painted as just another authoritarian African president (Stearns, 2012). After this election, his two main competitors, longstanding historical opponent Etienne Tshisekedi, and former ally and speaker of the parliament, Vital Kamhere did not accept election results but chose not to escalate street protests in the name of peace

Since then, Kabila has struggled to regain credibility and legitimacy both internationally and among Congolese. In 2013, Kabila announced 'national concertations' which resulted in a 'government of national unity' announced in December 2014. Facing a serious internal challenge to his rule, Kabila took the time to consult, lure and threaten and managed to come up with a government including some opposition figures but none of the most vocal and historical opposition forces.

The next presidential and legislative elections are planned to be held in 2016 and former members of Kabila's camp like Vital Kamhere and Moise Katumbi are preparing their campaigns. It will be interesting to see whether 'Matata II', i.e. Kabila's new government under respected Prime Minister Ponyo Matata will be able to show enough results to make the case for a change of constitution to allow Kabila to run for president again. The main opponents like Kamhere and Katumbi, however, will most probably not let this decision pass easily. Overall, it is not even certain that Kabila is willing to change the constitution. Although it seemed the Kabila camp was planning in late 2014 to allow him a third term by undertaking a national census over the next two years in order to lay the groundwork for an adequate voter register and to postpone election for about two years, Kabila ostensibly dropped this plan and announced not to run again. Given Kabila's legacy of smart tactics of rule, he might even allow for a democratic transition because he knows anything else will not be accepted by his powerful competitors and the Congolese people.

Kabila's ways of dealing with conflict and displacement in the east have been consistent from the start. This consistency has been largely overlooked by intervention actors such as think tanks, the UN and humanitarian NGOs. While there are surprises, his overall strategy is clear. When we look at the way Joseph

Kabila approaches governing the Congo today, there is a discernible pattern. He deals with conflicts in the Kivu when they escalate to the point where they could threaten him. Apart from these moments he gives his momentary allies and supporters free reign.

So when the successive eastern based rebel movements of the Forces de Libération du Rwanada (FDLR), the Rassemblement Congolais pour la Démocratie (RCD), the Conseil National pour la Défense du Peuple (CNDP) and the Mouvement du 23 Mars (M23) wreaked havoc on the population and voiced their opposition to the Kinshasa government Kabila tended to respond slowly but ultimately decisively.[21]

The RCD was integrated into the 2003 transitional government and ceased to exist after that. In the 2006 elections its constituency supported Kabila. The RCD-successor organization CNDP under Laurent Nkunda threatened to take the North Kivu capital of Goma in 2008 and 2009 and was dismantled in the run-up to the 2011 elections just to be born again in the Mouvement du 23 Mars which ultimately managed to occupy Goma in late 2012. Described as an embarrassment by international observers (International Crisis Group, 2014: 6), it took Kabila a few diplomatic moves to scapegoat Rwanda for the M23's rise and to end up with a Rwandan government tarnished diplomatically because of its obvious involvement. His approval rating also soared once his army had beaten the M23 in concert with the African Intervention Brigade headed by his new ally South Africa. His regional politics was ultimately successful. This will allow Kabila to focus on the national arena in the coming years.

In the national arena, Kabila has focused in the past years on prestigious infrastructure projects and high visibility economic projects like the 20 industrial agriculture parks recently announced by prime minister Matata. In the meantime, Kabila has occasionally limited the freedom of expression, jailed critical reporters and fed his presidential guard well. Macroeconomic growth is sound, as a recent World Bank report triumphantly wrote (2012).

Given these continuities and partial successes, it seems paramount to consider Joseph Kabila as a ruler of a structured political economy who quite ably deals with the dilemmas of rule he is faced with. Yet, there is barely a scholar who analyses the governmental strategies at play in the Congo.[22] For the last 14 years conflict analyses have colonized research on the Congo. This is a remarkable tendency given the stability of Joseph Kabila's reign since 2001. The Congo's government is not just engaging in 'malevolent politics' (Koddenbrock, 2014a) but it is obviously genuinely trying to move forward on a number of fronts, be it agriculture, mining, infrastructure or foreign policy.

This short history of ruling the Congo highlights that challenges of rule and political economy are immense and that substantial changes will inevitably take time. The short-term perspective of UN peacekeeping and NGO humanitarian aid barely touches on this reality that international intervention in its contemporary forms is part and parcel of Congolese strategies of rule and a co-constitutive feature of Congolese statehood in the east should be taken into account when reflecting on the use and legitimacy of humanitarian intervention in the Congo.

In the following chapter, I will dig more deeply into the way contemporary policy papers and individual interveners analyse the Congo. Throughout this analysis, I will show that there is a powerful discourse of pathologization at play. Instead of a nuanced political economy view of the social structure of the Congo, this discourse is highly detached and reductionist. Several dominant conceptions of the government, the state, the economy and the Congolese interrelate to enact a reality of the Congo ripe for intervention. This helps sustain the practice intervention.

Notes

1 For a recent example of this approach, see the article by Neal Ascherson in the New York Review of Books, *How Millions have been dying in the Congo*, 5 April 2012, available at: www.nybooks.com/articles/archives/2012/apr/05/how-millions-have-been-dying-congo/?pagination=false, last accessed 11 February 2015.

2 Joseph Kabila has repeatedly threatened to throw MONUSCO out of the county. Most recently in February 2015, see www.rfi.fr/afrique/20150215-rdc-joseph-kabila-hausse-ton-face-communaute-internationale/, last accessed 22 February 2015.

3 www.cia.gov/library/publications/the-world-factbook/geos/cg.html, last accessed 11 April 2014. Nobody knows the exact numbers, however. For this reason, the Kabila government has tried to do a national census since 2009 but has so far not delivered on its promises. This national census has in early 2015 led to riots in Kinshasa when people assumed Kabila would use the time it would take to complete a census to extend his term beyond the end of his tenure in 2016.

4 According to the 2012 World Bank study, subsistence agriculture currently contributes 40 per cent of the GDP and 'engages 60 per cent of the workforce' (2012: 35).

5 From 1885–1926, Boma was the capital of the Belgian Congo.

6 How much profit he made from this property is not well established because his private pockets remained beyond public scrutiny. According to an estimate by Jules Marchal however, 'Leopold gained up to 50 million francs of annual profits between 1900 and 1908' (Marchal, 1996: 353). It is well known, by contrast, that the Congo colony provided all the funds needed for the Belgian war effort during World War II (Nzongola-Ntalaja, 2002: 29).

7 See Vansina (2010) for a critique of these numbers.

8 The Belgians exploited mines through newly founded concessionary companies like the Union Minière du Haut-Katanga, founded in 1906, partly owned by the Congolese state and the Compagnie du Katanga, a private enterprise based in Brussels (Lumumba-Kasongo, 1992: 26). Congo became one of the largest copper producers worldwide (Jewsiewicki, 1972: 233).

9 Radical opposition, however, continued to be rare as the famous memorandum from a group of *évolués* in 1944 showed. In this memorandum the *évolués* consciously distinguished themselves from the 'backward masses' by pronouncing: 'We ask that the government recognise that, alongside the native mass, backward or little developed, a new social class emerges, [the *évolués*, KK], which is becoming a kind of native bourgeoisie' (Young, 1994: 257; Depelchin, 1981: 25; Nzongola-Ntalaja, 2002: 79).

10 MONUC and MONUSCO's progressive loss of neutrality and alignment with the Congolese armed forces is an interesting reversal of the role played back in the early 1960s. The UN mission now actively privileges the elected government over its opponents. The 'vacuum' trope, by contrast, continues to be deployed in the same manner. As the analysis in the next chapter will show, state failure in the Congo is often discursively framed as a 'power vacuum' despite obvious government action and regulation.

11 Götz Bechtolsheimer has recently shown that the relationship between the US and Mobutu was highly conflictive and that a lot of the successes in mustering US support Mobutu achieved were very much the results of his efforts and not only a result of US interests or their hegemonic Africa policy (2012: 233).

12 The role of powerful businessmen in challenging central government rule is still at the heart of the current conflicts in North Kivu. Recurrent fighting is essentially an expression of the shifting calculus the implied parties make whether it is worth fighting or not at this particular point in time.

13 The main rebel force behind the Shaba rebellions were the Katangan Gendarmerie, former Mobutu allies which had played an important role in putting down the Simba rebellion in Katanga when Mobutu seized power in 1965. Moise Tshombe, their leader, had played a key part in the assassination of Lumumba. After using their help, however, Mobutu sidelined them and drove them to exile because he considered them as dangerous competitors to his rule. Tshombe died under dubious circumstance in an Algerian prison in 1967 (Odom, 1978: 8). Using the Angola of the civil war as their rear base – Angola was at the time the epicentre of Cold War proxy fighting in Africa (van Reybrouck, 2012: 440) – the Katangan Gendarmerie staged the two Shaba rebellions in 1977 and 1978. The rich copper province of today's Katanga was in danger again. Mobutu's army was humiliated twice because only with the help of American, Belgian, French and Moroccan military and logistical support was he able to put down these challenges to his rule. Crucially for the structure of Mobutu's rule, these episodes highlighted a number of things. First, the army was weak and could easily be beaten. Second, Mobutu could count on international support when he needed it. Third, Mobutu was able to secure this support even under daring circumstances (van Reybrouck, 2012: 441). But there is evidence that Mobutu only managed to mobilize Belgian parachutists and the French Legions when he had ordered European captives shot and made it appear as though the rebels did it (van Reybrouck, 2012: 441). According to David van Reybrouck, Mobutu knew his history: 'Kill a few Europeans and you will have a European Army at your sides as long as you manage to blame the others for it' (ibid., my translation). The United States under then President Carter seemed reluctant to support Mobutu during Shaba I. Belgian was also not enthused with Mobutu at the time because parts of 'the Belgian business community had hardly forgiven Mobutu for his nationalization programmes of 1973 and 1974. Aside from additional supplies of small arms and crew-served weapons, Mobutu received little else from his ex-patrons' (Odom, 1978: 8). As a consequence, Mobutu had to look for support in Morocco and France. Luckily, Giscard D'Estaing, then president of France, was intent on furthering French influence, meeting French business interests across all French speaking countries worldwide and pleasing his wealthy family. US and Belgian restraint provided a perfect opportunity for France to step into this void.

14 The former rebel Rwandan Patriotic Front was renamed Rwandan Patriotic Army (RPA) when the RPF became ruling party.

15 The story of the Congo wars has been told many times. Please consult Prunier (2009) or Reyntjens (2009) for a detailed account.

16 For example, Kabila granted a diamond monopoly to the Israeli company IDI Diamonds (Braeckman, 2003: 112). A monopoly has the disadvantage of pleasing one and displeasing a lot of others.

17 Stearns and Prunier both point at disgruntled child soldiers and Angolan acquiescence to the plot. Because of a lack of cash, Kabila had apparently started to trade with the Angolan UNITA rebels, a red line not to be crossed for the Angolan government (Prunier, 2009: 254).

18 http://data.worldbank.org/indicator/NY.GDP.MKTP.CD/countries/CD-zf?page=2&display =default, last accessed 14 January 2015. Data in current US$.

19 See http://content.undp.org/go/newsroom/2006/july/drc-elections-20060721.en, last accessed 18 January 2015.

20 On the more recent South Korean deals see: www.consultancyafrica.com/index. php?option=com_contentandview=articleandid=801:south-korea-in-africa-understanding-south-koreas-interest-in-africa-part-iiandcatid=90:optimistic-africaandItemid=295,   last accessed 13 March 2013.
21 See Rachel Strohm's blog at http://developmentdaily.files.wordpress.com/2012/11/ rebellion.jpg for a great illustration on how the RCD, the CNDP, the M23 and others intersect, last accessed 24 May 2015.
22 See von Billerbeck (2012) for a rare exception, and my recent analysis in Koddenbrock (2014a).

2 A Congo ripe for intervention
The pitfalls of knowledge production

Intervention actors rely on information and knowledge production to devise their activities. They require knowledge for programming and project development and they need a general discursive environment and public debate that is conducive to their cause. Since most intervention actors like the UN peacekeeping force, and development and humanitarian NGOs, are large bureaucracies, they require knowledge that suits their bureaucratic logic. Knowledge has to be actionable and digestible.[1] For this reason, intervention knowledge does not usually focus much on historical analysis and doesn't try hard enough to understand current governmental strategies and rationalities. To the contrary, the policy departments of big NGOs, UN agencies and donor governments, as well as the anglophone and francophone think tanks catering to them, produce short and easily digestible reports. These reports often do come with a few historical sections but they rarely situate the formidable challenge of ruling the Congo in its broader context.

Think tank reporting and intervention bureaucracies' knowledge production and interveners' own way of making sense of the Congo show how intervention actors 'practise' the Congo, how they relate to 'it' by enacting their own version of it. In line with Annemarie Mol's dictum that 'the reality we live with is one performed in a variety of practices' (1999: 74), these knowledge practices help create the reality intervention is able to operate in.

The challenge of analysing the Congolese political economy, the reasons of conflict and displacement consists in the multiple layers to be taken into account simultaneously. And it is the compartmentalized nature of knowledge production that prevents more comprehensive understanding. Humanitarian organizations will produce statistics on IDPs, refugees and malnutrition rates. The UN peacekeeping mission, in turn, produces knowledge on rebel groups, their location and the risk levels connected to this. Policy papers have a more general outlook and nurture an underlying discourse on Congolese politics and political economy which the more specialized agencies are then tapping into.

The following analysis of policy papers between 2008 and 2012 and interveners' responses from Goma and New York shows that intervention actors often pathologize the Congo and social life in the country by turning the government, the state, the economy and the Congolese themselves into deficient and malfunctioning entities. This is based on a dismissive reading of Congolese actions. The government turns into a weak and destructive government, the state into a failed state, the economy into a criminal, illegal and unproductive mining economy and the Congolese themselves appear as violent, under the yoke of a vicious history and rather incapable of shaping their future constructively.

This way of enacting the Congo has one chief effect: it legitimizes Western intervention by making the Congo ripe for intervention. If what is happening in the Congo is pathological, the Congo and the Congolese people need a doctor and medic. If there is no or bad agency in the Congo, intervention needs to step in to fill this void. The Congo is thus enacted as filled by pathological presences or as a container for a wealth of absences. These lend credence to the self-evidence of Western intervention.

A malevolent government

In their UN study on the protection of civilians, military analysts Victoria Holt and Glyn Taylor inadvertently showcase these pathologizing perceptions among intervention staff. They quote one MONUSCO (then called MONUC) staff member as saying: '[I]n creating our mandate, the Security Council's biggest mistake is presuming that 'Government' is a reality in DRC. It is not. How do you support nothing?' Another MONUC staffer comments: 'We just saw a deal between Kabila and Kagame. When MONUC is not involved, how do we really understand [our own operating, KK] context?' (Holt and Taylor, 2009: 167). For the first senior MONUSCO staffer, there is a nothing instead of a government in the Congo. The second staffer is angry because s/he does not understand what is going on and seems to point at something indecent about that deal between Kabila and Kagame. These two statements are clearly at odds with each other but sum up the problematic for most international observers: the government is either absent or engages in malevolent politics. The rational strategy of alliance building and deal-making is not appreciated among these UN staffers.[2]

Among intervention actors, the Congolese government is mostly portrayed as unable to enforce Congolese laws, provide security and other state functions. It is in general seen in terms of absence rather than presence (Institut Français des Relations Internationales, 2009: 13; International Crisis Group, 2010a: 6; International Peace Institute, 2011). Nevertheless, there is a countervailing analysis focusing on the destructive or questionable acts of the Congolese government and their lack of legitimacy. Since the government's growing partnership with China and increasing willingness to oppose Western prescriptions, this focus on government malevolence has been gaining ground (for example, Paddon and Lacaille, 2011).

Being destructive, however, requires means of influence. When policy papers criticize the government because some of its moves have had detrimental effects, there is an obvious paradox: either the government is weak and cannot shape policy or it is strong but directs policy in the wrong way. Assuming the Congolese government is powerless or even inexistent can lead to surprises. In fact, contrary to the underlying discourse of a lack of governmental capacity, the government seems to work with a consistent strategy of alliance-building and divide and rule tactics, if needed (Koddenbrock, 2014a).

There have been numerous examples of government power and effectiveness beyond the episodes recounted in the previous chapter. Because of intervention actors' clear focus on the east of the country, however, there is a decisive conflict bias in the knowledge they produce.

For example, when president Kabila announced a mining ban, in the fall of 2010, which was to stop all mining activities in the Kivu and Oriental Province, the FARDC troops that were frequently regarded as beyond Kinshasa's reach, swiftly left the important Bisie mine. A similar process had occurred when Kabila ordered the non-integrated 85th brigade to leave in 2008 when a deal with Rwanda was struck (United Nations, 2009a), replaced by the first brigade mostly composed of former CNDP rebels (United Nations, 2010a). In early 2011, Global Witness reported that there were no armed groups near the mine, only the mining police (Global Witness, 2011a: 8). The UN Group of Experts, by contrast, asserted this was not yet the case (United Nations, 2011a: 21). What is more, customary authorities are said to have an important role in distributing mining and land rights in the area (International Alert, 2010a: 70). Taken together, these pieces of analysis indicate that the government may indeed shape mining control but that its exact geographies and hierarchies remain hard to understand.

There is considerable research, too, on the elite networks spanning from the Kivus to the Congolese capital Kinshasa or the Rwandan capital Kigali but who controls whom where has not been convincingly shown yet. Analysis fluctuates between ascribing a destructive 'politics of the belly' (Bayart, 2006) to the Congolese government and showing that they are just utterly unable to exert authority over these mines and the resulting trade. This ambivalence could give analysts pause when using the lack of so-called resource governance as a straightforward call for intervention. In case mining is much more regulated and remains within the reach of important elites either in Kigali, Kampala, Goma or Kinshasa, regulation would not be a panacea. In fact, the power of these elites would have to be broken in some way or the other. Governance initiatives and certification schemes do not pose a serious threat to these power structures.

As indicated in the previous chapter, striking deals with its neighbours is one of the key skills a Congolese government has to master. Kabila has been repeatedly successful at that. In November 2008, the Congolese and Rwandan governments decided to leave their competition aside for a moment in order to pacify the Congo's east and to provide a more fertile ground for president Kabila's re-election in 2011. They agreed to arrest the CNDP rebel leader Laurent Nkunda, who had nearly occupied Goma, the capital of North Kivu, and to integrate the CNDP rebel forces into the Congolese army and join forces to fight the FDLR. The FDLR has been openly hoping for regime change in Rwanda and has continuously been regarded as a threat by the Rwandan government. This deal with Rwanda constituted a major step towards better cooperation and ensuing military operations temporarily weakened the standing of the FDLR at the time.

Although Congolese president Kabila had used similar tactics in 2005, when he surprisingly sided with the Rwandan-supported former RCD rebels to secure votes in the 2006 elections, some influential Western analysts were caught off-guard by these developments (International Crisis Group, 2010b: i). They could neither believe that agreements were founded behind their back nor that cooperation between former supposed enemies was possible. These political moves showed the extent to which the Congolese government is shaping Congolese politics, if strategic interests are at stake. A very similar process occurred with the CNDP successor organization M23 in December 2012. The M23 did manage to take over Goma in early November 2012, but pulled out again after just ten days when Kabila, Ugandan president Museveni and Rwandan president Kagame had started negotiating in earnest. Every time a more consolidated rebellion flares up in the east the story goes: Kabila is weak, he will fall. This repeatedly erroneous assessment is usually quickly brushed under the carpet once it is obvious that he has not fallen at all.

Among the Western policy world, the 2008 deal with Rwanda was read as unfavourable for the Congolese government. It was assumed tough concessions had to be made because the government was believed to have negotiated from a position of weakness. The CNDP rebels were given guarantees that they would not to be taken to court for crimes committed, that they could retain their parallel administration structure over parts of North Kivu, were awarded control over important mining areas, and Tutsi refugees in Rwanda were to be allowed to eventually return to the Congo. The International Crisis Group bemoaned in this regard: 'that commitments had also been made regarding access to grazing land in North Kivu for thousands of cows belonging to Congolese Tutsis and Rwandan military' (International Crisis Group, 2010b: 32–33), a rare glimpse into another important pillar of the Kivu economy beyond mining.[3]

The logic of these deals remains highly opaque and there is occasionally a sense of respect for how ably the Kabila government has kept Western donors at bay in this (Paddon and Lacaille, 2011: 20). This does not prevent some think tanks from giving specific recommendations towards the respective governments and international organizations. The International Crisis Group, for example, reacted to these surprising developments with a call for more transparency but did not argue *why* secrecy cannot contribute to solving complex diplomatic challenges:

> A strategy based on secret presidential commitments, however, will not bring peace to the Kivu: the present approach must be re-evaluated and broadened in order to engage all local communities and prepare the future of the region in a transparent dialogue that also involves neighbouring countries.
>
> (International Crisis Group, 2010b: i)

Experts of diplomacy might well assure this ICG analyst, that secrecy has at times played a fundamental role in moving international relations forward.

Not only did policy reports paint the Kabila government as non-transparent and incapable of diplomacy, in another episode they also naturally assumed that its approach to internally displaced persons (IDP) in the east was malevolent and indecent although there was little to no evidence to support this claim.

Prior to the 2011 elections, Kabila possibly wanted to convey the impression that the region was getting more stable. During a visit to the refugee camps around Goma, he personally told the IDPs around Goma to go home because it was purportedly safe. Tens of thousands immediately did. The international representatives in Goma were outraged by this display of governmental power because they argued it wasn't safe (Human Rights Watch, 2010: 53). But they could not do anything but acknowledge the fact that most of the camps were suddenly empty.

In Goma, the issue of IDP return in the fall of 2009 created a stir.[4] Numerous emergency meetings were held during which NGO country managers expressed their anger about what they regarded as irresponsible and dangerous. NGOs accused the UNHCR of being in cahoots with the government and as collaborating in forcing IDPs to leave. By reducing the IDP camp inhabitants' daily rations, NGOs argued, UNHCR provided strong incentives for them to go home. UNHCR, by contrast, responded that they had conducted wide ranging surveys and that most of the IDP had expressed their *will* to return. Furthermore, school had started again and families did not want their children to miss any more schooling because of being stuck in a camp.

Among these discussions which I witnessed during and after UN OCHA coordination meetings in Goma and which I discussed during interviews with UNHCR, NGOs and the provincial minister of planning, a strong sense of entitlement was tangible. NGOs presented their case in a way that seemed to imply that 'their' IDPs were leaving and that they were unfortunately not able to deal with them outside of camps. The issue of IDP return and dealing with IDPs in host families has continued to preoccupy humanitarian NGOs and the UN. However, as Brookings Institution's Stacey White argues, there remains a 'lack of vision and funding for these kinds of activities' (White, 2014: 2).

In Goma, I witnessed the strong administrative and managerial components to this controversy. Some of the intervention actors specialize in camp management, others have increasingly started to support IDPs among host families and even the host families themselves. Among humanitarians and in policy circles, it has slowly become obvious that most IDPs prefer to stay away from camps and prefer to live with family or acquaintances if they can. This often puts a strain on host families' ability to fend for their daily needs as the number of people to cater for has increased. Organizations more adapted to this pattern tended to be less vocal about the issue of obvious IDP return. Their business model was not in danger. Those who were only equipped to deal with camp situations suddenly faced a challenge, as they could no longer operate in as convenient a manner as before.

This controversy shows that the question of government authority is always read through one of the two lenses – weakness or destructiveness. During the IDP return episode, NGOs suddenly assumed a very strong but destructive government because it had forced 'their' IDPs to go home. Moreover, they painted the UNHCR as a dangerous government ally. NGOs often take pride at working around the government as much as they can because of their humanitarian principles. UNHCR, by contrast, seemed to cooperate well with the provincial authorities. Overall, in Goma, it was obvious from this episode, and during the even more controversial one about a law on humanitarian aid that was to be passed in the provincial assembly (see conclusion), that interveners had to interact and negotiate with government authorities all the time.

In the policy world, this version of reality did not feature prominently. At key moments the government is reported to make announcements, issue decrees or order some of their citizens to move, and this shows important results. These signs of authority and influence would, in theory, render the weak and dangerous government lens problematic. Yet the implications of these incidents are not dealt with. These events are presented as marginal episodes, if at all, so the overall narrative remains one of governmental incapacity or malevolence.

Based on the regularity of these episodes in key policy papers and the evidence from field research and interviews it is reasonable to assume rationality and strategic government behaviour. Instead of turning the government into a weak or irresponsible institution it would seem rational to scrutinize their strategic calculus. This would imply questioning numerous tacit assumptions present in these episodes: for example, IDPs are normal people. Usually, they do not want to live in camps. As a consequence, calling on people to leave these camps is not a malevolent act per se. The way NGOs talked about 'their' IDPs in Goma and the extremely meagre evidence presented by the main report on the issue (Human Rights Watch, 2010: 52ff.), suggests that they were very reluctant in even considering the rationality of the government's decision to send IDPs home.

Pathologizing the government was also a prominent practice among the interveners when we discussed Congolese politics and politicians in particular.[5] Among some of the interviewees the Congolese government is not seen to possess adequate human material for politics. The Congolese politician is egoistic and lacks a sense of responsibility.[6] Foreign intervention should educate them to exert leadership and to stop pursuing anything else but personal enrichment.[7] In addition, Congolese leadership should adapt to the requirements of today. Things have changed. And yet, as a senior EU official laments:

> It's a pity but Congolese politics is still in the 1960s here. That's the case with the head of state in particular because he was educated by his father who was a bit blocked in his thinking. He continues to have a perception that is not at all representative of the outside world anymore and which is still the perception of the Lumumba epoch, of imperialism, of the two blocks. Today, the two blocks it's the same; but it's China he imagines, it's China and the Western World.[8]

As we have seen in the previous chapter, for Congolese governments, there is good reason to think geopolitically. The way Congolese politicians are described here pays no attention to the possible inner logic of this kind of calculus. Playing off external actors against each other has been an integral and existential part of Congolese governmental strategies in dealing with the outside world. Europe calculated in terms of balance of power, mutually beneficial trade in Europe and the exploitation of the colonies. Today, some European politicians most certainly think in different political and economic blocks again because of the rise of China and they certainly engage in alliance politics. However, with the view to the Congo, for some interveners this signifies being stuck in the past.

The failed state effect

Next to a broadly condescending attitude towards the Congolese government, the Congo of today is often captured as a weak or failed state ranking high on failed state indices and low on development indices.[9] These indices influence media reports and come up frequently in policy papers and in the interviews. Christian Büger and Felix Bethke have shown how the 'failed state' has spread widely and how the number of publications on the issue exploded in early 2000 in academic publications and in 2005 in non-academic publications (2014: 44). The failed state has provided jobs for a lot of analysts.

Various analyses of the state in the Congo have been provided since the 1960s (Lemarchand, 1964; Young, 1965; Callaghy, 1984; Young and Turner, 1985; Schatzberg, 1988; Nzongola-Ntalaja, 2002; Vansina, 2010). Steeped in the debates among comparative political science[10] of the time and often with a Marxist background, these wide-ranging studies focused on class relations and elite formation in postcolonial Mobutist Congo and Zaire. During the last 20 years, this perspective has disappeared. Most recent literature instead deals with the Congo wars, apart from a few works by Théodore Trefon (Trefon, 2009b, 2011) and nobody has attempted to study Joseph Kabila's state yet. During nearly 15 years of Kabila rule the Congo has not been considered a real state worthy of academic attention.

The state concept serves as one of the key 'devices' (Aradau and Huysmans, 2014) pathologizing the Congo in intervention knowledge production. The status of the state is paramount for legitimizing different components of international intervention. After all, statebuilding is needed when the state is deficient. The way the Congo is pathologized here differs from the pathologization of government because a central concept nurtures it: the state. What the Kabila government does is not simply neglected or overlooked or turned into something malevolent or pathological. By contrast, Congolese political life is measured against a universal standard of statehood. The deployment of the state concept functions as a yardstick which turns the Congolese state almost automatically into an underdeveloped, deficient pathology. I call this the 'failed state effect' (Koddenbrock, 2013a).

There are two main understandings of the state among intervention. Sometimes the state is simply seen as absent; sometimes it does not function properly. It does not provide the state functions it is expected to provide. This means there is, on the one hand, a conception of some overarching entity at play which could be traced back to the Hegelian conception of the state as supreme idea. On the other hand, there is the more functionalist perspective on the state being an actor with specific capacities to fulfil state functions. The failed state, then, which is one of the core terms used to capture the lack of statehood identified in the Congo, is closer to the state actor with capacities model. The failed state does not function properly.

The 'failed state effect'[11] among Western interviewees comes about through a number of ways to enact the Congo by using the state yardstick. With the help of some illustrative examples from my interviews in Goma and New York, I will show that there are different ways of using this state yardstick. I call these modes of using the state yardstick reification, juxtaposition and contextualization. Reification is the most widely-used one.[12] During 'reification', the state is simply presupposed and the lack of identified statehood in the Congo proves its failure. It takes the state as a natural requirement of political organization and posits its absence in the Congo. Alternatively, serious attempts are made to stay clear of the state yardstick and to give the Congo some sociology of its own, just to suddenly resort to the state again and cause another 'failed state effect'. I call this 'juxtaposition' because an analytical reading is suddenly juxtaposed to a pathologizing one. In juxtaposition, there is no logical link between the description of what is happening and its downgrading as non-statal. The third approach I identified during the interviews with interveners sees the Congolese state as deficient but doubts whether this deficiency is based on the lack of capacity or willingness of the Congolese. It takes account of some of the material and historical circumstances of Congolese social order. This can usefully be termed 'contextualization'.

In 'reification', for example, slow decision-making and parallel chains of command are used as indicators for state weakness because an implicit understanding of the state asks for it:

> The current situation is difficult. There has been some progress recently but obviously, until now, the expectations of the Congolese population were exaggerated and what the Congolese leaders achieved is without doubt even less than we hoped. The Congolese state remains extremely weak. The Congolese leaders take their time in making decisions especially with a view to security which is essential to build state authority. Although there is a Congolese army, at the moment there currently is no real Congolese army, there are men in, but it's also not a disciplined army in which there are several parallel chains of command.[13]

Heterogeneous governmental practices like parallel chains of command in the army indicate a weak state for this EU official. That slow decision-making, competing centres of power around the presidential circle and concentrated around hubs of economic activity might be a particular and rational form of statehood is not an option here.

The following statement by US adviser in Goma operates along similar lines. He posits the Congo as a dysfunctional para-state first – inherited from the Belgians – and describes actual governmental practice and reason in a second step:

> I think it's very difficult and you know Congo is a highly dysfunctional state given to it by the Belgians basically and reinforced strongly by Mobutu. They have a genuine para-state really. The norm of the institutions is that they find ways to make money off the population that's their imperative and they do not provide services, they do not act in the interest of the population, they act in their own interest to take from the population on a whole.[14]

Instead of describing the way government takes place in the Congo, para-stateness provides the frame and automatically makes the state appear dysfunctional. This kind of reasoning among interveners does not take governmental logic and practice at face value to understand more deeply what overall principle of intelligibility this might lead to. Instead, the state as a device of intelligibility comes into play and endows the observations made with a particular performative effect. It sustains a pathological Congo.

Other interviewees are willing to give Congolese governmental practice some credit but nonetheless turn it into a failed state. In contrast to taking the state as a given from the start, as in reification, the state comes in as clearly in tension with preceding analysis. I call this 'juxtaposition'. To what extent this can border cognitive dissonance shows this interview with a senior NGO manager:

KK: What is the Congo for you?

RESPONDENT: A country with quite a few, I mean, an extremely fascinating, very complex country with plenty of non.-, at first you think non-functioning structures, but somehow they do function but differently than you imagined. I mean, there are, it is not chaotic, there are ways of functioning and structures of power which here, which work very well here, which are not always the ones one would like or expects.[15]

This NGO manager is clearly not at ease with the usual perception of utter dysfunctionality. He concedes government takes place. Yet, not usually in the way foreigners expect it. This is an analytical approach to government in the Congo. This perceptiveness notwithstanding, in a different context he makes use of the classic pathologizing register which turns the Congo into a failed state above all else. Discussing the challenges Western intervention deals with, he responds:

> How do I build a functioning state from this pile of cow shit? You have that in Afghanistan, in Iraq, you have it here, you have it in many of these failed states. How, how do I do statebuilding?

This imposes an implicit understanding of the state on governmental practice in the Congo. Earlier, the NGO manager chose to take a more complex route. The

Congo is now a 'pile of cow shit' and it is one of these failed states like Afghanistan and Iraq. This short-cut approach does not manage to link social observation to the state or to state failure in a coherent way. This is one of the core features of the state 'device': People do not develop it but suddenly pin it to their observations. Interveners often cannot resist thinking in terms of failed statehood.

The third approach to the Congolese state I identified among Western Congo interveners – 'contextualization' – sees it as deficient but doubts whether this is based on the lack of capacity or willingness of the Congolese. It takes account of some of the material circumstances of the Congolese state and struggles with the reasons and responsibilities for this challenging state of affairs:

KK: And what are the current main challenges for the Congo?
RESPONDENT: It's to restore or even install some state authority and then security. There are so many things that need to happen at once. Because you need to have security but you need to have a justice system but then, you know, what happens to people after they've gone through the justice system. The prisons. I mean it's just so many things that need to happen at the same time.
KK: Do you have the impression that the state has no authority actually?
RESPONDENT: No, not no authority but it's too weak in too many places. But it has also to do with the size and the resources. And sometimes, for example, I've been to the north-east and, I think sometimes it's just the geography of it. It's so far away and it will be so expensive. It hasn't been a priority. But I don't think it's something like someone sat in Kinshasa and decided, we are not going to care about this area. It's more, you know, it's just the way it happens.[16]

This UN staffer deploys two potentially distinct ways of looking at government in the Congo. The opening paragraph contains the unexamined term of state authority – the failed state lens. However, she goes beyond government capacity or willingness to explain the lack of 'state authority' when she theorizes about the size and geography of the country. Despite her terminology of 'weakness', she considers the fact that this might not be due to some kind of conscious choice by the government but due to structural and material factors. Government of the eastern part of the Congo might be patchy. Congo's geography might play a role in determining governmental reason. Whether state weakness or failure is the most adequate label for such a situation remains in doubt.

The recent World Bank flagship report on the Congo's resilience and potential adopts that exact approach. It does not simply pathologize the Congo but contextualizes its challenges and its statehood:

Developing effective state institutions is difficult in a postconflict environment. Institutions establish their credibility gradually over time. But in a postconflict environment, rapid results are needed, and these often require bypassing certain natural steps. For example, the Democratic Republic of

Congo established temporary project implementation units in an effort to side-step limited capacity in national institutions. To stabilize, the country must shift from these immediate, short-term arrangements to ones that support the nation's institutional capacity to deliver results. For such a shift to be sustainable, it needs to be grounded in the political economy.

(2012: 103)

This is a nuanced analysis. Although the terminology of 'postconflict environment' connects to the widespread and ahistorical conflict approach to the Congo, this World Bank report mentions the Congo's political economy and the need for time. It thus calls for more scrutiny and more grounded concepts.

This illustration of the failed state effect among interveners has shown how the state operates as self-explanatory prerequisite for any conception of order in the Congo, how it is examined more closely occasionally but relied on nonetheless among Western intervention staff – as the failed state. This way of pathologizing the Congo has the side-effect of legitimizing foreign intervention in the Congo – among foreign interveners. Were the Congo as state not seen as failed, it would be harder to uphold the self-evident need for intervention.

A criminal, illegal and unproductive economy

Just like the 'state', the 'economy' works as a device turning the Congolese economy into a locus of pathologies and dysfunctions. Three broad themes have dominated views on the Congolese economy in the last decades and among interviewees: the resilience of the people despite the troubles of the formal economy, the enormous economic potential of the Congo given its wealth in natural resources,[17] and the daring challenges resulting from its natural resource and mining economy.[18] Which of these themes dominate and where has been shifting constantly.

The resilience trope was and is very prominent in economic anthropology as well as among many of the intervention staff interviewed in Goma and New York. Resilience tends to be stressed as something remarkable and as an antidote to more widespread pathologization of the Congo's economy. In her influential book *The Real Economy of Zaire,* Janet MacGaffey provided captivating anthropological insights on the way Congolese cope despite faring low on growth and income indices. Her take on a 'second economy' which is not simply informal or illegal but has a 'high degree of organization' (MacGaffey, 1983: 355) and even allows people to be upwardly mobile and become rich was widely read in Africanist circles in the 1980s. In his *Reinventing Order in the Congo*, Theodore Trefon recently provided another take on the resilience of the Congolese, the *Kinois* (inhabitants of Kinshasa) in particular (Trefon, 2004), and Maria Eriksson Baaz and Ola Olsson have contributed to this approach to the economy stressing the agency and rationality of Congolese economic actors. Building on anthropological research among the Congolese police they show, contrary to widely held beliefs on the Congolese economy, how codified and organized income distribution within the police is. Income is largely generated by so-called corrupt practices like roadblocks and 'property violations', but indeed serves to stabilize the police forces and allows them to provide services that the population actively asks for (Baaz and Olsson, 2011: 226–227). There is thus an important strand in the academic literature stressing that the Congolese economy 'works' (Chabal and Daloz, 1999). It works because there is rational and productive behaviour, not only anarchy and irrationality.

A countervailing position, however, has become more and more influential since the late 1990s with the ubiquitous debates about the 'resource curse' and the role of 'greed and grievance' for the onset or duration of conflict. Paul Collier's work was most influential in this regard and Paul Collier's *The Bottom Billion* made their ideas available to a larger public (Collier, 2007; Sergiou, 2012: 27–44). This position has contributed to a perspective on economies in Africa as resource economies and places of predation, violence and lack of development. This conception has been overwhelmingly influential among recent policy reporting on the Congo.

As a consequence, the Congolese economy in Western policy analysis and the interviews conducted in Goma and New York is largely seen to be constituted by natural resources and mining.[19] Resources serve to explain the persistence of conflict, as 'resources are a liability'[20] and 'invite exploitative interests',[21] and operate as one of the key explanations of state and government weakness (see further Autesserre, 2012; Koddenbrock, 2012b).

In policy paper descriptions, the Congo's economy is represented by mining alone because the Kivus and their mining sector dominate policy reporting.[22] This conveys the image that the Kivus' problems stand for those of all of the Congo. Rarely is the attempt made to provide a more varied picture of the different types of capital accumulation in which land, cattle, other commodities and services could feature prominently.[23] Their potential economic importance remains beyond the scope of most policy analysis.

A 2011 Global Witness report illustrates this approach:

> [t]he trade in tin, tantalum, tungsten and gold has been fuelling the conflict in eastern Democratic Republic of Congo (DRC) for over a decade. Rebel groups and members of the Congolese national army have made millions of dollars through illegal control of mines and trading routes, while inflicting appalling suffering on the local population.
>
> (Global Witness, 2011a: 4)

This statement may indeed be accurate, but it is one-sided. The report enters the topic of the Congo's economy through these minerals only, and the complexities of social, political and economic situation in the Kivu provinces, and the Congo as a whole, remain beyond its scope. Not only 'tin, tantalum, tungsten and gold' may be fuelling conflict. The trade in timber, hemp, cattle and cheese, as well as the taxation of citizens, may also provide the income and incentives needed to engage in violence. Perhaps the Kivus' business elites have an interest in prolonging conflict, and it is their conscious choice that fuels conflict (International Peace Information Service, 2008: 26). Even the government may have an interest or an important role in conflict. According to the KfW Development Bank, mining only contributes 10 per cent to GDP, and the export of coltan and copper only constitute 16 per cent of overall exports (KfW, 2007: 15ff.). Policy papers and think tanks understandably focus on specific sectors and issue areas. However, if not made transparent, this selectivity too easily lends itself to stabilizing Western intervention's self-evidence which currently assumes that resource governance shall be improved with the help of Western supported certification schemes.

The same de-contextualizing pattern is apparent when the Global Witness report gets into detail: '[t]he cassiterite (tin ore) mine of Bisie, located in North Kivu's Walikale territory … is hugely significant because it accounts for 70 per cent of the cassiterite produced in the province of North Kivu' (Global Witness, 2011a: 8). Without providing information about the tax base of the province or the overall contribution of cassiterite to the North Kivu economy, this paragraph conveys little information despite its authoritative style. The same report quotes the North Kivu finance minister as saying that a mining ban imposed by the Kabila government in September 2010 reduced monthly provincial revenues from US\$600,000 to 400,000 from then until March 2011. The report does not argue the ban was ineffective. To the contrary, the ban is described as effective, as many miners lost their jobs and sources of livelihood. However, the underlying tax revenue indicates that resources other than mining might actually be twice as important for the province because the revenues have only gone down by US\$200,000. This possibility and the potential implications for analysis are not scrutinized (Global Witness, 2011a: 16).[24] They do not fit the dominant discourse on the Congolese economy.

The Congo's economy is not only enacted as a mining economy. It is also seen as criminal, illegal and unproductive and inimical to development. The assertiveness of this kind of knowledge production is surprising because, at the same time, there is recurrent reporting on the opacity of the mining sector. Some reports mention that the tracking of locations, conduits and profits, actors and power structures is extremely challenging: nobody really knows (International Alert, 2010a: 72, 2010b: 7; World Bank, 2012: 28; 2011: 19). The logic of policy recommendations, however, obscures this. That much of this opacity remains unacknowledged can be seen in the way policy papers shift their strong judgments on the existence of certain minerals. While a 2008 report, for example, assumed that artisanal mining focused on coltan and cassiterite but not on gold in the Kivus (World Bank, 2008: 8), another report now assumes that gold is mined by myriad actors (International Peace Information Service, 2009a: 11).

In addition to the global end-users a variety of local actors have stakes in mining: thousands of artisanal miners (called *creuseurs*); soldiers involved in levying taxes along transport routes; prostitutes serving the miners and soldiers; high-ranking military officials making a fortune at the end of the chain of taxation; owners and pilots of transport planes; local farmers selling produce to the workers; and traders affiliated with mining products, refineries and international companies. Current policy papers do not represent this variety. Instead, they produce an easily grasped image that might stimulate outrage among readers. First, they highlight which armed groups control which areas, and tacitly imply that they fuel conflict (United Nations, 2011a: 17; Enough Project, 2009; Global Witness, 2011a: 6). Second, reports often highlight a specific mine – the Bisie mine in Walikale – and the scandalous mining activities that take place there (CASM, 2008; Global Witness, 2010a; Enough Project, 2009). Thus Western policy papers suggest that contemporary mining in the Kivus is bad in three respects. Mining is criminal because the army or other armed groups are involved. It is illegal because it does not adhere to the stipulations of the 2002 mining code (passed by the transitional administration). And it does not contribute to development because artisanal productivity is low and opportunities for capital accumulation are lost.

This approach conveys an image of lawlessness and violence based on the fact that armed actors are involved, not based on the way they behave. Although there is evidence of violent behaviour from armed actors (Global Witness, 2011a: 26), they act predominantly like participants in a trade rather than peace spoilers. Harassment and violence seem to be exceptions rather than the rule. The fact that regularly unpaid armed forces dig minerals themselves supports this (ibid.).

A broader perspective comprising national, regional, continental and international trade components is also used to paint the economy as criminal:

> [t]he trafficking networks based in Uganda and Rwanda, usually heavily military themselves, intertwine with informal, powerful Congolese structures, reaching back to shadowy, powerful figures, often military, based in Kinshasa. These trafficking networks then link in a crazy quilt to international networks of trade in Congo's resources.
>
> (World Bank, 2011: 18)

The wording of this report is utterly literary, close to a Shakespearean drama (Koddenbrock, 2014a). Shadowy figures lurk in the background. In these accounts, criminality, the report insinuates, originates from the fact that some of the overseers of the trade are somehow 'military'. In addition, since trafficking is both criminal and illegal, and it is assumed that much of the minerals are trafficked, the entire enterprise must be criminal. It is not mentioned in this report that the mineral trade also provides substantial revenues for the provincial administration, and can also be seen as a form of outsourcing of army pay. It is particularly rational from the perspective of the national government in Kinshasa if it meets the government's need to deal with elite inclusion (see previous chapter). Providing economic opportunities to potential competitors to its rule is certainly a rational way of dealing with elite inclusion.

Next to the criminal character of the Congolese economy, policy papers often invoke its illegality. The notion of illegality is used in a peculiar manner. For example, in 2002, the transitional government under new president Joseph

Kabila issued a code declaring artisanal mining illegal. Hundreds of thousands of miners broke the law by continuing with what had been a legal activity. Yet, this law is not enforced by the national or provincial governments, either because they see no use in enforcing it or because they lack the capacity to do so. However, policy papers do not hesitate to term these popular sources of income the 'illegal exploitation of natural resources'.[25] Technically adequate, this terminology does not describe the social processes at play, but instead criminalizes the Kivus' economy and legitimizes Western support and intervention.

An exception to the rule, one report by International Alert cautions:

> It is near impossible for artisanal mining to conform to the 2002 Mining Code. It stipulates that artisanal activity must be carried out in an area of exploitation 'demarcated as to its surface and to its depth'.... But no such areas have so far been defined in eastern DRC.
>
> (International Alert, 2010b: 16)

Given that up to 200,000 people earn their living as miners in the Kivus, and that both governmental and non-governmental actors are involved, this perspective on the socio-political processes connected to mining in the Kivu seems more balanced:

> Although the artisanal mining is considered to be part of the 'informal sector', it is nonetheless highly organized. All economic actors take part in a system with its own internal coherence and its rules, even if it functions in the margins of official legality, with the force of armed groups. Various contradictions flow from this, particularly between the customary and administrative authorities, but it also creates hybrid forms of management linking tradition and modernity within the framework of local institutional improvisations.
>
> (International Alert, 2010b: 16: 25)

But while artisanal mining may indeed be an important source of income for all social strata of the North Kivu's population other sources are not discussed in that report.

Artisanal mining is not only criminal and illegal for a majority of Western policy analysts. It also does not do anything for poverty reduction, or so the assumption goes. The non-development narrative about artisanal mining identified in policy papers, here paraphrased, runs as follows: the big Congolese state mining company Société Minière et Industrielle du Kivu (SOMINKI) fell apart during the demise of former president Joseph-Désiré Mobutu. Consequently, artisanal mining has boomed since the mid-1990s (CASM, 2008: 12–13). Yet, artisanal mining is less productive than industrial mining and a 'poverty trap' for the diggers (International Alert, 2010b: 57).

The narrative is backed by various data. Some reports argue that miners do not even earn money and have a negative income over the entire year (ibid.: 58).

Others assert that they earn between one and ten dollars a day (CASM, 2008: 2; Pole Institute, 2011: 16). For some, this is a decent income, compared to teachers who are paid worse; for others, this borders on slavery (International Alert, 2010b: 31). Despite its nuanced view on the 'hybrid forms of [mine] management', International Alert's report struggles to substantiate its poverty-trap claim. Even while making the claim, it recognizes that '[o]nly with solid quantitative data – as accurate as possible – will it be possible to correctly measure the economic and social impact of artisanal mining' (International Alert, 2010b: 59).

By contrasting current artisanal mining with industrialized mining during Mobutu's reign, readers are led to assume that state companies were productive, and that workers earned a better living before going in for artisanal mining. But evidence on salaries and standards of living during Mobutu's time is not provided. In addition, the Mobutu narrative usually maintains that he and his entourage usurped the state for personal enrichment (see previous chapter), which entailed neither decent wages nor high rates of productivity. For Western analysts, the Congo economy is deeply problematic. It is 'mono-cultural' because based on mineral extraction, it is dangerous, and it is unproductive.

The pathologizing structure at play in enacting the Congolese economy does not go unnoticed among Congolese observers. The Pole Institute, a Congolese think tank based in Goma, bemoaned in this regard:

> Nonetheless [despite the impression of lawlessness in the West, KK], many initiatives were taken in DRC by the sector stakeholders themselves, the Congolese State, Civil society and even the international community, to formalise the mining industry, ensure transparency and traceability [...]. But it appears that all these efforts were neither known about nor acknowledged, as if there were a kind of law of silence about everything positive that is done in this domain and that only the alarms and alerts of the NGOs, which are systematically hostile to the mining economy in DRC, should be taken into account.
>
> (Pole Institute, 2011: 77)

A well-substantiated critique of the 'resource curse' lens is made by Ann Laudati who argues that: 'contrary to the popular discourses on the oft-cited link between minerals and conflict, minerals are not the source of conflict in the Congo'. Instead: 'minerals played a rather minor and in some cases no role in facilitating the activities of some armed groups (2013: 32–33). Pessimistic assessments like 'ending the mineral trade will therefore not break the link between trade and armed groups rather it will simply create links with other commodities' (Johnson 2009, quoted in Laudati, 2013: 34)' are not particularly welcome.

Laudati makes the convincing claim that:

> scholarship must be cognizant of the ways different commodities are configured in widely divergent socio-economic and geographic ways, as these differences will lead to very different trajectories of war based on a multiple

and variable set of existing incentives and opportunities provided for would be warlords in resource rich environments. The use of pillaging by low level fighters may in fact contribute to a greater landscape of fear and violence for surrounding communities rather than the acquisition of minerals. Taking up arms reduces the efficiency of mineral exploitation while it promotes the efficiency of plundering activities. Furthermore, the period of hemp production is often associated with a cessation of violence as groups must collaborate and labor during the brief harvest season.

(Laudati, 2013: 46)

Analysing the Congo economy this way entails no simple resource curse, but a complex set of socio-economic relations that perpetuate conflict in the Congo. Resources may even foster temporary peace and collaboration, as seen in the case of hemp. Enacting the economy as simply a place of mining, criminality and lack of development is useful for the particular and possibly waning trend of mineral certification schemes in intervention, not necessarily more.

Nevertheless, alternative approaches to the Congolese economy have entered the debate. The World Bank report *Resilience of an African Giant* (2012) has attempted a reorientation of the debate on the Congolese economy while retaining some of its pathologizing registers. In contrast to the wealth of policy papers analysed above, agriculture now receives its due and is even credited with being responsible for the modest growth the Congo has witnessed over the last five years (World Bank, 2012: 8):

Subsistence agriculture generates some 40 percent of GDP, engaging about 60 percent of the workforce. Linkages with urban and international markets are limited as a result of poor infrastructure; lack of security, especially in the eastern provinces; high fees; and harassment, particularly at international borders.

(World Bank, 2012: 35)

This focus on agriculture runs counter to the predominant mining economy lens. Suddenly, it becomes imperative to build on the potential for GDP growth and employment creation offered by this sector of the economy. At the exact moment when the policy cycle, from identification of the resource governance issue with the UN report 2002 and the widespread implementation of policy initiatives of Western supervised certification mechanisms during the years until 2012, has come full circle, a 'new' crucial pillar of 'the' Congolese economy comes to the forefront.

The renewed focus on agriculture promoted by some donors and the World Bank in particular seems to indicate a new way of going about the Congo. Yet, more integrated analyses of the global economic links impacting on the Congo continue to be absent. When the World Bank deals with the international aspects of the Congolese economy, it is strikingly selective. For example, while the report acknowledges that the West did indeed support the Mobutu regime because it was a bulwark against communism on the continent, it stresses more prominently how generous the 'international community' was in continuing to support the regime despite the economic downturn starting in the late 1970s. These two statements are obviously at odds with each other. Above all else, the World Bank celebrates its intervention and chooses to downplay the problems with the regime it actively propped up.

Although the exploitative interests of neighbouring Rwanda and Uganda have come up repeatedly in interviews and policy papers, there is a notable absence of more global approaches to the Congolese economy. This is similar to the way Congolese governments' regional and international alliance-building has not been systematically researched. Congolese economic processes are almost exclusively analysed from a national container perspective.

During the coltan boom around the year 2000, when campaigns about cell phones and their contribution to conflict in the Congo mushroomed, there was a brief period of more comprehensive analyses. The first UN group of experts report on the exploitation of natural resources scandalized practices by German companies like HC Starck, a Bayer subsidiary, which bought large amounts of coltan during the conflict (United Nations, 2002: 16). Some of these more global approaches continue to feature in the group of expert reports when it comes to arms trading.

In the wake of these more global analyses, Canadian scholar Patrice Martineau mapped the entire coltan trade from diggers to end users. Martineau's report shows how coltan gets marketed from the village to the negotiating centre, crosses the border, gets processed for the first time in smelters owned by HC Starck, for example, and gets sold to condensator producers in order to end up in electronic devices like cell phones and laptops manufactured by Nokia or Apple (Martineau, 2003: 35). These kinds of meticulous analyses are rare. They contributed to a host of policy approaches to these issues like the OECD Code of Conduct for Multinational Companies or the UN Global Compact. Yet, the analytical approach of analysing the Congolese economy as integrated in regional and global markets has not been maintained.

Next to this lack of attention to global connections, the neglect for the question of international debt in analyses of Congolese political economy is striking. Arnaud Zacharie has shown the staggering levels of debt the Congo has acquired since decolonization with the active support of its Western supporters. Drily stating that the Congo remains at risk of 'debt distress' (World Bank, 2012: 36) excludes from view the important role Western donors have played in increasing this debt. After actively contributing to his military coup, Western governments supported president Mobutu's early 'white elephant' projects, lent him several hundreds of million dollars annually which became a heavy burden in the mid 1970s (Zacharie, 2009: 106ff.). When the newly independent Congo negotiated the take-over of some shares of former Belgian companies engaged in the mining sector the terms were less than beneficial: 'In reality, [this, KK] meant that a newly independent country would be paying colonial debts.' (Lumumba-Kasongo, 1992: 34). Including these legacies that continue to play a role today despite the several rounds of debt relief the country has gone through would constitute a more comprehensive way of analysing the Congo, one that would require serious auto-criticism from the West.[26]

The most glaring absence in analyses of the Congolese economy is the role of Western or foreign financing of the Congolese annual budget. None of the policy papers I analysed or the interviews I conducted brought up this topic although there are sources claiming that up to 50 per cent of the Congolese budget expenditure are financed by donors, including China.[27] Aid is the single-most source of income for the Congolese government and thus it's the economic 'sector' it is most dependent on.

As has become clear, intervention actors enact a particular Congolese economy they choose to work on. Between 2008 and 2012, the resource curse and mining has been in focus. Once this limited focus and the resulting intervention activities have proven to be ineffective, a new focus came in sight: agriculture. The ironic advantage of these shifts lies in the fact that, after some time, those issues that have fallen through the grid can become prominent and the new policy focus. Since agriculture was neglected for some time, the case may now be made that it is absolutely paramount to start focusing on it more. Overall, these shifts are highly productive for intervention because they reinvigorate the need for it (see next chapter).

The Congolese and their character

Among individual interveners, assessments of the Congo and the Congolese are highly problematic too. Sexual and gender based violence is the dominant lens through which policy analysts and interveners look at Congolese social life. Postcolonial and other critical approaches to intervention have repeatedly highlighted the racist conceptions at work in intervention. Maria Eriksson Baaz, for example, showed how development workers in Tanzania looked down on their so-called partners (Baaz, 2005). Gayatri Spivak's assessment that much of the urge to intervene originates in the desire to 'save brown women from brown men' (1988a: 296) continues to be relevant today. Despite the reflexivity I experienced among many of the interviewees in Goma and New York, talking about people and their interaction in a society or a collective seems to bring up more immediately racist reflections than discussing the state or the economy.

This last section of the chapter on pathologizing the Congo among intervention thus focuses on the assessments of Congolese society and the Congolese themselves circulating in the policy and media worlds and among intervention personnel. The criminality trope which was shown to be central to the economy overlaps with the overwhelming ascription of Congolese as being prone to violence. This takes place in a lot of policy and media reporting, but just as well among intervention staff that had immediate contact to victims of this violence in Goma.

Congolese society today is turned into a place of barbarism and violence among intervention. This has very real consequences. The programmes against sexual and gender based violence in the Kivus reconfigure their social reality. Not only do Congolese turn into irrational and brutish people for intervention, but this way of approaching them also provides incentives to Congolese to confirm these stereotypes by using rape accusations, for example, to get access to UN or NGO medical treatment.[28]

When recounting the longstanding troubles in eastern Congo, two 'facts' feature prominently. First: more than five million people have died as a result of the turmoil since 1995, and, second: the Congo has the highest prevalence of rape in the world. Five million casualties amount to six times the genocide in Rwanda. Although there is considerable scientific controversy about this figure, most think tanks continue to quote it, sometimes accompanied by a footnote mentioning the controversy (International Rescue Committee, 2007; Human Security Report Project, 2011: 15ff.). Until 2002, 2.5 million was the number provided by the International Rescue Committee, an American NGO with considerable presence in the Congo, and which commissioned the reports on high mortality during and after the Congo wars (Human Rights Watch, 2002). In policy reporting, Congolese society suffers in two respects: horrifyingly high levels of mortality, and the atrocities of sexual violence, which are conveyed by vivid eyewitness-accounts in NGO policy and advocacy reports.

Sexual violence has high media and advocacy value. The media can sell their products, and NGOs and governmental organizations get more attention when talking about something as appalling as a 'rape epidemic' (Harvard Humanitarian Initiative, 2010) or a 'femicide' (Ensler, 2007). Treating victims of sexual violence is also one of the main activities of many prominent humanitarian organizations (Duroch, 2004). Policy papers on sexual violence in the Congo portray women as mothers and victims, and tend to conceptualize violence as brutish, irrational and despicable. It is also presented as intimately connected with the mining-economy image, as '[t]he link between conflict minerals and mass rape here is crystal clear. So the first and foremost priority for ending the war here is to set up a system to regulate the minerals trade' (Enough Project, 2011: 1).

Sexual violence in eastern Congo is certainly a serious problem. Yet, reductionism prevails when analysing it. Explaining mass rape warrants serious scholarly attention, but policy papers mostly blame it on evil strategizing – rape as a weapon of war – or on barbarism. Historical, sociological and psychological approaches are largely absent.[29] The army, one of the main perpetrators of sexual violence, has been an instrument of repression since its inception in colonial times. The Belgian-installed *force publique* wreaked havoc on the populations under colonial rule, and Mobutu upheld this tradition during his reign (see previous chapter). Large parts of policy thinking leave history aside and resort to naturalizing essentialism devoid of historical or sociological context.

The UN-commissioned report on the protection of civilians quoted earlier in this chapter reasons that:

[m]otivated by ethnic sectarianism, economic opportunism, political manipulation, strategies of barbarism, and, in some cases, apparent nihilism as a

consequence of societal breakdown, belligerents have subjected the Congolese population to looting, ethnic cleansing, torture, mass rape, sporadic massacres, and, in some instances, attempted genocide.

(Holt and Taylor, 2009: 242–243)

The *New York Times* goes a step further by ending an article on the Virunga National Park in North Kivu hosting FDLR and other rebel forces: 'There used to be a lot of gorillas in there. But now they've been replaced by much more savage beasts' (Gettleman, 2007).

Maria Eriksson Baaz and Maria Stern have analysed sexual violence in a more nuanced fashion (Baaz and Stern, 2010). They depart from the racist terminology of weapons of war and barbarism, and attempt to make these processes of violence intelligible without defending them. They not only show how portraying men as strong perpetrators and women and girls as the only victims reinforces gender roles that may actually serve to uphold current behavioural patterns. Men may suffer less from sexual violence, but they suffer more from abuse and torture as participants of armed conflict. A more nuanced approach to violence in eastern Congo would weigh these different aspects.

In line with the practice approach to performativity adopted in this book, Baaz and Stern describe what reality the prioritization of sexual violence in the Congo helps to bring about. With their both symbolic and material capital deployed in Congo Western intervention, NGOs are highly influential in Congolese society. Baaz and Stern show convincingly how a kind of 'commercialization of rape' has appeared in Kivutian society (Baaz and Stern, 2010: 56). Because of its discursive ubiquity and the amount of funds available for international programmes to combat sexual violence, Congolese have started to make strategic use of these funding opportunities. Rape accusations are now used increasingly as a way to extract money from those who have some. False rapes are also on the rise to get access to health care provided by Western intervention (Baaz and Stern, 2010: 53). This in turn, inflates the number of rapes recorded and lends further credence to the perception of the Congo as the 'rape capital of the world'.[30]

At the same time, the strict prioritization of assistance to victims of sexual violence over other forms of intervention is questioned by Congolese actors who are at the receiving end of these interventions. The level of 'victimcy' needed to be regarded as 'legitimate recipients' of humanitarian aid (Utas, 2005: 409) is seen as problematic. One respondent, interviewed by Baaz and Stern reports: 'if you discuss too much, and try to get in other things that they don't think are important, you might miss the funding [laughing]. So you avoid discussing too much with them' (Baaz and Stern, 2010: 55).

Reflections on the Congolese surfaced during various parts of the interviews with humanitarians and peacekeepers in Goma. I asked explicit questions about the role of Congolese staff in their organizations, and on perceptions of the way internationals are interacting with the Goma population.[31] Furthermore, interviewees freely came up with their views on the Congolese during various interview sections.

The way the Western interveners I interviewed think about the Congolese can be subsumed under two categories. First, many statements refer to Congolese social character. Social character denotes observations of Congolese behaviour accompanied by tentative 'sociological' explanations for it like the legacy of the civil wars, of the Mobutu years or, at times, colonialism. The second category 'natural character' comprises more essentializing views on the Congolese character, ascriptions rooting their personality in some kind of Congolese nature or mentality. Although many of the interviewed show sympathy towards the Congolese which are quite similar to the optimistic assessments presented in the passages on potential and resilience in the economy section above, a grim picture results from observations of Congolese learned behaviour.

In terms of social character, Congolese are both seen as very patriotic and not patriotic enough. The Congolese passionate attachment to an undivided Congo in all its immensity features prominently.[32] But their perceived lack of engagement to get the country back on its feet is seen as unpatriotic.[33] The first understanding is presented as bordering the pathological when it comes with a ubiquitous fear of secession which is purportedly very important among Congolese. 'Balkanizer' is a swear-word in the Congolese policy scene. If you are seen to sympathize with those forces assumed to be backed by Rwanda you are in danger of being called one.[34]

What could be called an 'obsession with the outside' is the most recurrent theme running through interveners' assessments of Congolese social character (also by numerous of the Congolese interviewees). This obsession with the outside comes in various shades. Some identify Congolese aid-dependency which prevents them from doing things themselves, as they expect the internationals to do it for them.[35] Others describe how Congolese still assume they are being exploited by the West which is seen as off the mark given that the Cold War is over and the Congo has, it is said, lost most of its strategic value.[36] Congolese analysts are also said to be stuck in Cold War categories, as mining companies are no longer exploiters, but have become potential development partners. Congolese are seen to overlook this.

This way of analysing the Congo's relationship with the international realm, in particular Western countries, is clearly pathologizing and gives little credit to the reasons why this kind of analysis still predominates among Congolese. As I showed in the previous chapter, poverty, intimidation and violence have been recurrently fuelled or supported by the West and regional neighbours.

Some interviewees, then, regard Congolese attitudes towards international support and intervention as overly instrumentalist and not committed enough. Not working weekends or trying to make the most out of one's job at an international NGO or UN organization is frowned upon. A MONUSCO human rights officer relates one of these episodes:

[Context: The officer found out something new about some small local defence groups and wants to document this with the help of a Congolese colleague speaking the language.] So I wanted to document so I can argument strongly. So I was rushing to do it and then my colleague [name rendered anonymous, KK] didn't come because he was stuck for the weekend, it was a Saturday and I asked my colleague, a Congolese colleague who always comes with me and I said, look, I really think we should carry on working because there is so much here. And she said my office is closed, we are on a weekend, I'm probably not going to be paid for this so no way. And I very gently asked again on a Sunday. I said, what are your plans for today, me I'm going on a patrol do you want to join, I'd love you to come. She didn't. So that's again, for me that's a bit painful because I've been so tired and I came home and then I was in a coma and I was hurt, and it was hurting eve-rywhere, I work over my strength and there was so much to find and then I was with a Congolese colleague who said, look, I'm not receiving money for it so I don't work.

But sometimes I also understand her attitude because she's been here for years, she's probably seen one white enthusiast person, another white enthu-siast person, a third one. They all come, they write fantastic papers and nothing changes. And then she thinks ok, I want to rest. I want to be a human being, I want to enjoy my husband when I come back and stay with my kids, I don't want to, you know, work over power for what? You know. So I actually completely understand her attitude.

But then you also have to understand the attitude of the internationals. We are just on very different levels and you have to admit that we are on different levels. And I really try very much to understand their way of because this is their country. But still there is a different way of thinking and of doing. And I, I desperately try [pause]. And I'm very sad for them because I try to imagine like, you know, we go on massacre sites and we see all these people that have been killed and we see bodies. Or we see burnt villages then I can imagine, you know, I cannot imagine seeing a village in my country like this. I just cannot imagine. So I don't even want to imagine...[37]

The MONUSCO staff member vividly describes her committed fight for the better in the Congo. While she does not directly criticize her Congolese col-leagues for their different work ethics, she posits two distinct 'levels' of engage-ment. Since she portrays her own level as 'white' and 'report writing' and 'enthusiast' the other level implies a more distant and less motivated approach. She 'completely understands' this approach after all these years of Western intervention with limited results, but the immensity of the atrocities she wit-nesses in her job do leave her wondering if this Congolese way is really the ade-quate way to go about 'their country'.

During the interviews I witnessed many attempts among Western interveners to put themselves in their Congolese colleagues' shoes. Despite this commitment to understand, Congolese colleagues seem to remain strange. For example, inter-viewees calmly report that Congolese staff members with much more work experience and who are 20 years older are probably intrigued by the fact that some junior European is to supervise them 'but make the most out of it' without turning to resistance to this set-up.[38] Some interviewees describe their frustration about the difficulties involved in delegation of power within their organization. If Congolese staff members do not fulfil the tasks assigned to them in the way it is expected by superiors, one may hypothesize there is a lack of identification with the organization's aim or way of doing things. Explanations are not sought, however. It is just 'hard to delegate power here'.[39] There are also assessments of Congolese behaviour which interviewees connected to colonialism. Some of them describe Congolese colleagues' behaviour as cool and distanced, or as overly docile and passive. Congolese staff members are said to be 'shocked' if they were supervising white staff because they have been used to the contrary for decades.[40] Also, the traumas lived through have caused a lack of imagination among Congolese to develop their own solutions to their conundrum.[41]

When it comes to the statements on Congolese 'natural character' there is no escaping the fact that racist statements are highly prevalent among humanitarians and peacekeepers in Goma.[42] Next to the slightly more context-rich conceptions of Congolese learned behaviour, here, essentializing and racializing concepts are alive and well.

A short enumeration of statements: you cannot trust the Congolese, they lack the capacity to absorb funds, the Congolese is gentle, sometimes subservient, possesses a mediocre intelligence, is endowed with a lot of resilience, maybe too much resilience to change the Congo's ways, they have a bad mentality, no sense of the common good, no long-term vision, no integrity, no entrepreneurial spirit, they are egoists interested in individual aggrandizement, their horizon is limited, they have great etiquette and humour and are generally a lot of fun. They retain a remarkable degree of happiness despite the hardship they go through.[43]

In contrast to learned behaviour, ascribing a natural character that is an intrinsic character to a people is racist in itself. The genealogy of this 'scientific racism' has been chronicled and dissected elsewhere.[44] 'Scientific racism' loses sight of social patterns, history, constraints, strategic decisions and tactics which might explain the behaviour identified by interveners. Yet, the 'lazy but simple and happy' trope existing since slavery seems to have remained the blueprint many interveners implicitly build on.

The enumeration above indicates essentially two ways of talking about the Congolese: stressing their deficiencies or stressing their values. The first approach is used by quite a few more experienced people who seem to have grown warier over time because their expectations for change do not appear to have been met. The other approach wants to remain positive and sympathetic towards the Congolese. The happiness and resilience trope, however, easily evolves into an infantilizing move when the remark is made, that the Congolese are too nice to change things, or that dancing and making music distracts them from real politics. This is not a general digression, but a frequent one among Congo-supporters. The genuine 'Congo fan' might be talking like this:

And I think, you probably discovered this in your interviews, but Congo is very attaching in a strange way. And I think maybe it's being so, everything being so out of proportion. You come to the size of the country, the scale of the problems, you know, Goma is like, it's not only like, 'Oh we have a problem with sexual violence and conflict'. 'Rape capital of the world'. Or you know just the nature, it's so big. You've probably seen this Congo is as big as Western Europe. And all of these countries fit in. Or the Congo River second largest in the world. Forest. Yes. Completely impunishable. Or rebellions. Yeah! We have a lot of them. Or. Just, it's something really fascinating in a way. And the Congolese are, you know, really strong people. Especially in Kinshasa. I would often think about how these people get by. It's so impressive. Nine million people or how many in this, with the infrastructure it's impressive. And often with such a good sense of humor and with music and going out drinking and dancing and you know it's something very impressive about it. I find.[45]

The opposite position is exemplified by a Belgian EU staff member who told me the following in response to my 'mars question' designed to spur imaginative thinking about the Congo:

KK: And the last question: Imagine you were on Mars and you saw the world and next to you there is ET and you see the world with the Congo and the links between the Congo and the world and what is happening there. How would you explain the situation to ET sitting next to you?

RESPONDENT: In the Congo? In the Congo?

KK: Yes.

RESPONDENT: I have never asked myself this question. That's difficult. At the same time, it's a really likeable people you know. They are a bit like children who are recurrently naughty and you have to sanction them again and again. And even that role of sanctioner, I am not sure why we should adopt this role. Because they are entirely respectable. At the same time they are not mature yet. They mix up their public coffers with their own pockets. The money of the state, that which comes from taxes is for the people. You need to distribute it. They have not understood this yet, you know. They are not mature or I am hesitant to acknowledge it, and it is genetic. That means it is going to take a long time. We have a certain responsibility however. Because we know very well what is going on. It's in the papers. You knew before coming here that there is a lot of corruption here.[46]

These racist, paternalist and condescending attitudes certainly do not go unnoticed in the Congo. Onesphore Sematumba, one of the heads of Goma's Pole Institute, related an episode about Jacques Chirac and Joseph Kabila to me to sum up his take on the relationship between the West and the Congo:

[Joseph Kabila after his inauguration, KK] goes to Jacques Chirac and Jacques Chirac says: 'But this young man is marvellous. He is learning fast.' Ha, right. They say he is learning fast. We are talking about the head of state, ha, he is learning fast. Others, I don't know who exactly, say: 'But this young man has an extraordinary capacity to listen.' They are finding him qualities and they say them out loud. As if it was … I do not see president Sarkozy saying about Obama that he is learning fast.[47]

This chapter has shown two things: First, in the policy world, reductionist and pathologizing ways of enacting the Congo dominate. The government is malevolent, the state failed and the economy criminal and unproductive. Second, among intervention personnel there is serious scrutiny and attempts at understanding but condescension and racism persist nonetheless. Whenever the potential of the Congo becomes more prominent as in recent approaches to the economy, this is intimately tied to the 'natural' dimension of the Congo not the 'social' one. The Congo has a lot of potential because of the fertility of its soil or the power of its rivers. When human institutions are required which need to be built by people, very little potential is left. These assessments provide a fertile ground for humanitarian and peacebuilding actors to legitimize and perpetuate their work in and for the Congo.

Notes

1 See the 2014 Third World Quarterly special edition on knowledge production by the International Crisis Group (Bliesemann de Guevara, 2014).
2 See previous chapter on Kabila's strategies of rule.
3 See further Ann Laudati's illuminating piece on the 'economies of violence' in the Congo (2013).
4 This passage is based on field notes taken in Goma between August and October 2009.
5 NGO New York 1, 18 November 2011; UN Goma 11 October 2009; UN Humanitarian Goma 1, 4 October 2009; MONUSCO Civilian Goma 3, 25 September 2009; Donor Goma 3, 12 September 2009.
6 NGO Goma 19, 18 September 2009.
7 Donor Goma 1, 5 October 2009.
8 Translated from the French, Interview Donor Goma 3, 12 September 2009.
9 The Congo ranks 2nd on the failed state index after Somalia and 187th and last on UNDP's Human Development Index (www.foreignpolicy.com/failed_states_index_2012_interactive; http://hdr.undp.org/en/statistics/, last accessed 26 February 2015).
10 Jan Vansina is a historian.
11 See Koddenbrock (2013a) and Koddenbrock and Schouten (2014) for a more extended discussion of this effect.
12 For example UN Humanitarian 6, Donor Goma 1, MONUSCO Goma 5, NGO Goma 3, UN HQ New York 6.
13 Donor Goma 3, 11 September 2009.
14 Donor Goma 1, 5 October 2009.
15 Interview NGO Goma 2, 22 September 2009 [translation from the German, KK].
16 Interview UN HQ New York 5, 23 September 2011.
17 NGO Goma 3, 5 October 2009; NGO Goma 19, 18 September 2009; NGO Goma 16, 16 September 2009; Donor Goma 3, 12 September 2009.
18 NGO Goma 3, 5 October 2009.
19 See selection of reports in the annex.

20 MONUSCO Civilian Goma 6, 6 October 2009.
21 MONUSCO Civilian Goma 9, 7 October 2009.
22 See, for example: World Bank (2008, 2011); Institut Français des Relations Internationales (2008); Global Witness (2009, 2011a).
23 For exceptions, please consult International Peace Information Service (2008), United Nations (2011a).
24 See also Pole Institute (2011); CASM – Communities and Artisanal and Small-scale Mining Initiative (2008). These papers also contend that the Bisie mine contributes 70–80 per cent of cassiterite exports from North Kivu but do not explain what share of overall exports or even tax revenues this corresponds to.
25 Among others United Nations (2010d); International Crisis Group (2009; 2010b). The UN's first panel of expert's mandate was to investigate the 'illegal exploitation of natural resources' starting in 2000, underlying the importance of the issue and probably contributing to a path-dependency in thinking about the Congo (United Nations, 2002).
26 On the other hand, it shall not be disputed that the Congo, as noted by Franck Baku, potentially does not live up to its agricultural potential. Instead of importing 100,000 tons of rice from Vietnam a year, it could produce the same amount in the Congo basin (Baku, 2009).
27 See the analysis by Jason Stearns on his blog. Stearns quotes the 2010 budget expecting US$2.1 billion of foreign budget support. Importantly, in 2010, China is the biggest donor with US$980 million ahead of the World Bank with 927. http://congosiasa.blogspot.de/2009/10/how-much-is-congo-getting.html, last accessed 15 March 2013. The annual budget provided by the budget ministry indicates for 2011 an even larger amount of foreign budget support of US$2.4 billion (Government of the DR Congo, 2011).
28 See interview with Laura Heaton on Jason Stearn's blog at http://congosiasa.blogspot. de/2013/03/interview-is-there-too-much-focus-on.html#comment-form, last accessed 15 March 2013.
29 A notable exception is a report by the Netherlands Institute of International Relations Clingendael (2011).
30 This expression was coined by UN Special Representative on Sexual Violence in Conflict Margot Wallström during a briefing of the UN Security Council in April 2010, see www.un.org/apps/news/story.asp?NewsID=34502#.UUN3bhfaPh4, last accessed 15 March 2015.
31 See the appendix on method for the interview guide.
32 See also Weiss and Crayannis (2004); NGO Goma 19, 18 September 2009.
33 Donor Goma 3, 12 September 2009.
34 NGO Berlin 1, 29 July 2009.
35 MONUSCO Civilian 5, 2 October 2009.
36 Donor Goma 3, 12 September 2009.
37 MONUSCO Civilian Goma 4, 29 September 2009.
38 UN Humanitarian Goma 6, 20 September 2009.
39 NGO Goma 17, 16 September 2009.
40 UN Humanitarian Goma 6, 20 September 2009.
41 MONUSCO Civilian 5, 2 October 2009.
42 Pioneering work on racism and racializing concepts in UN missions, and development work has been done by Baaz (2005) and Razack (2004).
43 NGO Goma 2, 22 September 2009; NGO Goma 19, 18 September 2009; NGO Goma 17, 16 September; Donor Goma 3, 12 September 2009; Donor Goma 4, 26 September 2009; MONUSCO Civilian Goma 4 29 September 2009; MONUSCO Civilian Goma 5, 2 October 2009; MONUSCO Civilian Goma 2, 25 September 2009.
44 See John Hobson's instructive analysis of Western 'International Theory' from 1760 to 2010 in which he argues: 'While the discursive *form* of scientific racism has not

re-appeared in international theory, it is nevertheless striking how much of its *content* finds contemporary voice in offensive and defensive Eurocentric institutionalism', Hobson (2012). For a good genealogy of 'scientific racism' see also Kerner (2008) and an influential argument on neo-racism by Etienne Balibar (1991).

45 UN HQ New York 5, 22 September 2012.

46 Donor Goma 3, 12 September 2009. Translated from the French, KK: 'KK: Et la dernière question si vous étiez sur mars et vous voyez le, le monde et à côté de vous il y a un martien et vous voyez le monde avec le Congo et les liens entre le Congo et le monde et qu'est-ce qui se passe là. Comment vous expliquerez, expliqueriez la situation au martien à côté de vous; Respondent: Au Congo? Sur le Congo? KK: Oui. Respondent: La je me suis jamais posé la question. Ca c'est difficile. En même temps c'est un peuple qui est si attachant tu sais. C'est un petit peu des enfants qui font des bêtises à répétition et qu'il faut réprimander à chaque fois. Et même ce rôle de faire la réprimande tu vois je ne vois pas pourquoi on prendra ce rôle-là. Parce que ce sont des tout à fait respectables. Et en même temps ils ne sont pas mûrs encore. Ils confondent le trésor public avec leur cassette personnelle. L'argent de l'Etat, l'argent qui est prélevé pour les taxes est pour le peuple. Faut le distribuer. Ils ne ont pas compris ça encore tu vois. Ils ne sont pas mûrs ou alors, ou alors ils ont ou alors je me fais des illusions et c'est c'est génétique quoi. Et c'est génétique c'est rare. Ca veut dire que ça va durer. Nous on a une responsabilité quand même. Parce qu'on sait très bien ce qui se passe. C'est dans les journaux, c'est dans la presse. Tu le savais avant de venir ici qu'il y avait la corruption ici.'

47 Onesphore Sematumba, Goma, 29 September 2009. '[Joseph Kabila après son inauguration, KK] va chez Jaques Chirac et Jaques Chirac il dit: mais ce jeune homme il est merveilleux. Il apprend vite. Ha voilà. On dit qu'il apprend vite. C'était le chef d'Etat ha il apprend vite. Bon, d'autres je ne sais pas qui, ils disent mais ce jeune homme là il a, il a une capacité d'écoute extraordinaire. On est en train de lui trouver des qualités et on les dit à haute voie. Comme si c'était … Moi je ne vois pas, je ne vois pas le président Sarkozy de dire d'Obama qu'il apprend vite.' Translation from the French, KK.

3 Managing the two faces of intervention

NGOs and the UN between public proclamations and operations

Intervention actors not only produce and rely on knowledge about the Congo as object of intervention. They also need specialist knowledge about their core business practices. Intervention actors are constantly rebuilding and reproducing their field. Specialist knowledge is essential in two ways: one, it informs operations; two, this knowledge is the United Nations' peacekeeping and humanitarian departments and NGOs' genuine contribution to specialist and public debate on intervention. Both of these are essential parts of the practice of humanitarian intervention.

While public debate on peacekeeping and humanitarian aid is rather restricted to times of large-scale disasters like the Tsunami in 2004, the Haiti earthquake in 2011 or Islamist attacks in Mali in 2013 the professional and bureaucratic fields of peacekeeping and humanitarian aid have expanded massively over the last 20 years. The funds spent on humanitarian action have risen from about US$6 billion in the 1990s to US$22 billion per year in 2013 (Development Initiatives, 2014: 4), those on peacekeeping from US$800 million to US$8 billion, and the number of peacekeeping soldiers and staff deployed across the globe, but primarily in Africa, increased from 14,000 to 124,000 (Benner and Rotmann, 2010: 115). The number of humanitarian field staff at the UN and NGOs is estimated to be 274,000 working for more than 150 NGOs with an annual budget of more than US$10 million a year (United Nations, 2013b: 11). With the rise of organizations and personnel came an increase in meetings, workshops and conferences to coordinate and move discussions forward. The reports analysed in this chapter fulfil this double-function. They orient the organization and serve as contributions to these professional forums.

Further to this professional field, it is important to highlight that intervention actors operate in a project market, giving shape to the 'NGO-scramble', as Cooley and Ron famously called it (2002). No UN peacekeeping or humanitarian aid could take place without funding. Apart from MSF and World Vision which are very good at attracting private donations, most intervention actors are primarily state funded. 'Donors' are thus a prime audience of intervention actors. Without legitimacy with donors there would be no funding. The project market's core is that donors 'buy' theses projects by funding them. NGOs and the UN know this and allocate resources based on their calculations about this project market, i.e. on how these organizations think they will get the best deal between getting funded and fulfilling their professional and moral aims. 'This means that some of the poorest populations in the world are in competition against each other [...] to become part of projects'. As a prerequisite for funding, then, NGOs and the UN enjoy the 'symbolic value [...] extracted from [beneficiary populations] in exchange for some of them getting help some of the time' (Krause, 2014: 173).

This project market is hardly dependent on operations in the theatre of intervention.[1] As long as the UN and NGOs manage to keep the perceptions right, legitimacy and funding remain sufficient. What happens in the field during operations is thus of limited importance to intervention unless big scandals become public like the support to former Rwandan *génocidaires* in eastern Congo in the mid-1990s or the diversion of food aid by Somali Islamists in 2012. Managing the organizations' image and potential threats and 'reputational risk' (United Nations, 2015: 2) is thus one of the most important pillars of intervention practice.

Apart from the general ability to deal with this market, actors also need to differentiate their products to distinguish themselves from competitors. The humanitarian aid and peacekeeping business is not just one of philanthropy and solidarity. A lot of jobs depend on them and international NGOs have become sizeable bureaucracies with budgets up to more than a billion US dollars annually.[2] Differences between NGOs and UN programmes and agencies are influenced by this structural need to distinguish themselves (Autesserre, 2014: 271). Of course, moral and political considerations have played a role in this, but the bureaucratic and economic logics of intervention have received too little attention (Cooley and Ron, 2002; Krause, 2014).

In order to highlight the logic of this market operating on funding and legitimacy, this chapter zooms in on the ways in which intervention actors deal with the disconnect between operations in the theatre of intervention and their knowledge and public relations practices. In a second step, I will show based on my field research in the Congo that many of the principles, norms and concepts used to legitimize their work and to attract funding are highly contested conceptually and implemented in quite a messy and contradictory manner on the ground.

This book argues that humanitarian and peacekeeping products are also in such high demand because they are judged according to their public face and without taking into account their messy operational face. The public face is essential because it is the focus of analysts, donors and the media. Its look serves to instil legitimacy and thus contributes to fundraising, it helps to symbolically differentiate various intervention products and organizations, and it creates the impression of constant evolution and adaptation to changing trends and circumstances. Operational intervention is decidedly less important. The often criticized neglect of 'the beneficiary' and its participation in decision-making is a logical consequence of this priority. What happens in North Kivu as part of operational intervention practice is much less decisive for the legitimacy of intervention.

Disciplinary debates on intervention

Heavily shaped by the general approach to research in the disciplines, intervention scholarship in IR, anthropology and development studies has differed substantially. In IR, debates about peacekeeping, humanitarian aid and development largely take place on a conceptual terrain, undisturbed by the messiness of intervention reality on the ground. In IR, scholarship does not need deep immersion into the object of study to be published. Anthropology mostly requires exactly that. Without about one year of field research, one cannot become a proper anthropologist. Development studies and peace and conflict studies, unburdened by overly hermetic discussions about their disciplinary identity, have traditionally straddled the divide between abstract theorizing and field research.

In IR, intervention scholarship like the liberal peace debate (Chandler, 2010: 22–42; Sabaratnam, 2013, Heathershaw, 2013; Andersen, 2012; Cunliffe, 2012) has thus adopted a very conceptual approach to intervention. The operational face of intervention hardly matters. When David Chandler identifies the rise of post-liberalism or resilience, he 'finds' these in academic and policy discussion and policy reports. Meera Sabaratnam, by contrast, in her decolonial critique of the liberal peace debate, builds on some field research but ultimately engages in a conceptual juxtaposition of decolonial thinkers like Fanon and Cabral to the white, male, anglophone, liberal peace debate. In anthropology, quite the opposite. Influential scholars of humanitarian aid and peacekeeping study the intricacies of humanitarian operations in their different localities be they in Caracas, Paris, Conakry or Beirut and have often tried to link them to biopolitical global governing rationalities (Fassin, 2012; Agier, 2008, 2010; Ticktin, 2011; Redfield, 2013; Kosmatopoulos, 2012).

Yet, an increasing number of studies with a less definite disciplinary character has been published on intervention. Building on the tradition of participant observation initiated by Barbara Harrel-Bond's *Imposing Aid* (1986), a study of refugee assistance in South Sudan in the early 1980s, several works of scholar-practitioners have highlighted the disconnect between claims and reality between the public and the operational face of intervention (Waal, 1997; Terry, 2002; Duffield, 2008; Marriage, 2006; Autesserre, 2010, 2014). Examining this literature inevitably reveals that there have been changes in degree, but the business of humanitarian aid and peacekeeping have essentially struggled with two main problems since their inception: their longevity despite their short-term approach and their unknown or even detrimental long-term effects on social and political order in the places of intervention.[3]

In his most recent work on the 'bunkerization of aid' (2012) Mark Duffield has provided evidence that intervention looks much less shiny on the ground than glossy PR might make us think. In her widely-read *The Trouble with Congo* (2010), Séverine Autesserre tried to show why peacekeeping in the Congo has not worked yet and has provided recommendations on how to achieve that. In her recent more global perspective on *Peaceland* (2014), Autesserre describes the milieu of peacekeepers and builders in several locales like Afghanistan, the Congo and others to show how they work and what works for them.[4]

My argument about and approach to intervention in this chapter has been inspired by these works but is most in tune with Monika Krause's work who recently published *The Good Project* (2014) and Zoe Marriage's *Not Breaking the Rules, not Playing the Game* (2006). Built on Pierre Bourdieu's field theory and based on headquarters interviews in Paris and London, Krause shows how humanitarian organizations like MSF or Médecins du Monde *actually* work. She is not driven by the normative urge to improve humanitarian aid or peacekeeping but calmly analyses the logics of the humanitarian aid field beyond their public proclamations. Marriage, in turn, based on Festinger's psychological theory (Marriage, 2006: 10) explores the ways NGOs deal with cognitive dissonance, i.e. the fact that their work does not match their proclamations, and how the invocation of rules and the disregard for not adhering to them allow humanitarian assistance to go unabated.

This is what I do in this book, but with a focus on two things that go beyond these works: the history and politics of the Congo, and the interveners' lived experiences and reflections. I focus on a single object of intervention, the Congo, in order to be able to put humanitarian aid and peacekeeping and the surrounding policy scene into historical and postcolonial context. This book relies explicitly on the reflections of humanitarians and peacekeepers to make the practice of humanitarian intervention more tangible, to give the analysis texture.

As I will show in this chapter, intervention thrives on the disregard for operational practice, for the messiness and contradictions during operations go unnoticed if critics mostly focus on normative debates, doctrine and policy declarations. As anthropologists David Lewis and David Mosse put it most poignantly:

> the disjuncture arising from the autonomy of practice from rationalizing policy is not an unfortunate 'gap to be bridged' between intention and action, but is instead necessary and must therefore be actively maintained and reproduced. Since 'success' demands that action be interpreted as the execution of official policy, competing logics and contingencies of action become necessarily hidden.
>
> (Lewis and Mosse, 2006a: 6)

In line with what Lewis and Mosse are arguing here, I consider the divide between the public and the operational face of intervention as useful and essential for Western intervention practice to remain legitimate and stable. A holistic view of intervention has to find a way of thinking both as simultaneously constitutive of humanitarian aid and peacekeeping. Promoting operational, rather anarchic assistance practice to the same level of attention as the lively conceptual and normative debating practice leads to a more nuanced view of humanitarian aid and peacekeeping and contributes to making their utility less self-evident. Legitimizing intervention on a normative level is one thing, legitimizing it with a view to messy assistance practice is another. Intervention, however, is both.

Not only does intervention produce projects but it aims to produce its overall legitimacy by providing symbolically differentiated products. The constant renewal of products – akin to a capitalist process of innovation – works by packaging intervention work in constantly evolving normative-conceptual clothing.[5] To render this symbolic differentiation controllable it is highly useful to manage conflicting evidence from operational practice and keep it under the radar. This is the reason for the very selective surfacing of evidence from the operational side of intervention. If normative and conceptual debates are lively and successful the other face of intervention, operational assistance provision, is able to operate relatively freely. Operational assistance statistics, the number of people reached or the timeliness of a response, do feature in annual reports and some degree of accountability towards donors and taxpayers is necessary, but all of the involved know that these data are malleable and not set in stone.

The importance of the public face of intervention for the UN and NGOs

That catering to the public and donors is essential to keep intervention legitimate is no secret. This CARE-sponsored report argues:

> As agencies struggle to assert humanitarian values, improve accountability and enhance their effectiveness within an increasingly politicised aid system, consistent, impartial and objective data will become increasingly important. On its own, this will not change the political economy of humanitarian aid. But it will help agencies rationalise their decision-making, and in the process provide a compelling justification and strong moral authority on which to build a more just, equitable and humane international relief system.
>
> (Oxley, 2001: 30)

This quote clearly articulates what is at issue here. In the year 2001 already, the analyst sees agencies struggling 'to assert humanitarian values'. This means two things: first, asserting these values is important for them and with it the moral terrain and quest for legitimacy; second, it has become more difficult because the aid system is 'increasingly politicized'. More actors populate the humanitarian field and make it harder for humanitarian agencies to articulate their humanitarian value. Because of this, 'objective data' will become important to enable humanitarians to regain that moral high ground. This implies that, previously, this objective data neither existed nor was it needed because humanitarians were free to act anarchically and did not have to report on the assistance level of their practice.[6] This data, then, will enable the agencies to make more informed decisions (they were apparently more haphazard before) and will contribute to greater legitimacy and increased 'moral authority' for humanitarian relief.

The CARE manager quoted here thus inadvertently articulates the two faces of intervention and their relative importance. The key to success is moral authority gained through public perceptions. Humanitarian aid strives towards the ethical high ground. What is happening on the ground only features as 'data' which is instrumental for moral authority but not the most important concern in itself.

The UN, and with it UN peacekeeping, operates in a similarly moral project market nowadays. Although the UN has in the past played an important role in diplomacy and foreign policy, its importance for peace and security has been declining since the 2000s. The UN is now essentially a big NGO, servicing the poor and poorest with its large peacekeeping, development and humanitarian apparatus. It comes as no surprise that the UN study on the protection of civilians[7] expresses the same need for moral authority:

> There is no more compelling or credible stance for a mission than to advocate for the most vulnerable. This is deeply tied to assisting the host State in fulfilling its protection responsibilities, and in speaking up if that is not a responsibility that the government can meet. That role is the basis of the UN's moral authority, and a powerful tool in winning over reluctant peacemakers, in speaking truth to the abusive, and in building credibility with both the local population and those worldwide concerned for civilians caught in conflict. Such moral suasion can have a tangible result: this apolitical but firm stance will help deliver credence to the mission's authority and determination to use its impartiality against those who challenge its efforts. In the end, this approach to protection of civilians does not guarantee success. But the effort to protect will engender respect and stave off those who would consider challenging the United Nations in the future.
>
> (Holt and Taylor, 2009: 16)

Advocacy for the most vulnerable and reminding the state of its protection responsibilities serves here as a tool to increase respect for the UN and 'stave off' future critics. The moral register and its instrumental use for the overall organization's legitimacy are at the forefront. Actual military or humanitarian protection practice only features in an indirect and curiously ambiguous manner. An alternative focusing on operations on the ground gets more tangible if one considers the following *hypothetical* wording: 'Robust and immediate deterrence of peace spoilers and the comprehensive use of its mandate to use all military means will help deliver credence to the mission's authority'. This choice of words would highlight hands-on operational action not public relations.

Consider also the number and order of recommendations given by this key report (Holt and Taylor, 2009: 9–13). There are eight recommendations lasting from understanding threats to civilians better to more clearly defining protection and building better partnerships to managing expectations better. 'Doing more' to protect civilians in theatre comes last. While this does not mean that is considered unimportant, it is clearly not prioritized. It is one among many concerns for the peacekeeping bureaucracy. Conceptual clarifications and alliance building dominate because the public face of intervention is the main focus of 'doing' peacekeeping. Conceptual debate is the most successful strategy to legitimize intervention.

Since Western intervention consists of both faces and sets of practices, their relationship is crucial. In what follows below I will show that operational practice often plainly contradicts the proclamations made about key issues in policy papers, strategies, resolutions or media statements.[8] These contradictions render the analytical judgment about what intervention actually *is* more difficult. Is humanitarian aid principled because it proclaims so, or is it not principled because it constantly violates the principles during operational practice in the Congo? The strategy here is not about scandalizing the obvious disconnect between proclamations and the operational, or between words and deeds, but it consists of taking seriously both sets of practices in order to highlight the inherently difficult decision about the *being* and character of intervention. With this ambiguity, its legitimacy is also no longer guaranteed. Taking operational practice just as seriously forces analysts and critics to deal with a more ambiguous and negotiated practice of intervention.[9]

Positioning humanitarian aid: principles, space and need

The conundrum of humanitarian aid has always been this: can humanitarian aid come to the rescue of those in need of life-saving support without tackling the root causes of this need? Since the establishment of large-scale aid bureaucracies with the end of colonial rule in the early 1960s, humanitarian aid has been at pains to distinguish itself from development work and even more transformative endeavours like military occupation. With the boom in military intervention, the strong belief in democracy promotion and the rise of human rights organizations of the 1990s, this act of distinction had become more vital. 'New humanitarianism' and civil–military relations have thus become core topics among the humanitarian scene (Chandler, 2002; Slim, 2002; Reid, 2010). Because of the increasing number of military actors acting alongside or in concert with humanitarian NGOs and humanitarian branches of the UN since the US occupation of Afghanistan, and the large-scale military relief operations during Tsunami relief, this quest for distinction has moved back to centre stage. The market of aid and intervention products has become so crowded that distinctions have become both harder and more essential to make.

Several attempts have been made to label how different humanitarian organizations position themselves on this continuum of transformation from 'emergency' to 'alchemism' (Barnett, 2011), i.e. working on causes or disregarding them, or from 'Wilsonians to Dunantists' (Krause, 2014: 111). In essence, these distinctions are necessary for the intervention market to function, to be visible to donors and to retain necessary levels of moral integrity for the inside of these organizations themselves.[10]

The 'humanitarian principles' in their varying interpretations have formed the core capital of distinction for humanitarian aid organizations. The ideas at the heart of the principles were already enshrined in the 1864 Geneva Conventions but they were only explicitly formulated in 1965 by Jean Pictet's legal commentary for the ICRC (Pictet, 1979).[11] The principles were then included in the MSF charter when it was founded in 1967, and partly taken up by the UN landmark General Assembly Resolution on humanitarian aid 46/182 in 1991 and by various other organizations and donor proclamations like the *EU Consensus on Humanitarian Aid* (European Commission, 2008). Jean Pictet at the time proposed seven principles among them the five most important ones universality, humanity, independence, neutrality and impartiality.

The legal status of these principles is weak. In fact, they could be termed bureaucratic operating procedures or even slogans. Whenever humanitarian organizations provide assistance they *claim* to adhere to these principles. The principles of universality and humanity indicate the global ambition enshrined in them. The principles thus call for a universal and global opportunity to live up to them. This essentially tries to bring about a global operating space for UN and NGO humanitarian aid. The fact that various humanitarian donors and actors define these principles in a different way underlines that these differences also serve to distinguish themselves on the project and funding market.

The ICRC as the initial doyen of the principles, for example, defines neutrality as 'in order to continue to enjoy the confidence of all, the Movement may not take sides in hostilities or engage at any time in controversies of a political, racial, religious or ideological nature' (ICRC, 1996: 7). They consider impartiality as:

> it [the ICRC, KK] makes no discrimination as to nationality, race, religious beliefs, class or political opinions. It endeavours to relieve the suffering of individuals, being guided solely by their needs, and to give priority to the most urgent cases of distress.
>
> (ICRC, 1996: 4)

Independence is for the ICRC to: 'always maintain their autonomy so that they may be able at all times to act in accordance with the principles of the Movement' (1996: 9). These principles thus posit humanitarian aid as focusing on need, staying clear of politics and being autonomous of other broader concerns, and of not favouring any party to the conflict.

Organizations' understanding of the principles varies and expresses gradual or even fundamental differences as part of their positioning in the project market. The UN has not adopted the independence principle, for obvious reasons. The UN as a whole could hardly claim to stay clear of other political objectives. The EU, another political actor, however does include independence. Oxfam has dropped neutrality and so forth. This indicates the performative function of these principles. Adopting one principle and abandoning another helps to position the organization on the market of intervention.

The divide between public and operational practice, between what is made visible and what is happening below the radar of attention in the field becomes obvious during field research. Operational intervention practice is negotiated and part of an intricate field of social relations in North Kivu. While it shall not be disputed that some humanitarians and peacekeepers try their best to live up to the norms and principles they defend in public, there is a wealth of evidence on the essential disconnect between these two core practices of intervention. However, as argued above, as long as operational practice is not scrutinized, interventions will be judged according to their public face in which Congolese social life and the messiness of assistance practice plays virtually no role. In what follows, I will provide a reading of the conceptual tensions on the public face of intervention itself and on the negotiated and messy character of operational intervention practice to allow for more informed judgment on what intervention in the Congo is.

The principles in practice

The MSF manager in Goma was infamous for her critical remarks. She was also regarded as an 'arrogant isolationist' (Bradol and Jézéquel, 2010: 11) that did not take part in the UN cluster system which was set up in 2005 to respond to more demand for coordination among the ever-growing humanitarian scene. 2009, however, was the time of recurrent rebellion in eastern Congo. It was not the RCD of the early 2000s or the M23 of late 2012. The group was then called CNDP. In the weekly humanitarian information meeting hosted by UN OCHA, the MSF manager exclaimed towards the MONUSCO spokesperson who had just given a presentation: 'We don't want your patrols. But we want your information. We are about to set up an operation in Ntoto[12] and we need to know more about the security situation there. What can you tell us?[13]

MSF is one of the organizations which mostly refrain from using military patrols to highlight that they are independent from the regime change or statebuilding agendas of occupation forces or UN peacekeeping missions. However, asking for military information is not in line with the independence principle which calls for complete autonomy. This is a less pure, more grounded approach to independence than some public MSF proclamations on the evils of military humanitarianism insinuate (Weissman, 2010). Overt cooperation in the open public through military convoys is off limits but profiting from MONUSCO's capacity of information gathering is seen as sufficiently independent. A very principled approach would have to stay clear of all kinds of cooperation with military actors like the UN peacekeeping mission. Yet, there is a lot going on under the radar of seemingly free-standing principles.

Whether an organization of Western intervention pursues longer term political aims or not, and thus strays from the independence principle, often depends on where you look and who you talk to among this organization. The American NGO International Rescue Committee (IRC), for example, is among the largest organization in terms of funds spent in eastern Congo. On its website, it presents itself as a humanitarian relief organization, coming to the 'rescue' of the Congolese. In Goma, this humanitarian impression is first confirmed by an IRC staff member talking about the virtues of her work in contrast to more developmental, transformative approaches (see further Koddenbrock 2012a):

I wouldn't say that we are solving the situation or that we are preventing the future situation. I mean we do our best but I don't see it as a solution to the problem. But I do it because I think someone needs to do it. Particularly for me I have evolved from doing general development work into emergency work, and the reason I went up there is because it is actual life-saving work. It is actually urgent. It needs to be done or there will be mass problems. And development, I see it sort of more long-term, it might work, it might not work. You could probably make a case that the Congolese should be doing it themselves rather than us doing it for them. Whereas emergency work, if someone doesn't respond that's the end of it. So for me it's in my own head more justifiable.[14]

This IRC staff member engages in relief work that, for her, can and should be clearly distinguished from development work. Another staff member, this time based in New York, says just the opposite about the IRC:

IRC presents itself as a humanitarian but it's like one per cent of what we actually do. You know we're doing so little well drilling and blanket distribution. It is one per cent of our budget in Congo. There are countries where that is a bit higher but it's by no means what we're doing. When we're working it's always working with local NGOs, working with local partners. Working through governments where possible. Strengthening governments, strengthening institutions.[15]

It is obvious from these quotes that public proclamations and operational realities may differ. There are two realities of intervention. The New York staff member posits the IRC as a development NGO which consciously does not follow the principle of independence from political structures. The Goma staff member says the opposite. How principled humanitarian aid is in practice is contested. Among the same organization you find staff members working in and on the Congo who are happy about its development approach and others who are glad that the IRC is really a humanitarian and not a development organization. To determine the reality of intervention, public proclamations thus have to be taken with a grain of salt.

A similar indeterminacy is sometimes visible in public self-descriptions. The ICRC's 2009 *Mission Statement* indicates how important it is to position the organization between humanitarian principles and the 'new humanitarianism'. In the statement, the ICRC tries to rhetorically square the circle between dealing with causes of problems and being neutral and independent at the same time:

Analysis provides a basis for deciding on an overall strategy, with specific priorities and objectives, and determines the types of problem and/or the categories of needs on which the ICRC is going to concentrate its efforts and its resources. It is then a matter of developing a strategy aimed not only at addressing the direct consequences of problems, but also – as far as

possible within the framework of neutral and independent humanitarian
activities – their origins and causes.

(International Committee of the Red Cross, 2009a: 13)

As we have seen above, principled humanitarian aid requires absolute independence of any other aims than helping according to need. Yet in the current predic-
ament, this position has become harder to justify. That's why humanitarian
organizations try hard to have the best of both worlds.

The disconnect between public and operational practice is no secret among
intervention organizations. They do not actively trick their customers. A specific
dose of disconnect seems to be useful, however, for two main reasons. First,
many interventions take place in conflict zones. Interveners need to manage their
perceptions. Situations may arise where they need a particular image to be
allowed to work. This is particularly relevant for humanitarian organizations
which assume that without adhering to the humanitarian principles they will not
get access to some conflict zones because the power brokers of the area might
regard them as threatening. Second, ambiguity in normative debates may be
useful because it allows defending all kinds of activities in case somebody ven-
tures to scrutinize them to check whether they are in line with their mandate.
Yet, overt ambiguity might damage their unique selling proposition. Clarity
legitimizes and shows customers what they will get. Ambiguity or paradoxical
approaches, by contrast, serve to shield operations from criticism. Public proclamations thus always need to strike a fine balance between these two options.

The recent flagship report by Oxfam entitled *Crises in a New World Order*
(2012) also features the normative turmoil many humanitarian organizations find
themselves in because of conflicting expectations directed at them and the
crowdedness of the field. Oxfam entered the humanitarian field late because it
acted as a classic development NGO at first. It diversified its development portfolio in the wake of the 'new humanitarianism'. Oxfam is now at great pains to
preserve their position in both the humanitarian and development fields which
translates into highly ambiguous normative and conceptual proclamations with
regards to the principle of impartiality. Impartiality, as indicated above, has
come under fire after humanitarian agencies treated former Rwandan *génocidaires* equally to the victims of the genocide (Waal, 1997: 204–212; Terry, 2002).
The presence of Islamists in Somalia now constitutes a similar moral imbroglio
for humanitarian organizations. Oxfam writes:

> The dilemmas that humanitarian workers confront in crises like Somalia
> cannot be ignored. That does not mean that impartiality should be comprom-
> ised; it means accepting that peace, development, and environmental
> sustainability are as noble ambitions as humanitarianism. Humanitarians
> have sometimes forgotten that truth. All those aims must be pursued,
> without compromising the humanitarian imperative to save lives, but with
> the humility to accept that there are difficult choices between different strat-
> egies. In Somalia, for example, 'taxes' to armed groups may not constitute

ethical pragmatism to get aid through. Rather, they may fuel the violence that largely created the crisis in the first place. In the long term, they may cause more suffering than the aid agencies' relief can reduce. In that case, they are far from humanitarian or principled.

(Oxfam, 2012: 22)

It is obvious from the quote above that Oxfam does not dare to express clearly what they are saying here: sometimes the principle to offer aid to everyone who needs it (impartiality), and particularly to those who need it most, may prolong conflict and should thus be disregarded. This means, in these situations, impartiality should indeed be compromised after weighing costs and benefits. The report, however, explicitly argues that 'impartiality should not be compromised' while proposing the opposite a few lines later.

This strategy of ambiguity, in case it is a strategy, has a welcome side effect. Whenever donors or the public wonder about Oxfam's position on humanitarian principles they can point to this: we take the principles very seriously, but we acknowledge that difficult choices have to be made in specific situations. Operationally, Oxfam retains its leeway because both being taxed by rebels and refusing to be taxed and abandoning operations can be explained within the framework set out in the report. This report allows them to act in a principled and in a less principled manner whenever they deem fit. This is pragmatic and underlines nicely what public NGO proclamations are: a useful performance.

An alternative way of dealing with the conflicting normative demands of the humanitarian principles and 'new humanitarianism' on the project market has recently been tried by UN OCHA. In contrast to the paradoxes and ambiguities among the IRC, ICRC and Oxfam proclamations above, OCHA embarks on a strategy of rallying the troops for the purity of the principles again. This entails not to allow the obvious challenges and ambiguities involved in contemporary humanitarian aid to surface in their reports.

One of the masters of mobilization and advocacy for humanitarian principles, former UN Under-Secretary General for Humanitarian Affairs Jan Egeland, begins the UN OCHA report entitled *To Stay and to Deliver* in the following way:

Because humanitarian work has become so widespread and so visible, peoples all over the world now expect that the needy should get immediate relief when conflict or disasters strike. All major religions, ideologies, and humanistic philosophies prescribe that the sick, the suffering, and the starved should be helped irrespective of race, creed or culture. But this expectation, shared by heads of state and the public at large, that humanitarians will rush to the neediest irrespective of circumstances, is not supported by a corresponding unconditional political and military support for the basic humanitarian principles that are a precondition for secure and unrestricted access by our impartial humanitarian workers.

(United Nations, 2011b: viii)

This is a strategy of rallying the troops because it tries to reinsert the principle of universalism through the back door and because it does not problematize the impartiality of humanitarian aid at all – contrary to what the Oxfam report did. For Egeland, the observation that people in need deserve help globally amounts to an expectation that 'humanitarians' come to the rescue. He thus ably inserts the well-known figure of the humanitarian where villagers or ordinary people could have featured. The humanitarian is not the natural and self-evident figure to implement a universal imperative to help those in need. The municipality, regional government or associations, so called 'first-responders' living in the area, would be alternative candidates. However, they do not feature at the expense of the abstract 'humanitarian'.

The deployment of impartiality in this passage deserves closer scrutiny. Egeland posits that, in principle, humanitarian workers are impartial. However, since people like the Union of Islamic Courts in Somalia (see Oxfam report above) tax these workers when they want to deliver their aid, he identifies a lack of unconditional political and military support for the humanitarian principles. He implicitly grants that in a situation like the Somali one, humanitarian principles become hard to adhere to. By posing the problem this way, Egeland asserts that the principles only work if they are allowed to work. This is a rare glimpse into operational practice of humanitarian aid. Normative debates on the principles convey the image of free-floating normative principles. In fact, they are bound by context and practice. This is only acknowledged tacitly and privately by humanitarian organizations and Egeland attempts to gloss over it.

Always trying to be the avant-garde of humanitarian aid, MSF has recently decided to adopt the opposite strategy, a strategy of transparency and honesty. This strategy amounts to acknowledging openly the tension between the publicly said and the operationally done. MSF has begun to highlight how entangled humanitarian aid is with local power structures and institutions. This strategy can most usefully be analysed with a view to another core concept that works to enable humanitarians to do their work – humanitarian space – a concept that MSF has coined and remodelled for many years.

Humanitarian space: appealing to abstract humanity

Like the principles, the concept of humanitarian space has a self-empowering function for humanitarian aid: 'Indeed, the two feed on each other, as claims about the need to preserve a space beyond politics are intimately tied to the argument about the importance of upholding humanitarian principles as a means to secure access' (Sending, 2010). Originally enshrined in the Geneva Conventions of 1949 and 1977, humanitarian space was an operating space granted by warring parties of inter-state conflict which 'should enjoy special protection even amidst ongoing conflict' (Esteves, 2010: 622).

Paulo Esteves describes how this space moved from a state-sanctioned space to a self-empowering notion in the 1990s. Former MSF-President Rony Braumann played an integral part in redefining humanitarian space. For Braumann, humanitarian space amounted to a 'space of freedom in which we are free to evaluate needs, free to monitor the distribution and use of relief goods, and free to have a dialogue with the people' (quoted in Esteves, 2010: 622). Freedom is the key term here. Braumann tries to bring about a free humanitarian space that is not explicitly dependent on any party's consent but implicitly refers to some abstract humanity that humanitarian aid should be able to deal with freely.

Not surprisingly, in 2011, we witness yet another conceptual shift away from the notion of a free humanitarian space. Remember: constant evolution and soul-searching performs an essential legitimizing function because it indicates a continuous quest for the best solution on the public face of intervention. Marie-Pierre Allié, acting president of MSF-France, positions MSF as the new avant-garde of an entirely different understanding that is in effect a reversal of Braumann's. It is not ambiguous (Oxfam, ICRC and IRC) or mobilizing for the principles (OCHA) at all. Instead it is about honesty, making transparent that the purity of the principles is a utopia:

> Contrary to the 'shrinking space' theory – which frees aid actors from any responsibility for conquering and defending their own sphere of activity – there are no legitimate perimeters to humanitarian action, valid at all times and in all situations, which become clearly visible once the mists of 'military-humanitarian confusion' have lifted and humanitarians are protected from any political fallout. There is, however, a space for negotiation, power games and interest-seeking between aid actors and authorities. MSF's freedom of action is not rooted in a legal and moral 'space of sovereignty' that simply needs to be proclaimed in order to be automatically acknowledged and respected. It is the product of repeated transactions with local and international political and military forces. Its scope depends largely on the organisation's ambitions, the diplomatic and political support it can rely on and the interest taken in its action by those in power.
>
> (Médecins Sans Frontières, 2011: 3)

MSF is adopting an honesty approach to analysing their work here. Note, however, that the beneficiaries of humanitarian aid do not feature in this new account. But this is not the main point I wish to highlight. President Allié actively questions the notion of an abstract legal and moral space, and argues that what MSF is and does takes place in a complex theatre of intervention which is populated by a number of actors with different interests. In a sweeping move, she even declares as normal the diversion of aid. This was one of the major scandals in the nineties (Waal, 1997) that recently flared up again because the UN World Food Programme (WFP) was accused of losing half of their food aid to Somali rebels.[16] She thus questions one of the main sources of legitimation for humanitarian aid that 'your money reaches the beneficiaries', a rhetorical device aid organizations have been carefully cultivating by shielding the public from the intrusions of the more operational.

This break comes very close to acknowledging interventions' operational practice and of lifting the veil on the often hidden face of intervention. However, it is not the shifting content that stabilizes intervention per se but the practice of conceptual shifting in itself. By constantly bringing up new strategies of positioning the market of intervention is reinvigorated.

The importance of 'need'

Next to the legitimizing function of the principles and the discussion on humanitarian space, a key source of legitimacy lies in the concept and negotiation of beneficiary 'need'. The concept of need is the third of the core vehicles of legitimation of humanitarian action. Despite all talk of risk, vulnerability (Darcy and Hofmann, 2003) and resilience (Chandler, 2012), 'need' continues to be the core rallying call for humanitarian aid. The constant quest of humanitarian actors for more adequate needs assessments serve as important tools of justification and fundraising towards donors. The UN Inter-Agency Standing Committee's integrated needs assessments and UNHCR's global needs assessments are just two examples. Performing a continued search for the adequate measurement of needs has become ever more important since the humanitarian field has grown and become more publicly visible.

Essentially, need operationalizes the principle of impartiality. The existence of objective physical needs[17] makes the practice of impartiality appear possible. It has been repeatedly shown, however, that need is only one among several potentially more decisive factors in humanitarian decision-making (Darcy and Hoffman, 2003; Rubenstein, 2008; Krause, 2014; Binder, Koddenbrock and Horváth, 2013). This is usually decried as a lack of honesty and calls are made to return to real needs-based delivery. Yet, in line with the approach adopted here, this misses the function of performing the quest for needs measurements. Organizations try to foreground the quest and the invocation of need, not the operational practice.

As shown above, donors and organizations alike continuously stress that humanitarian organizations get active 'according to need', 'solely based on need'. Human need is an equivalent to the 'threat to international peace and security' legitimizing peacekeeping. Given its potential breadth there are multiple understandings of human needs deployed to trigger and legitimize humanitarian operations. This was not always the case. The first classic humanitarian organization – the ICRC – simply tended to those wounded in war (Krause, 2014: 101). Needs beyond wounded soldiers were beyond the reach of the ICRC at the time.

As Monika Krause has shown, in contemporary humanitarian aid there are myriad triggers of a specific humanitarian operation in a specific place.[18] There is a multitude of factors next to the apparent purity of need, as Krause proved in her interview-based analysis of decision-making among MSF-France and Action Contre la Faim (Krause, 2014: 22ff.). Krause argues that organizational identity matters, as MSF will cater to medical needs and Save the Children to children's' needs. Continuously changing programme priorities from sexual and gender based violence, to HIV and AIDS, to shelter and education, play a role in shaping who goes where and when to do what. National borders are also decisive as different national standards of living are taken into account to judge on the urgency of an emergency. Need is thus not an absolute category but will be weighed against nation-state statistics. These are fraught with methodological difficulties. Organizations also take great care to be present in a perfect number of countries. Operations in too many countries create too much overhead so operations become hard to manage. An insufficient number of operations might by contrast create an image of too slim a 'portfolio' (Krause, 2014: 28–30). Moreover, donor preferences and media attention matter greatly and the possibility of access to the places of identified need. This extends to security conditions and existing infrastructure like roads. The presence of a military (occupation) force might compromise staff security, because one is perceived as in bed with them, which also strongly discourages NGOs to go where the need is. Then there is the notion of 'added value' which means that it is more attractive to go to places where there are no other organizations or where one's set of skills is not yet available. The character of the populations served also plays a role. If it is very spread out, the cost-benefit ratio of an operation will be less positive, because a smaller number of 'beneficiaries' for each aid dollar invested will be reached. This means camps offer ideal environments to reach people quickly. Camps thus tend to be prioritized over remote and sparsely populated areas, as observed in Goma during the IDP return episode explained in the previous chapter, although this is not warranted by absolute need. Finally, the existence of a strong state and government matters. When they are seen to exist, they are considered responsible for helping their populations in the first place. Needs in failed or weak states will thus be prioritized over needs in the US after hurricane Katrina, for example.

The wealth of these non-principled factors impacting on where needs will be served indicates that similar to the principles, need primarily works to stabilize humanitarian interventions because continuous debate creates the impression of soul-searching and the quest for better work (Binder, Koddenbrock and Horváth, 2013). Being more attentive to the operational level, however, reveals it is much more complicated than that. Need has never shaped humanitarian aid alone. Humanitarian assistance practice is based on a bundle of bureaucratic considerations and operates within an intricate web of power relations and social structures. The strong focus on the conceptualization and measurement of needs and principles occupies analysts and policy makers and keeps them busy with concepts that operate beyond these self-interested concerns and beyond power structures and governments. Analysts are led to think along abstract lines that are based on assumptions of 'void', 'vacuum' or state failure, clearly a notion with a long colonial legacy – think 'terra nullius'. The reality of operational intervention practice is different because there is no void in humanitarian aid on the ground.

MSF's renewed strategy of negotiated humanitarian space full of social relations has been a long time coming. Former MSF-president Bradol now acknowledges, for example, what James Darcy had already indicated in 2003: agencies tend to assess situations in relation to their own programmes (Darcy and Hofmann, 2003: 6). Bradol and Jézéquiel reveal that:

> we are [sometimes, KK] choosing our areas of operation by virtue of their potential for experimentation with new approaches related to early treatment or prevention of malnutrition. [...] Once again, this is not necessarily a problem, but it is helpful to recognise what really influences our operational decisions. In this case, they are related to a particular view of malnutrition as a global issue: our local operations serve as arguments in a series of negotiations over global food and nutrition policies.
>
> (Bradol and Jézéquiel, 2010: 12)

Xavier Crombé was an early advocate for the position MSF adopts publicly today:

> It is part of both humanitarian and peacekeeping public relations to make the role of the welcoming state appear smaller than it is. Need and humanitarian principles are all devoid of any engagement with the public authorities or other de-facto authorities. In forums of reflection or in private, humanitarians tend to stress the multiple dependencies they find themselves in. The work of humanitarian NGOs does indeed not take place in a vacuum. We are compelled to negotiate with a certain number of actors, including Western armies, as well as 'rebellious' armed groups, factions, governments or local authorities that are more or less legitimate, in order to have access to the civil populations that we intend to assist. We should therefore acknowledge in a pragmatic way that we are in fact dependent on these interactions to successfully carry out our activities. This is why, rather than talking about independence to describe our position in the relations of force and domination that characterizes our areas of operation, it seems to me more realistic to talk about the ongoing attempt to balance our dependencies.
>
> (Crombé, 2006: 5)

MSF has started to challenge the abstract need and humanitarian space approach publicly but, in operational practice, is far from taking existing power structures seriously beyond the necessities of negotiation. MSF acknowledges these power structures are there but are often unwilling to cooperate with them. In Goma, an MSF manager told me how this dependence plays out. It is a nuisance to the capacity of self-directed assistance provision.

The manager had been sceptical about the utility of the operations MSF currently pursued in North Kivu. The hospitals and health centres they served were not the ones where need was greatest, according to her. But when they came to the area and had to decide where to engage they had to negotiate with the provincial ministry of health which tries to manage NGO and UN service provision as good as they can. The British NGO Merlin, for example, will get the hospitals around Rutshuru, the German Malteser a little health centre on the road towards Rutshuru and MSF a hospital behind Sake, etc.

KK: And the other question, not about the moral duty but do you think that you have the right to work here?

RESPONDENT: Yes and no. Yes because we're here to provide the assistance to the local population which would otherwise not have it and they don't have a voice to ask for it. Then yes, I think, we do have a right to be here. Again, I think sometimes we get to this blockage where we feel that the right to be here is done through the authorities who as far as we may know do not represent whatsoever the people we're actually trying to help. So you're sort of working in two ways. You're trying to make the authorities happy so you can physically have the legal right to stay. But at the same time we're trying to target the population which we think is most vulnerable and sometimes there is a clash between the two. When we first got here we had a long debate over where, which health centres we are allowed to support. We felt that we had the right to go out to the most remote health centres, again not necessarily the highest numbers but maybe the more vulnerable ones. Areas where they have stock ruptures like essential drugs every month. The authorities didn't want that. The authorities wanted us to stay on like the main access roads which is where the numbers are much higher because for them that was more their priority, you know. The numbers look better at the end of each month. So in the end we kind of had to make a compromise. We did refuse to go to their ones but we ended up going to ones who had maybe higher patient numbers but are still further away. So yeah I think we have a right to be here if we actually respond to the needs of the population. But I think often we mistake that right by thinking, well, the authorities have given us the right to be here therefore we can do whatever we like. I think there is a missing link between the authorities and the local population.[19]

There is a lot going on in this interview passage. On the one hand a complex negotiation of morality takes place. On the other, it shows how MSF calculates and negotiates with the dependencies it finds itself in. The 'right to work' question during my interview served to gauge interviewees' attitudes towards well-known aid criticisms, colonial legacies or the general moral foundations of their work (see next chapter). This MSF manager argues there are two levels of right: a formal level which is expressed by the authorities giving them work permits and visas and a material level where the legitimacy of the authorities is in doubt because she does not feel they are representing their people. She deduces from this distinction that organizations are not free to do whatever they like just because they were granted operating permits. They should be striving to do morally sound work all along.

On the other hand, the intricacies of need and their relationship to negotiations with existing power brokers surface clearly here. The MSF manager assumes that their principles require them to go where the most 'vulnerable' are. Vulnerability is a recent variation on the concept of need. MSF's dependence on local political authorities prevents them from doing so. Negotiations lead to a situation both can live with. This is what Crombé has argued for and that which President Allié turned into the official MSF position in 2011. Obviously, humanitarian aid never happened in a void despite the normative proclamations made. Yet, it is obvious from this interview that accepting the role and priorities of the actually existing government structures is a hard pill to swallow in operational practice, despite the progressive tone of the new public MSF performance about the dependence of assistance.

Seen from this angle, it makes intuitive sense that there is not a single external evaluation of MSF operations available publicly. These evaluations might show how hesitant or even hostile MSF often is to these negotiations. All publications potentially straddling the disconnect between public claims and hidden reality have been undertaken by their own high-level or research staff. The short pieces by former or acting presidents Rony Braumann, Hervé Bradol or Fabrice Weissman, the flagship report on *MSF and Protection: Pending or Closed?* (Soussan, 2008), as well as the book-length volumes on *Humanitarian Negotiations Revealed* (MSF, 2012) and *In the Eyes of Others* (MSF, 2011) all bear witness to this. Analysts have to rely on these non-independent sources or the annual reports which feature an introduction by the acting president summarizing the conceptual debates and challenges taking place throughout the last year and charting the way forward. This fact indicates that acknowledging dependence and the intricacies of decision-making remains part of the public performance at the expense of real scrutiny.

Peacekeeping in question: protection and the robust mandate

Legally, a UN peacekeeping mission is one of the possible reactions to the Charter provision of a 'threat to international peace and security' (UN Charter, Chapter VII). This threat can be brought to the attention of the Security Council by the UN Secretary General, the UN General Assembly and individual UN member states (Bellamy and Williams, 2010: 42). It is noteworthy that early peacekeeping missions like UNEF I (United Nations Emergency Force 1) in 1956 (Suez crisis) and ONUC (Opération des Nations Unies au Congo) 1960–1964 (Congo crisis, see Chapter 1) were mandated by the General Assembly. These mandates predate the massive expansion of UN membership after decolonization. Because of this, the more democratic General Assembly was still used by the Security Council veto powers to pursue their interests. Once the permanent members of the Security Council and their allies were outnumbered in the General Assembly, the Security Council turned into the prime decision-making body on peacekeeping operations.

A UN peacekeeping mission is thus triggered by the impression of the UN Secretary General, the General Assembly or a member state (or a coalition of member states) that international peace and security is under threat or that it

might be in order to claim so. The mission is then dispatched by majority decision in the Security Council (without any veto). What counts as a threat has been
quite varied over time, i.e. the increase in peacekeeping operations went hand in
hand with a broader notion of this 'threat to international peace and security' to
the point of it becoming something of an 'empty signifier' (Laclau and Mouffe,
1985).

As Alex Bellamy *et al.* note, various phenomena were used to identify a 'threat
to international peace and security'. They argue that while initially designed to
cover aggressions of state against state, it came to cover a rebellion in South Rho-
desia (1965) and South Africa's nuclear weapons programme (1977) during the
Cold War. According to Bellamy, the landmark resolution turning the 'threat' into
an essentially empty signifier was Security Council Resolution 688 which identified the flow of Kurdish refugees across the Iraqi border during the First Gulf War
in 1991 as a threat to *international* peace and security. Since then a wealth of
events have served as legitimation to invoke Chapter VII responses: state collapse
in Resolution 794, the overthrow of a democratically elected government in Resolution 841, HIV-Aids (1308), international terrorism (1373), nuclear proliferation
(1540), humanitarian suffering (770), massive human rights abuse (1199) and the
massacre of civilians (1674) (Bellamy and Williams, 2010: 49).

Endowed with a different history, institutional embeddedness and partly
military mandate, peacekeeping has dealt with two main issues in recent years:
protection of civilians and the robustness of its mandates. The UN peacekeeping
mission MONUSCO has served as the most important laboratory of reform of
peacekeeping. Soft, intelligence measures of information gathering have been
tested here first as well as the first ever Intervention Brigade as part of
MONUSCO since 2013 boasting the UN's first explicitly 'offensive' mandate
(Breakey and Dekker, 2014).

The practice of protection

Initially a provision of the Geneva Conventions that the life of civilians needs to
be protected during conflict, 'protection' has increasingly permeated all kinds of
debates on peacekeeping and humanitarian aid. UNHCR employs protection
officers, humanitarian organizations 'do' protection, there is a protection
'cluster' in the UN humanitarian cluster coordination system and most new
peacekeeping mandates since UNAMSIL in 1999 have contained a protection of
civilians mandate.[20] The UN Secretary General publishes an annual report on the
protection of civilians and humanitarian NGOs like MSF or Oxfam, and organizations like the ICRC partake actively in this conceptual discussion (Soussan,
2008; Oxfam, 2011a; International Committee of the Red Cross, 2008b).

In the last decade, we witness a merger of peacekeeping and humanitarian aid
around the notion of protection. Protection had always been one of the key
notions of the ICRC and the UNHCR (Barnett and Finnemore, 2004: 101). Back
in the 1960s, it was essentially a legal concept. Granting asylum, for example,
was a protection activity (Barnett and Finnemore, 2004: 75). In 2012, protection

has been redefined and broadened to include the direct provision of security, the protection of livelihoods in an area of conflict or statebuilding and development activities. Yet, according to a UN DPKO staff member in New York, the UN does in fact 'not have a clear view of what protection is yet'.[21]

Another UN DPKO staff member in New York was delighted about the cooperation between humanitarians and peacekeepers during innovative protection approaches.

> But it's always been a central issue. It's just the way we've done it, has changed somewhat. So that we've got the forces in widespread bases, you know, commanders don't actually like to have their forces spread out in this way but we have to do that. We have joint investigation teams with human rights and civil affairs etc. The humanitarians are involved with deciding on what are the 'must protect', 'should protect' and 'could protect' zones which I think is really good and is quite actually cutting-edge that the humanitarians work very closely with the force on this.[22]

There are multiple potential genealogies of this trend of convergence. The move from state security to human security as a new core concern in global politics certainly played a role (Chandler, 2008). The ubiquity of the notion of the 'responsibility to protect' since the Kosovo investigation in 1999 and the International Commission on State Sovereignty report in 2002 have also contributed their share (Chandler, 2002: 243–248). Yet, since its endorsement at the World Summit in 2005, the 'responsibility to protect' has been in decline, reinvigorated briefly by its invocation in the course of the NATO attacks on Libya in 2011 and its invocation to remove president Gaddafi from power (Paris, 2014).

Protection operates as the same kind of public performance for peacekeeping as the humanitarian principles and the concept of need for humanitarian aid. Its conceptual status, however, is even more unstable and multi-faceted than need or principles so it provides a welcome ground to engage in conceptual debate among intervention. Protection is understood as an activity, an objective or state that is reached when peace or development arrive (Holt and Taylor, 2009; Sending, 2010: 20). Protection of civilians, in turn, is a 'specific legal framework' (Soussan, 2008: 8) in International Humanitarian Law.

Thanks to this conceptual openness, protection can be promoted as a part of multi-dimensional peacekeeping missions which are essentially statebuilding missions. At the same time, they can be used as showcasing a very narrow and 'apolitical' approach to intervention. This leads to complex conceptual debates. Yamashita, for example, clearly posits protection as part of a larger agenda:

> Humanitarian protection has not been established as a principle that expresses new impartiality on its own. Instead, it has become a functional component of peacekeeping mandates, which, however, focus on wider objectives concerning the extension of state authority and the restoration of stability.
>
> (Yamashita, 2008: 622)

In the Congo, the protection of civilians mandate initially also operated as an antidote to the clearly transformative statebuilding approach of fighting alongside the national army which continues to commit serious human rights abuses. By showing that the mission also protected civilians, the mission could claim that in fact the individual and its survival was at least equally or even more important than building the state by defeating its enemies. Simultaneously, it could be seen as part of that statebuilding strategy because in counterinsurgency doctrine, protection is an instrument to win the hearts and minds of the population (Friis, 2010: 52). In this view, protection is not about individual survival as such but about the individual as a supporter of new social order.

Similar tension between public proclamations and actions on the ground exist among the UN peacekeeping mission MONSUCO in the Congo. MONUSCO consists of a maximum of 22,016 uniformed personnel and about 4,000 civilian staff.[23] Roughly 3,000 military personnel constitute the Intervention Brigade mandated by Security Council Resolution 2098 in March 2013. Civilian staff is organized in various sections in the Kinshasa office and the numerous provincial offices of which Goma is the largest. The main sections are: Political Affairs, Civil Affairs, Human Rights, Public Information, Rule of Law, Child Protection, Disarmament, Demobilization and Reintegration (of combatants) and Demobilization, Disarmament, Repatriation, Resettlement and Reintegration (of foreign combatants)[24] plus many more like logistics, aviation etc. Public Information, for example, runs a large radio network called Radio Okapi which has turned into one of the most popular radios in North Kivu.

Because of repeated episodes of non-protection, MONUSCO has turned into the most innovative laboratory for new instruments of peacekeeping. Next to the first ever robust 3,000-men strong Intervention Brigade, it boasts 49 community liaison assistants and has deployed joint protection teams (JPTs) on 52 missions. JPTs consist of civilian staff from the sections on human rights, civil affairs, rule of law, translators and military personnel.[25] They serve to gather information before immediate protection needs arise. Moreover, MONUSCO has established 20 community assistance networks which have supplied villages in isolated areas with means to contact the authorities or MONUSCO in case of violent incidents.

All these innovative approaches have been developed after the so-called Kiwanja massacre of late 2008 during which MONUSCO remained unprotective despite its mandate. In this massacre, CNDP rebels allegedly executed 150 Mai-Mai fighters and UN peacekeepers stood by three kilometres away without interfering. Their joint human rights office reported in late 2009:

In the aftermath of the Kiwanja killings, MONUC was strongly criticized for not having protected the civilian population, a task explicitly stated in its mandate and international law. The need for peacekeeping missions to operationalize protection is relatively new, and implementation methods are still very much in the developmental stages. Further training of military personnel in peacekeeping operations would be required. Further, the formulation of clearer criteria for exactly when peacekeepers are to intervene in order to protect civilians must take into account both the need for peacekeepers to possess knowledge of the dangers faced by civilians in a given situation, and the capacity of peacekeepers to make a positive difference in that situation. Evidence gathered during the UNJHRO [UN Joint Human Rights Office, KK] investigation suggests that the military personnel who were present in Kiwanja at the time of the killings were not aware of the nature or magnitude of the situation, due to language and cultural barriers or lack of effective communication with civil society leaders in Kiwanja.

(United Nations, 2009c: 3)

This account is quite upfront if looked at closely. The need to operationalize protection suggests that, in fact, it has not been properly operationalized and thus not implemented consistently yet. Until 2008, protection was thus only a public performance. According to this self-assessment, MONUSCO lacked 'knowledge of the dangers faced by civilians' and the basic language skills to acquire that knowledge through personal communication.

The UN tries to prevent these fundamental lacunae with the novel instruments listed above. However, it is not the first time UN peacekeepers do not manage to protect populations despite their presence. This is the old Somalia, Srebrenica and Rwanda trauma and it keeps happening. Managing expectations is thus one of the main preoccupations of leading figures of peacekeeping.[26] This serves to underline that peacekeeping claims to protect civilians but operationally often does not. Protection of civilians is also a public relations device.[27]

Because of the breadth of the concept, protection can become a contradictory affair in operational practice. Situations may arise where the humanitarian urge to treat and stay clear of justice directly contradicts the justice approach to protection taken by the MONUSCO human rights section, let alone the military approach to protection. A MONUSCO human rights officer, for example, related an episode to me where her approach to protection through justice clashed with the MSF approach to protect through the provision of care only:

Honestly. Sometimes I find it's violating people's rights. You see I was faced with a situation in which I came with a magistrate to a village. And there were two rape victims. I knew that there were victims and he found one and the magistrate interrogated her and I think for her for her as victim she was extremely happy because it was a magistrate coming to her to listen to her story, to take up her case. And when we were going to listen to the other one she wanted to, she really wanted to. I mean, we just said, we spread the word that we are here with a magistrate very discretely to one woman who knew the women. And the victims came deliberately! She really wanted to testify. Then some NGO supported by some health facility came in between and said, I'm sorry to harass the victim and almost threatened her to not testify. Well, it's the victim's right. And she was saying it in Swahili and the judge was understanding this way. He was telling me she was basically intimidating the victim to not testify. I mean this is obstruction to justice. I have all the right to arrest for what she is doing [laughing] this NGO lady. And indeed also, you know, in the same village we came with the magistrate and we went to MSF to ask them if they could facilitate the contact with the victims: No, no, no it's complication, you know, ta ta ta. Ok, but the victim has the right to file a complaint if she wants to. Sometimes it's the only thing they want to. Sometimes they lose all they have; they lose their husband, everything. So for them it's gratifying to hear that the judge is condemning the person for what he's done. And then MSF oh no, no, no, we, ah, ah, ah. You know but then ok we don't ask them to share any information. We just ask them to ask the victims if they want to testify. That's different. I don't want information! I just want if they want to. There are here with a judge, you see. That's why it's a bit unfortunate, you know, what to do?[28]

During operations different understandings of protection clash. There are situations where care – MSF – and justice – MONUSCO – are completely at odds with each other. The administration of these issues by NGOs and the UN finds its limits when no central authority imposes its decisions. In this case, MONUSCO will have to find other means to inform the public about the presence of the magistrate than using MSF as intermediary. In operational practice, two legitimate approaches to protection clash as utterly contradictory. Protecting rights through legal redress or through medical treatment are fundamentally opposed by the people and organizations involved.

The robust mandate in practice

The second key issue in peacekeeping emanating from field research and relevant literature is the 'robust mandate'. Since the mid-1990s, the need for more robust mandates and an increased use of force by peacekeeping missions has dominated the strategic debates on peacekeeping. The 2000 Brahimi report and the 2008 Capstone doctrine are the landmark strategies of this evolution (United Nations, 2000, 2008b). Since 2000, missions tend to come in their robust Chapter VII variety authorizing the 'use of all necessary means', not only to protect themselves but also humanitarian workers and to dispel and overpower adversary forces.

The process leading up to the Capstone doctrine led to a reinterpretation of

> the three basic principles of consent of the parties, impartiality, and non-use of force except in self-defence. According to the new 'Principles and Guidelines', UN peace operations are to 'manage' the consent of the parties, including, 'as a last resort, the use of force,' and the limits to the use of force are expanded to include 'self-defense and defense of the mandate'.
>
> (Benner *et al.*, 2012: 22)

The defence of the mandate clause in particular provided the necessary freedom of action for UN peacekeeping missions like MONUSCO. If the mandate concerns a peace that is to be kept, all activities by actors threatening this peace can be countered militarily to nurture this peace. Consent of the parties is thus no longer the highest normative good. 'The mandate' has taken its stead. The Intervention Brigade, issued in March 2013, takes this further. There is now no longer any doubt that MONUSCO acts as a party to the conflict and is taking sides. Although the wording of the Security Resolutions cautions against taking this as a precedent (UN Security Council Resolution 2098, paragraph 9), it is quite probable that a more partial UN peace enforcement role will soon be more common.

MONUSCO, like most UN peacekeeping missions, has a history of dismal protection failure. The Kiwanja massacre was only the most recent one before the M23 rebellion (see Chapter 2) managed to take over Goma. At first, MONUSCO seemed to take their robust mandate seriously. In the fall of 2012 MONUSCO used its attack helicopters to fire at M23 positions. Humanitarians witnessing the scene wrote on Facebook:

> The MONUSCO is right now bombing the forest near Rugari, where civilians took refuge from the military attacking their villages – so people face the terrible choice of being shot by the military or by an armed group in their villages, or suffer the bombs of the MONUSCO in their hiding places ... just incredibly sad from any perspective.[29]

While the use of attack helicopters showed that MONUSCO adhered to its robust mandate, when the M23 rebels advanced in late November 2012 and the FARDC retreated, MONUSCO suddenly stopped fighting. Asked by journalists about the reasons for this retreat, former head of UN DPKO Hervé Ladsous said that the UN could not support an army that was no longer fighting.[30] In an interesting culmination of the difficulties with the MONUSCO mandate of simultaneously protecting civilians and building the state (Veit, 2012), MONUSCO suddenly decided to drop the protection of civilians mandate because there was allegedly no state army to build and support any longer. The civilians that were exposed to the rebellion in Goma were abandoned by the UN. The protection mandate became operationally void.

Obviously, there were strategic considerations at play too. UN leadership might have decided that president Kabila might need an embarrassment to finally do something about the volatility of the east. Alternatively, the UN might even have considered ending their support for Kabila. Or they were simply flabbergasted that from one day to the other the FARDC suddenly stopped fighting the M23 allegedly because the acting general was turned.[31] Speculations abound but nobody knows what was really going on.

As a reaction to this, after a number of diplomatic meetings, the Intervention Brigade was founded, fought back the M23 whose supporters in Rwanda had been shied away by diplomatic pressure, and is now, at the time of writing in early 2015, turning towards the longstanding FDLR problem. This has led to another round of diplomatic posturing between the Kabila government and

MONUSCO, because the government's motivation to solve the FDLR issue once and for all continues to be low.[32]

Protection and the 'robust mandate' obviously harbour many potential interpretations and allow a lot of operational leeway. The contradictions between different approaches to protection and the possibility of abandoning a protection mandate when seen fit indicates that intervention practice is much more then what is proclaimed in public. On the ground, protection and the robustness of the mandate prove extremely hard to implement.

Conclusion

In this chapter I have argued that public proclamations play an integral role for legitimizing intervention. By opening the black box of intervention, it became obvious that proclamations and operational practice harbour a lot of contradictions. Taking seriously the accounts of operational practice also shows that intervention is inherently negotiated, messy and sometimes highly problematic.

Promoting operational practice and the ambiguities of public proclamations themselves to a more visible position in studying intervention engenders two critical effects. One, because of the contradictions and messiness involved intervention needs to work harder to justify itself, the answer to 'why are we here' (Li, 2007: 281) has to be pondered again. The self-evidence of intervention decreases. Two, the social life taking place in the Congo inevitably moves to the forefront because operations are seen as continuously entangled with it. Capturing public proclamations as strategic positioning in a project market and operational practice as decidedly ambiguous and messy ultimately turns intervention into a practice in constant need of legitimation.

This chapter has argued with the help of strategy papers and policy documents taken from the UN and core humanitarian organizations such as ICRC, MSF and Oxfam, and the evidence gathered in Goma and New York, that managing the disconnect between the public and operational face of intervention is essential for intervention actors. Humanitarian principles like independence and impartiality are effective as rhetorical devices just as the concept of humanitarian space and the notion of need. What happens in their name, however, is a different story and it was the ambition of this chapter to consider these two practices together. Peacekeeping is also not simply becoming more protective or robust but oscillates from blatant non-protection to the haphazard use of attack helicopters to clear counterinsurgency operations although staff members acknowledge the fear – half jokingly – that they 'would be killed for saying this'.[33]

Organizations choose different strategies to deal with conceptual ambiguities and manage the intrusion of the operational into the public in different ways. The nuances between these organizations serve to differentiate them symbolically in the competitive project market in which intervention practice is situated. The UN, the ICRC, MSF and Oxfam position themselves in different ways in debates about humanitarian principles, humanitarian space and the concept of need. The UN struggles with the inherent contradictions within and between protection and a robust mandate. What intervention is and what is problematic or laudable among it can be seen best by having a closer look inside.

Notes

1 This is one of the reasons why Monika Krause's astute sociology of this market was reasonably based on NGO Headquarters practices (2014).
2 See Walker and Maxwell (2008: 120). More recent data from the financial reports for 2011 show the budgets have increased across the board (Médecins Sans Frontières, 2012a; International Committee of the Red Cross, 2012). They amount to an expenditure of US$900 million for 2011 (MSF) and US$861 million (ICRC). For Oxfam no all-chapter data is available.
3 In 1986, anthropologist Barbara Harrel-Bond already asked: 'are the same mistakes which have been made over the last 40 years about to be repeated?' (1986: xviii). This kind of language continues. In recent debates, the 1990s and 2000s are seen as an era of challenges and opportunities for improvement although most of them have existed since the inception of humanitarian aid. This historical amnesia is functional from a bureaucratic point of view because the impression of evolution and improvement is more easily generated without history.
4 There is a very prolific debate on intervention among German scholars. They show how rule on the ground changes by internationalizing and informalizing further in the case of intervention in Bosnia (Bliesemann de Guevara, 2009), how intervention entrenches pre-existing power relations (Veit, 2010) and highlight the limits to state-building from without in Kosovo (Distler, 2014).
5 There have been a large number of reform initiatives in recent decades which fulfil this exact function of constant evolution: at the UN these ever-novel bureaucratic improvement programmes were called 'humanitarian reform' from 2005 to 2012 and 'transformative agenda' since 2012.
6 See Barnett (2011: 217) on this issue.
7 This study was administered jointly by UN OCHA and DPKO.
8 The issues were identified through a grounded theory analysis of key publications produced by the ICRC, MSF, Oxfam and UN OCHA as well as UN DPKO and MONUC/MONUSCO from 2008 until 2012.
9 The edited volume by Michele Acuto on *Negotiating relief* (2014) unites a wealth of interesting contributions arguing for this exact perspective.
10 See Iver Neumann (2007) for an analogous argument about the way speeches are written in the Norwegian Foreign Ministry and how these speeches are essentially a hotchpotch of different constituencies within the ministry.
11 I am grateful to Claudia Meier for pointing this out to me.
12 This village is situated about 100 km north-west of Goma, secluded and far off from decent infrastructure.
13 Fieldnotes Goma, October 2009.
14 NGO Goma 4, 12 September 2009.
15 NGO New York 1, 18 November 2011.
16 www.wfp.org/node/21755, last accessed 18 February 2015.
17 Darcy and Hoffman argue that the needs concept originates in development 'basic needs' language and the Maslow pyramid (2003: 16).
18 For a discussion of these phenomena in the German context, see Binder, Koddenbrock and Horváth (2013).
19 NGO Goma 7, 16 September 2009.

20 Ongoing peacekeeping operations with protection of civilians mandates are: the three UN missions in South Sudan and the Republic of the Sudan, UNAMID S/RES/1769 (2007), UNISFA S/RES/1990 (2011), UNMISS S/RES/1996 (2011); MONUSCO S/RES/1925 (2010) in the Democratic Republic of the Congo; UNOCI S/RES/1528 (2004) in Côte d'Ivoire; UNMIL S/RES/1509 (2003) in Liberia; MINUSTAH S/RES/1542(2004) in Haiti; UNIFIL S/RES/1701 (2006) in Lebanon; and UNAMA S/RES/1974 (2011) in Afghanistan.

21 UN HQ New York 3, 9 December 2011.

22 UN HQ New York 2, 18 November 2011.

23 MONUSCO website www.un.org/en/peacekeeping/missions/monusco/facts.shtml, last accessed 28 February 2015.

24 The administrative structure is on file with author.

25 See   www.unv.org/en/what-we-do/countries-and-territories/france/doc/at-the-sharp-end.html, last accessed 18 March 2015, for a description of the JPT's work.

26 See interview with former UN Under-Secretary General for Peacekeeping Jean-Marie Guéhenno in the next chapter.

27 See Breakey and Dekker's interesting analysis of the 'Weak links in the Chain of Authority' playing an important role in making peacekeeping operations notoriously resistant to a forceful interpretation their mandate. They argue that the five pillar set-up from Security Council, to UN Secretariat to the mission to troop contributing countries and the force itself and the concomitant 'line of authority' is by no means a 'chain of command' and tends to privilege the most defensive link.

28 MONUSCO Civilian Goma 4, 29 September 2009.

29 NGO Goma 22, Facebook, 25 July 2012.

30 www.rfi.fr/afrique/20121121-rdc-herve-ladsous-rfi-monusco-m23-goma, last accessed 12 March 2013.

31 Then acting general Amisi has now been replaced by Francois Olanga and is under house arrest in Kinshasa, www.taz.de/!106154/, last accessed 18 February 2015.

32 See www.rfi.fr/afrique/20150215-rdc-joseph-kabila-hausse-ton-face-communaute-internationale/, last accessed 26 February 2015.

33 UN HQ New York, 2 December 2011.

4   The insecurity of legitimate and effective presence

The individual in intervention

Goma's city centre is replete with foreign humanitarians and members of the UN peacekeeping mission. Populated by between 500,000 and a million inhabitants, Goma is one of the veritable 'NGO-poles' (Büscher and Vlassenroot, 2010: 256) hosting at least 1,100 humanitarians and 1,500 peacekeepers (Koddenbrock and Schouten, 2014). The foreigners' cars dominate the main roads and the four roundabouts like 'Bralima' and 'Seigneur' which people refer to when they explain the way to you. The numerous restaurants, clubs and bars largely cater to their and to wealthy Congolese needs. During my research in 2008 and 2009, the 'Cocojambo' was the place to go, an open-air club with palm trees, decent steaks, a pool table and good drinks. Quality hotels and villas line the shore of Lake Kivu. The Ihusi, the Chalet, or the Nyara are the places foreigners on short-term missions chose to stay in. Not many of these visitors and 'experts' know who owns these places and profits from the wealth generated through daily room rates of US$80 to 150.

Doing research in Goma is exciting. To get to my interview appointments I had to rely on public transport which meant using motorbike-taxis, a means of transport reasonably forbidden to foreign professionals who use their own cars or drivers to negotiate the city. Parties happen virtually every weekend at one of the UN or NGO houses. During my two stays in Goma of about two months each, I went to parties hosted at the main houses or staff residences of Mercy Corps, Merlin, the ICRC, Solidarités, Première Urgence, the International Rescue Committee and others. They varied in their intensity but generally added to the addictive mix of beautiful young people from all over the world, great locations often by the lake and the touch of danger when being taken home in the Toyota 4 × 4, owned by the NGO, slightly intoxicated.

The day after, these people go about their business with dedication, drive out to the refugee camps, go check on the health centres they support in the sur-roundings of the city or further out in the province, or attend one of the myriad of coordination meetings that come with the UN cluster system. Others pack their expedition gear and drive out to secluded villages to investigate human rights abuses or board one of the few UN helicopters managed by the Indian peacekeepers to fly to rebel-held territory to convince them to disarm and return to civilian life.

Having experienced this, it is difficult to deny the attractiveness of the job as a humanitarian or peacekeeper – despite the apparent global inequalities enacted in them. Largely brought up and educated in the West, interveners come to the Congo for varying reasons. The job market and their individual motivations play an important role in triggering their excursions. Having arrived in the Congo, these triggers get complemented by individual experiences on the job. This leads to substantial modifications in reflection which this chapter sets out to analyse. Like the previous chapters, it contributes to a more holistic look at intervention by highlighting what is happening on the operational face of intervention in the Congo – at the level of the individual intervener.

The lived experience of intervention work and the gratification it offers play an important part in making intervention happen, in continuing to make it happen. Individuals carry out intervention practice and their reflections provide evidence on how they relate to their work, how they continuously perform it. Intervention practice not only consists of knowledge and organizations but also on individuals and their thoughts.

But individual motivations, experiences and reflections are completely absent on the public face of intervention. The carefully crafted press releases and policy documents convey the impression of a monolithic and convinced intervention scene. The public face of intervention consists of glossy UN and NGO reports and of a pathologizing Congo discourse. Yet subjective experiences are just as crucial as pathologizing the Congo is for perpetuating intervention. These people in Goma and New York – which offers in many ways similar rewards – embody intervention. Without them, it would not take place.[1]

Individuals in intervention scholarship

In contemporary IR, Ole Sending is one of the rare scholars who advocates the need to study individuals in intervention. Next to Paul Higate and Marsha Henry (2009), he is one of the few who regard performances among individuals including their reflections as important to get a more comprehensive view of what intervention actually is. Sending argues that:

> by shifting focus to the practices that the actors involved partake in, it is possible to identify the performative aspect of peacebuilding in terms, for example, of how peacebuilding emerges with its distinct meaning and significance in and through how peace builders categorize and understand the countries where they intervene in particular ways, how they judge different types of knowledge, and how they perceive of their own role.
>
> (Sending, 2010: 8)

Sending's practice-theoretical framework is tangible when he argues that 'peacebuilding emerges with its distinct meaning and significance in and through' the acts and analysis of peacekeepers. Peacekeeping practice is not simply given or preordained but is actively carried out by those doing and reflecting on it. The individuals carrying out intervention practice are part of what this practice is.

Despite the wealth of literature on humanitarianism, peacekeeping and intervention in general, sociologies or ethnographies of intervention personnel have only recently entered the discussion in IR (Baaz, 2005; Marriage, 2006; Autesserre, 2014). In social anthropology and development studies, the anthropology of aid has been a growing field of study for a long time (Crewe and Harrision, 1998; Mosse, 2011; Brigg, 2009). Most of these works, however, have dealt with development interventions because neither humanitarian aid nor peacekeeping had played an important part of intervention before the 1990s.

The most comprehensive study of humanitarian workers *Le travail humanitaire* was published in 2002 by the French sociologists Pascal Dauvin and Johanna Siméant. The study attempts to 'grasp concrete reality of humanitarian work' (Dauvin and Siméant, 2002).[2] In IR, there have been an increasing number of studies interrogating NGOs and UN organizations and their internal processes but the people carrying out intervention practice have remained mostly out of the picture (Barnett and Finnemore, 2004; Sending and Neumann, 2011; Benner, Mergenthaler and Rotmann, 2012).

Establishing the anthropological and sociological interest for the individual into IR remains to be done. Practice theory and a performative understanding of the world open up this research avenue. Zoe Marriage and Séverine Autesserre's work features the thoughts of individuals as part of their broader narrative of how aid doesn't work properly (Marriage, 2006; Autesserre, 2014). This chapter, however, provides a broader panorama of interveners' reflections more akin to the life-history research done by David Mosse (Mosse, 2011) and similar to the autobiographical reports written by interveners themselves (Smirl, 2012; Alexander, 2013). This book places a bigger focus on the details and depth of intervention experience, because only through these details the allure of intervention which helps perpetuate it becomes understandable.

Motivations and rewards

The 'international' in Goma has many embodiments. He, 24 and British, with a degree in International Relations from the London School of Economics, may write human rights reports about Congolese army atrocities for the UN peacekeeping mission MONUSCO (formerly MONUC). She, 21, from France, may work as a nurse for one of the big humanitarian organizations like Save the Children or Médecins Sans Frontières or smaller ones like Solidarités and Merlin.[3] He may also be an 'old-hand', 55, from the United States, having worked in many African countries and in Afghanistan or Iraq before, who now occupies the head of office position at one of the well-paid posts at UNHCR, the World Food Programme, or as head of the political affairs section at the UN peacekeeping mission.[4]

Among the intervention scene the saying goes that 'mercenaries, missionaries and misfits' (Stirrat, 2008) engage in humanitarian, peacekeeping and development work. This conjures up an image of a particular brand of outcasts, overly

motivated, ideological and somehow crazy people. However, the people I encoun-
tered and talked to did not appear outrageously different. They constitute a pretty
representative cut across Western mobile, internationalized middle-class life
worlds. It is thus not surprising that the reasons for engaging in this kind of work
are nearly as numerous as the people I interviewed. Yet, some aspects are recurrent and can be presented here as key motivations driving intervention practice.

Before presenting these findings, a few words on the survey sample: I explicitly targeted Western staff because I wanted to study this part of intervention
primarily. In Goma, a majority of interviewees were between 20 and 45 years
old, most in their late 20s or early 30s.[5] Goma is an important entry point into a
UN or NGO career. It is a high-risk duty station that provides disincentives to
more seasoned staff with families. The people I interviewed in New York tended
to be more senior, the age mix at HQ positions is more balanced.

The grounded theory analysis of the interviews shows that many humanitarians and peacekeepers do their job primarily because they are looking for personal fulfilment. The quest for a meaningful and fulfilling job permeated many
of the responses. The following is an excerpt from an interview with a senior
health care specialist from Australia who I shared house with when staying at
the residential house of the Congolese NGO called Heal Africa. This NGO,
renowned for the excellent community work they do and the hospital they
service in the city centre of Goma regularly brings in foreign volunteer experts
to contribute to their work. When I was staying with them, a sizeable group of
Australians composed of experienced nurses and doctors were offering their services next to a German student of medicine and a British nurse.

Working in the Congo is thus seen by some as a fulfilling way to enter the
retirement phase of their lives while at the same time giving some of the privileges they enjoyed over the course of their lives back:

> Yeah, why do I do it? It's a good question. I guess I was at a stage in my life
> – I am 62, my wife is 60 – we're at a point where we're retiring, we're
> winding down other activities to think of retirement. Our children are at an
> age where they're married and they had children of their own, they still need
> our attention so I mean one of the reasons we're here, we do have free time
> on our hands despite the fact that we need to look after our family back
> home. And I still do some consulting in health care mainly overseas but the
> motivation is that we're planning on retirement then we suddenly realized,
> well, what are we going to do for the rest of our time, you know. Maybe we
> can travel both within Australia and overseas but is that fulfilling? So we
> decided to postpone these sort of retirement plans for a few years and
> instead use our money as a volunteer team to come here. So rather than
> spending 10,000 dollars on holiday we decided we spent 10,000 dollars in
> coming here. […] I've got an easy life back home why shouldn't I impart
> some of my knowledge and skills that I have had and enjoyed in this indus-
> try over the years. So I'm trying to give back something that I've gained
> over the years in my working life.[6]

A young epidemiologist from the UK, at an entirely different stage of his career, expresses similar desires of doing something meaningful coupled with the opportunities the job offers to see the world and the curiosity it satisfies:

> For now it's, it was where I thought it was most meaningful to do work. Also because you probably can't do it, you can do it forever but much better to do this kind of work when you're young and starting out rather than getting stuck in London or Geneva. So like I say the fact that I was good at, quite good at it naturally and it was meaningful and it also allows you to travel. And for me that's really interesting.[7]

Junior humanitarians and peacekeepers have a clear conception of the way this particular job market functions. They know that in the early stages you need to spend some time 'in the field' to be able to get to the more pleasant posts in Geneva, New York or London. When you're younger, being in a conflict zone might even be more rewarding than 'getting stuck' in one of these Western cities, as the humanitarian above expresses it.

The quest for fulfilment seen in these interviews can be separated into varying sources: their perception of their home countries, political and moral considerations, a certain degree of voyeurism, the desire for intellectual challenges, and rational career and income calculations.

One interviewee stressed that she found social work in her native Canada even more rewarding[8] but the majority of respondents argued that they could not justify it to contribute to improving their home societies because they were too rich.[9] Making them even richer was morally questionable given the problems in countries like the Congo.[10] It is also less rewarding to build something when everything is already there. The satisfaction that can be drawn from this is clearly visible in the following quote from a seasoned NGO manager in Goma who told me how great it feels to build a school when it is the only one around, not one of 50:

> There is a road, people settle back in, farmers start farming again. The schools we have built, that's good, very motivating. You cannot have this kind of satisfaction in Europe. When you build a school in Europe there are already 50 or 100 of them in the same town, this is not very motivating. Here in the Congo if you build a proper school according to state standards which is clean etc. well it is unique in the entire town. This is very important, I find this very important.[11]

A young UN official from the human rights section expressed how she could never work in Belgium: 'Belgium is a too clean society, it's boring, there is nothing going on.'[12]

Interestingly, there is a more escapist variant of this assessment of home societies. Dauvin and Siméant had already argued that the perceived 'banality of the everyday' – 'banalité du quotidien' (2002: 145) – was a key motivation for humanitarians to leave their home countries. The problem with Western societies is not their standard of living. Life in the West is seen as too comfortable. A member of the UN demobilization programme who has already worked several of these high-risk and high-reward jobs told me how great it feels to build societies from scratch, to really create something that 'makes a difference'[13]:

> And you are going to make people even more comfortable? From lower comfort to higher comfort? There is stuff you can do I mean, you know, there is stuff in inner cities and things like that, community work but. Set like this you're working on national level, stabilizing, I mean in Palestine I was working creating a state from nothing. I mean how many people do that? Where are we going to build our capital, what's it going to look like, how is our infrastructure look like, where is our future habitation going to be, where is our economic centre going to be, how are we going to control our cultural centre? Like you're building a state from nothing. And here you're also building a state from almost nothing because it was a collapsed state so. We're recreating a state. You know like where do you go from there?[14]

Doing something substantial and essential, building from scratch and knowing that one contributed to something important seems to be a fundamental part leading to the personal fulfilment most interveners strive for.

A handful of interviewees couched their responses in more overtly political terms. A Belgian peacekeeper told me that she was grateful she got the chance to make up for Belgian colonialism through her work.[15] A French humanitarian said that he was convinced we were unable to do anything political on the global scale so the only thing left to fight against global inequalities was humanitarian aid.[16]

Apart from these more social or historical motivations, a substantial part of the fulfilment offered by humanitarianism and peacekeeping in the Congo is purely egoistic. Some interveners are motivated by this job because it gives them the opportunity to 'see a true conflict'.[17] Others enjoy the intellectual challenge the complexity of the Congo offers:

> It's a place I wanted to come to for a longish time. When I was in Congo Brazzaville I was reading, you know, it's impossible to find any information on Congo Brazzaville. So the only stuff you get about it is Congo. And I read King Leopold's Ghost and that was wow. At the same I was working closely with a charity called Anti Slavery International and so anything to do with slavery was interesting to me. And so to read about what happened here and so long after other countries it abolished slavery. Like this place started it. Which I found, I mean just the timelines are terrible. It's so bizarre. Anyway. So for me that was what hooked me. It was you know reading this book about Congo and also just hearing about the political machinations behind the scenes and there are so many minerals here that

everybody wants a part of it. So that was probably what interested me most.[18]

Being a humanitarian or a peacekeeper in the Congo can make you relatively rich – if you work for the right organization. The Norwegian Refugee Council, the UN, Oxfam and the ICRC pay best, small French NGOs like Solidarités or Première Urgence pay worst.[19] As a consequence many of the interviews were not shy to tell me that it was, on the one hand, a useful career step and on the other a handsome source of income. This is what brought them to this job in the first place:

I do my job here because this is a job, a well-paid job in parentheses, which I would not like to give up, for which I am ready to take certain risks and for which I am willing to pay a price like being separated from my family etc. I can deal with that but I would not say that I deeply care about the suffering populations, I am sorry to say that but they will keep suffering for decades.[20]

The job as a peacekeeper or humanitarian can also be gratifying because of the work variety it offers. This UN HQ staffer expresses her satisfaction with combining field and HQ deployments:

And then really wanted to go back to work at the field. So I went to work in Cambodia in a classic peacekeeping operation. And then I have sort of switched between being at headquarters and being in the field. Because that's really the most interesting kind of career path in the UN is to be in the field and then also be at headquarters but maintain, you know, ensure that you are in the field as much as possible as well.[21]

This panorama of motivations shows that people engage in intervention for all kinds of reasons from personal fulfilment to moral concerns, from being fed up with the comfort of their home countries to the attraction of the Congo as a challenging and historically unique place. Some interveners also rank mundane financial or work variety reasons above all else.

The key feature of intervention practice distinguishing it from other pursuits might be that it is a vessel for such a variety of motivations. Very few other jobs provide this plethora of potential satisfactions. What these satisfactions have in common is that they are never part of the public face of intervention. Why should tax payers fund the personal desires of well-paid adventurous Western middle-class individuals, people might ask.

Gratifications on the job

Once in country motivations get modified, extended, reinforced or weakened by experiencing intervention. The responses used in this section stem from interview passages about interveners' personal successes and about the reasons for doing this kind of job. In contrast to the analysis above, I chose to focus on the more immediate gratifications while doing this job, not the ones that made them try it initially.

While one of the 'old hands' in the Goma scene, a senior MONUSCO adviser simply told me that 'one of the things of working in places like this is that they do have a buzz, they are a drug',[22] there are broadly three aspects of this job that make it particularly rewarding. First, the job seems to offer lots of personal satisfactions because one's impact is quite visible; second, because living through it is simply very interesting and because it provides opportunities for learning.

It is clear to most of the interviewees that their impact can be extremely short-lived but there is a considerable sum of situations of impact which provides them with a degree of job satisfaction. For example, a MONUSCO human rights officer related a very short-lived success of her work to me which, however, also highlights the unstable nature of many of these successes:

RESPONDENT: Our negotiation did the demobilization of two child soldiers against a pack of biscuits for the rebel leader.
KK: [laughing]
RESPONDENT: No, I'm very sad because he got shot in the head, I'm very sad.
KK: Who?
RESPONDENT: The rebel leader.
KK: Oh.
RESPONDENT: He was an extremely sympathetic and conciliating rebel leader and he was full of child soldiers.
KK: CNDP?
RESPONDENT: No, Mai-Mai. And we told them that they had to disarm. And he was not sure. And I said, come on I give you a pack of biscuits. He said, ok. He brought the kids … he was so happy the next day he brought three others. And I had gone on vacation and I learnt that there's been a targeted attacked by the Kivu Mai-Mai group and they couldn't find the chief so they killed him. Shot with a bullet in his head. Very unfortunate.[23]

When interviewees talk about the impact they have, the researcher gets a very strong sense of what stabilizes intervention at a personal level. Similar to the triggering motivations about building something from scratch highlighted in the above section, the experiences humanitarians and peacekeepers make are extreme and provide a fertile ground for feeling needed and useful. I will quote a few passages at length here to convey an impression of how powerful this feeling of having an impact is.

When discussing other potential vessels of political engagement or work, I asked a MONUSCO staffer about what he thinks about working in a more indirect way to influence Canadian foreign policy, for example. He replied:

Yeah, yeah but it's indirect. You're working on trying to build a consensus with the international community. If you're from a middle power like

Canada you are going to have less impact on the overall situation. And you have no direct impact. But here I mean last night I carried a woman into a helicopter who was raped and her face beaten by a rifle back. You know, I brought her physically to a hospital. Where else am I going to get that experience, you know? Where are you going to go from there? I could be like a hospital worker or something like that. But you're not going to really see the same type of thing. It's an intense environment.[24]

A senior NGO manager who had worked as a paramedic before has experienced what it means to save lives in his home country. However, humanitarian work becomes extremely rewarding because it links the intellectual challenge of nego-tiating humanitarian principles and the political situation, and the feeling that you have had an impact on thousands of lives:

Paramedic, driving around, picking up people, stitching them up, or somehow pushing syringes into them, taking them to the hospital, I have done that, and I really enjoyed it but it was somehow not stimulating enough, intellectually. It is very mechanical and then I looked for something where I can link this practical, practical-useful with something intellectually stimulating. And that is the case in humanitarian aid, right? But as you say, all these dilemmas ad contradictions you have them here a lot. No matter where you look. But at the same time this practical, fulfilling part of it. So you think, man, now we did indeed increase the standard of this health centre, right? That is something, what do I know, this was useful for these 20,000 people. This is a combination which I find really exciting.[25]

A British MSF manager had a very different job trajectory. After a Master's in Business Administration at the London School of Economics, she somehow ended up in Darfur and has not left the field since then:

I don't know. It was never a sort of planned job path. I kind of fell into it. I did my first project in Darfur and loved it so decided to try another one and then it sort of snowballed from there. I love the variety of the work that we're doing every day. I love working for MSF. I find them a very principled organization to work for. And yeah, you're very much with MSF, you very much see the direct results of what you're doing, there is a much closer link between sort of cause and effect or assistance results. So on a personal level that's very satisfying to see. And then I suppose the more you do it the more you feel you have something to offer. Definitely the first couple of missions you're wondering slightly if you're being that helpful or not or why it is necessary for you to come out here in these con-texts. And then when you see more and more context you definitely start feeling that you have more to offer. So I think it's a mix now of feeling comfortable and doing a good job but mixed with like the variety of the work every day.[26]

The feeling of achieving something, of being helpful, of having something to offer is a key gratification of working in and on the Congo.

For some, intervention also offers a multitude of learning opportunities because you are challenged on so many levels:

> You question yourself much more here. You are in a completely different environment to the one you have been used to since you were a kid. You question yourself much more easily here. And the fact of questioning yourself allows you to advance much faster, you know. Well, I like all that.[27]
>
> ——
>
> It allows you to learn something every day, that is important. And to advance personally, and you get to know new cultures and countries and you can learn a lot from them, you get a lot of responsibility. I think in most of the humanitarian organizations you will find people, they are put there [laughs] and they have to fulfill very demanding functions I think.[28]

Working in a foreign country, having a lot of responsibility and saving lives or building a state or stable peace forces you to learn if you want to meet these challenges. Despite frequent negotiations with provincial authorities and rebels, the intervention scene has a lot of freedom of action so: 'I think it is worth coming to work here because we do have a certain freedom of action here which we do not have in Europe.'[29]

Crucially, like the intellectual attraction to the Congo's complexity shown in the previous section, many of the internationals just find their job incredibly interesting. This emotion counteracts the feeling of an overall lack of impact that can kick in if you look at the bigger picture:

> I just love it. There is many reasons. It's extremely interesting. It's extremely interesting. I've never done something so interesting. My work is my fuel. I mean, I never had this before. I'm waking up and I'm happy to go to work. I'm rushing to go to work sometimes because there is so much to do. But also I think it is a bit gratifying because honestly the situation here I've seen so many horrible situations and many times I've seen that we are the only ones that have the means to do something about it. And it is surely gratifying to think, now if we move ourselves, if we, we really can do something, we really can change something in this people's life, we really really really do something but it's usually small. I think in the big we don't do much.[30]

This prominent narrative of how 'interesting' this job is, here highlighted through a MONUSCO civilian, elicited criticism by more senior staff in New York. This is not surprising. Those who have been in this job longer and have decided to focus more on management and coordination at the expense of feeling their direct impact sometimes cannot relate to the enthusiasm of more junior field staff. However, intervention is both: critical reflection and the latent voyeurism of interestingness:

And that's where it comes back to that it's 'interesting', it's so interesting and I think that's, I mean, I don't know if I should say this on/I have sat in meetings and when it comes down to the whole issue of sexual violence in DRC in particular I have sat in meetings and have heard the horrendous accounts of what happens in terms of sexual violence in DRC. And I swear to God there are humanitarian workers who would lean back and say, 'Oh, my God, it's fascinating, oh, it's so interesting.' And I'm like/To me that is, it's for all the wrong reasons and it's/And this is exactly what Said is saying, it's this interest in seeing what, why, it's this interest in, it would be so interesting to categorize all the different women on the basis of how their hair is braided or it would be so interesting to do the whole, what's it called in English, positivism or whatever or the modernism. It's so interesting to do this. Do you see what I mean?[31]

This humanitarian manager in New York is not shy to articulate problems with her own milieu. Anybody working in and on the Congo can identify with the prior statement that this work is just incredibly interesting. The occasional obscenity and deep global inequality reproduced during this 'interesting' practice of intervention are however tangible here.

Negotiating duties and rights

While organizations have to do everything they can to beautify the public face of intervention and make their work appear necessary on the project market (see previous chapter), individuals in Goma and New York feel less of this pressure. During an interview under conditions of anonymity, one can get a glimpse what kind of normative concerns *also* animate intervention practice. The responses show that the self-evident necessity of intervention is much less consensual among interveners themselves.

Intervention in the Congo might be a routine practice shaped by the Western structural privilege of being able to do this job, by a pathologizing Congo discourse (see Chapter 2), and the requirements of the project market (see Chapter 3), but on the operational face of intervention there exists a lot of doubt. These concerns are often hidden because somebody else will take the place of someone who has left intervention because of these doubts. To develop a fuller picture of the operational face of intervention, however, it is important to take account of the scepticism among it.

Whether an agent of law enforcement *should* or *has to* do something depends on executive decisions and budgetary constraints. For example, whether the German police *have to* actively seek out illegal immigrants or whether they simply *should* or even could is not quite clear. While it is illegal for illegal immigrants to live and work in Germany, to what degree the forces of law prevent them from doing so varies. Administrative and budgetary constraints are clearly a real concern in law enforcement and prevent the absolute convergence of formal law and material enforcement in the context of illegal immigration.

A similar phenomenon is at the heart of intervention on a global scale. Peace-keeping missions *can* be triggered when the Security Council has identified a threat to international peace and security. They don't have to. There are other instruments like sanctions or simple negotiations available. Humanitarian aid, while appealing to humanitarian principles, similarly *can* be disbursed to places where need is identified (see previous chapter). However, there is no duty to dis-burse aid. Intervention is thus not a duty but a voluntary act by international organizations mandated through the Security Council or NGOs mandated by their own private decision-making procedures and the fact that the Congolese authorities have let them into the country and granted them work permits.

The broad discussions about the responsibility to protect since 1999 essen-tially evolve around similar issues. Like peacekeeping and humanitarian aid, it establishes no duty to protect but a call to protect. Governments should protect their populations. If they fail to do so, the so-called 'international community' (Bliesemann de Guevara and Kühn, 2011) should step in. It does not have to. There is no mechanism forcing any kind of decision on those countries involved in dealing with the challenge of the recalcitrant government at hand.

Essentially, duties only exist when there are sanctions and punishment in case they are not fulfilled. You have to respect the traffic lights otherwise you will get a fine in case the police catch you. The nature of human rights as claims without a corresponding *duty* to protect them is mirrored in the way humanitarians and peacekeepers relate to their work as (no) moral duty. The fact that intervention operates beyond the realm of legal duty might explain why very few respondents framed their humanitarian or peacekeeping work as a duty. There is even widespread resistance to the term. Many of the respond-ents stress that they want to refrain from the hubris involved in calling their work a duty. Instead, they see it primarily as a personal interest, a step towards self-fulfilment.

As we have seen above, intervention is animated and sustained by the indi-vidual satisfaction people draw from this kind of work.[32] It does not result from a moral duty: 'And I think that people who are telling themselves this, that sounds wrong. That sounds really wrong. Because this always depends on per-sonal interests.'[33] Or a seasoned UN adviser simply states: 'no, I have a personal interest and it's something I stuck up but I have no greater moral calling other than it satisfies me to try and do what I can to assist because I ain't living here.'[34] Some also describe that they were initially on a 'moral crusade' but have grown more pragmatic on the job:

I've already lost that sort of I'm doing this because it's the moral thing to do. And that was definitely a part of it. Not giving something back as I don't even know what that means. But just trying to find meaning in your own life. And yeah, something is interesting day to day. It's a combination. I think if you go into it only wanting to, only seeing that it's a moral and meaningful thing to do you are just bound to be eventually fed up and disil-lusioned cause it will never, there is too much crap that goes along with it.[35]

Apart from those who stress that personal interest animates them, there are some humanitarians and peacekeepers who simply state that it's not a question of duty but one of will. They are not obliged to do this kind of work but simply want to.[36] A more pragmatic notion of the call to work in or on the Congo is that they do it because they are a good fit for the job:

> No. It's a choice. No I don't think I have a moral duty but what I do think is what I said at the beginning I think that I'm a good candidate for this kind of job because of the flexibility coming from different backgrounds and therefore I fit in very well.[37]

A small minority of people I interviewed was more open to the notion of a moral duty. These internationals affirm there is a moral duty because those who have learned to do something about human rights[38] or are starting to be effective at their job[39] 'because I could do it there was a bit of a moral obligation to try to do it'[40]:

RESPONDENT: Moral duty. Yes, I think there is a moral duty. Absolutely.
KK: Why?
RESPONDENT: I think everyone that has a right to life in terms of humanitarian assistance, right to life, right to dignity. And then the right to development. And if we contribute a small piece of that pie then we should.[41]

The question on the moral duty to work in or on the Congo was designed to get at the moral and normative horizons people working in humanitarian aid and peacekeeping invoke. Taking into account some responses by African expatriates working in the Congo adds an interesting perspective on the insights provided by the Euro-Americans presented above. A senior Save the Children manager in Goma, for example, responded to the moral duty question in the following way:

> It's the notion of duty which creates, varies. It depends on history also. Me, for example, in the Congo, moral because it is Africans like me above all. Brothers, you know. From the same continent etc. etc. When I look at the Congo I am looking at a brother. Ok, we are from the same continent. We are all Africans. We share more things than others. I can tell them things and they can take it. If somebody else says it, he was a colonialist before etc. They cannot say this with me. How am I colonialist? Nothing. Racist. No, I am also not racist. Racist, how. You see? So it's easier for me to talk and I make use of this when the opportunity arises.[42]

This African intervener brings history and colonialism and different degrees of legitimacy for different continents to engage in this kind of work into the equation. This opens an interesting perspective on the question of moral duty. For this NGO manager, the fact of being from the same African continent, of being a 'brother' provides him with moral legitimation to engage with the Congolese. According to him, he is also more able to talk to the Congolese and argue with them because he cannot be called a colonialist or racist.

Solidarity and cooperation may thus also depend on the role of history. If Congolese chose to invoke historical legacies in their encounter with Western aid workers, this would clearly make it harder for Westerners to invoke a moral duty. The colonial *mission civilatrice* was sold as a moral duty back in the day. Most Euro-American staff members seem to be quite aware of that and make an effort not to paint their work as a moral pursuit.

There are thus two broad readings of the material presented above. On the one hand, it is quite accepted among the aid scene to see their work primarily as a tool for self-fulfilment. Morality does not necessarily have to come in. On the other, some people even regard it as hypocritical or dangerous to invoke this moral duty because of the colonial legacies or the overt idealism connected to it.

Just before asking the question 'do you think you have the right to work here?', I tended to get nervous because it was at this point that I opened myself up to being seen as one of these critics of intervention who pretend to know that it is clearly a neo-colonial business and nothing else. The interviewees' initial reactions tended to prolong these awkward situations. Some of them were that surprised that they said they did not understand the question.[43] Others asked me to clarify what I meant by it.[44] Those who answered immediately tended to stress that this was an 'interesting', 'tricky' or 'difficult' question.[45] There is obviously something touchy about the right to engage in humanitarian aid or peacekeeping in the Congo. Among the individuals doing intervention, this is not a self-evident practice. Its stability and legitimacy is potentially insecure.

Some of the respondents were openly sceptical about their overall right to be in the Congo.[46] However, the large majority of respondents were convinced that it is the right thing to do overall. The responses substantiating the view that internationals have the right to work in and on the Congo can be grouped into two different core assumptions. First, a right to do this kind of work existing *prior* to coming to the Congo or working on it from afar. Second a right that has to be earned *while* practicing intervention. This conception of procedural legitimacy can be further distinguished as to its sources. One group of people focuses on the way the work is done, patients are treated, or partners consulted. The other, minority group wonders about what the Congolese think of their work and see their judgments as essential for their right to work in and on the Congo. We can thus identify three sources of legitimacy that interveners see: a legalistic perspective and two kinds of legitimacy – a procedural one and one of recognition by the beneficiaries and hosts.

The legalistic perspective is straightforward. 'We have been invited by the government',[47] 'our organization has the mandate'[48] or 'as long as we get work permits'[49] or 'At any rate, there is no international legislation which prevents me.'[50] are representative ways of putting it. Most of those expressing their legal right to intervene complement this with the procedural view of legitimacy. Behaving the right way,[51] treating partners respectfully,[52] fulfilling the duty towards the patient,[53] being motivated[54] are some of the ways respondents capture this.

Another close reading of the interview with the MSF manager presented in the previous chapter serves to indicate the intricacies of the legalistic and procedural approaches to the right to work in the Congo. It also shows the lack of control mechanisms or rights of participation of the beneficiary 'populations'. Intervention is utterly non-democratic. The MSF manager, while very reflective on the sources of legitimacy and the power structures in the Congo, relates inadvertently that beyond the legal right to be in the Congo, none of her sources of legitimacy originate in the Congolese themselves. Instead, MSF gives legitimacy to itself by focusing on self-determined measures of quality care.

KK: Do you think that you have the right to work here?

RESPONDENT: Yes and no. Yes because we're here to provide the assistance to the local population which would otherwise not have it and they don't have a voice to ask for it. Then yes, I think, we do have a right to be here

Again I think sometimes we get to this blockage where we feel that the right to be here is done through the authorities who as far as we may know do not represent whatsoever the people we're actually trying to help. So you're sort of working in two sorts of ways: you're trying to make the authorities happy so you can physically have the legal right to stay. But at the same time we're trying to target the population which we think is most vulnerable and sometimes there is a clash between the two. [...]

So yeah I think we have a right to be here if we actually respond to the needs of the population. But I think often we mistake that right by thinking, well, the authorities have given us the right to be here therefore we can do whatever we like. I think there is a missing link between the authorities and the local population.

For this MSF staff member the problem with her operating environment is that those who grant them the legal right to work may prevent MSF from getting procedural legitimacy by treating those MSF deems most vulnerable. On the one hand, the authorities do not represent the people, she argues. On the other, they may have priorities that do not correspond to MSF's conception of what is a legitimate way of intervening. The interesting question becomes: what would she say if she had no grounds for questioning the chain of representation between Congolese voters and their authorities? Would it suddenly be acceptable to dispense with MSF's own priorities? Probably not. MSF's approach to procedural legitimacy is based on their own assessment of the quality of their care not on recognition by the Congolese. What matters most is that MSF treats the population 'which *we* think is most vulnerable'. From this perspective recognition by Congolese (authorities) would contribute to her conception of legitimacy if they had the same priorities. Furthermore, there is an implicit assumption that, given that beneficiaries are 'voiceless', they cannot be taken into account.

There are no formal channels of recognition or approval of intervention between its beneficiaries and its implementers. Two substitutes for active recognition and approval existed for those interviewees who worried about Congolese perspectives on intervention. First, an anecdotal approach which stresses that they have not come across anybody who told them to go home yet and, second, highlighting situations where MONUSCO support was actively solicited. In the excerpt below, the latter is clearly visible although this is not sufficient for this peacekeeper:

> 'The right?' No. No, that's a tricky one. No, and I don't know what deeply the Congolese think about it. Honestly, I just don't know, I just don't know. But what is helping me about this issue, it's true I asked myself this question ... I met so many Congolese who are so nice to us who are happy to meet us and I told you again, sometimes people just want the MONUC presence in order to protect them for the eventual attack that could occur this evening. And that's when I think, ok, it's good that we are here. But the right to work here I'm not sure.[55]

The second substitute for Congolese recognition of intervention is the fact that the government has not thrown them out yet. If they wanted to, they could just do it. At first sight, this is a very convincing approach. However, it is based on a very liberal conception of world politics without any global power differentials. On the other hand, the advocates of this position suddenly take a government seriously which they usually tend to portray as weak and malevolent (see Chapter 2).

The following longer quote from a senior UN manager in New York exemplifies this approach well. It also shows that he realizes the government's freedom of action might be smaller than he thought. This, however, is the point where these kinds of reflections usually stopped because power structures seemed a touchy topic and, furthermore, are apparently hard to pin down.

KK: What do you say to these people, well maybe it does not happen so much to humanitarians but to those in peacekeeping, that they say, come on leave us alone. I mean you were here 125 years ago, you are still here. You are meddling in our affairs. Do you think that is a legitimate question? They basically ask, is there a right to do this kind of work?

RESPONDENT: Well, I mean I think there, here there is a distinction between is it legal, i.e. has it been properly mandated by the Security Council which I think everybody would recognize has a standing in international law and so you can say, yes the intervention is legal. And in the eyes of the Congolese is it legitimate? That's an interesting question. The first part of the question is: who is speaking for the Congolese, in the same way that Mamdani up at Columbia who I used to study with...

KK: Yeah, me too.

RESPONDENT: He had this great line: 'The international community or those who claim to speak for them'. It's the same like the Congolese or those who claim to speak for them. Who is it that is saying you know why are you here etc? I do actually believe that if the Congolese want to say yeah you know what, we don't need your tutelage any more...

KK: They stop granting visas.

RESPONDENT: You know that is up to them. Yeah. I honestly believe that is up to them and to the government. Even though I might think it is not particularly legitimate, there is a government, there is an internationally recognized head of state, I think they have the right to do that. Oh sorry, the right, is that the right word? They *can* try to do that, they will inevitably come into some sort of conflict in that regard and then that's just a question of who prevails.

KK: You mean when they try to throw out the peacekeepers.

RESPONDENT: You know the Burundians did this three years ago with UNOBIR or UNOB I forget which version it was. But that's what the Burundians did. They said, well thanks a lot, we don't want you anymore. That's it. You know everybody went down there, SG [UN Secretary General, KK] calls and so on. You know. If the member state is like, yeah, thanks a lot. It becomes, it may you know there may be a different compromise then. You know what's really interesting, in the Congolese case there was, agh I forget what the name of that mechanism was, in 2003, 4, 5 there was this international mechanism to follow on the inter-Congolese dialogue. It was the p5 plus. And then after Kabila was elected the same member states said let's have the same mechanism to support the transition, he was like, no, no let's not. We don't need that. So, you know there is even in these situations considerable power that an individual member state has to structure its own relations. They are not simply supplicants. Regardless what we think of them.[56]

This interview is the only one of the 66 I conducted which directly alludes to the questions of Congolese leeway, the possibility of compromise and global power differentials. All the others bracketed these questions and focused on legality in a formal and legitimacy in a procedural way. The capacity for expressing Congolese priorities tended to remain outside the picture. What this seasoned UN manager is saying here is clearly at odds with the ways of enacting a pathological Congo as analysed in Chapter 2, because in his account, the agency of the Congolese government matters and shapes the outcome of political negotiations without being pathologized.

To posit the Congolese government as a source of legitimacy, interveners need to capture them as rational and goal-oriented. Lack of capacity and malevolence so prominent in the dominant ways of capturing the Congolese government would undercut this argument of the political leeway Congolese leadership enjoys vis-à-vis intervention (Koddenbrock, 2012b: chapter 2; 2014a). This underlines the paradox between the public and operational faces of intervention. On the one hand, intervention is made self-evident and necessary by turning the Congolese government into a weak and destructive one publicly. In private conversations, on the other, when pressed about their personal experiences, interveners describe the government as capable to grant or withdraw legitimacy from intervention.

A perspective on intervention which takes the operational reality of intervention into account by engaging with the individuals carrying out intervention in New York and Goma is able to pose numerous challenges to the self-evidence of intervention claimed on the public face of intervention. None of the policy papers analysed for this book cares much about the role of the Congolese government in endowing intervention with legitimacy. Some carriers of intervention practice do. An analysis susceptible to these carriers is thus able to consider both the public proclamations and the operational sphere of interactions and doubts simultaneously.

While there was already considerable soul-searching with regards to questions of morality and the right to intervene among interveners, the most destabilizing component among these individuals originates in the insecurities of impact many of the interviewed express, in the problems they associate with the 'aid game' as well as the personal consequences resulting from it. This last part of the chapter on the individual experience of intervention takes a look at these most destabilizing aspects. It is here that some of the reasons why people leave this job can be located. It is here that the disconnect between the public and operational face of intervention becomes most obvious.

Soul-searching and doubts

Unfettered enthusiasm among humanitarians and peacekeepers is hard to find. As we have seen above in interveners' assessments of their own motivations and rewards, many of the interviewed describe a gradual shift from idealism to pragmatism. Interveners' experiences contribute to sobering views on the benefits and problems of intervention. There is a lot of reflection, soul-searching and self-criticism among interveners. This insecurity of legitimate and effective presence is almost never part of organizations' public proclamations. One British humanitarian who had initially sought to find 'something pure' in his work life told me:

> I think quicker than I expected I got a little bit disillusioned and a bit bothered by the rubbish that goes with it. And not, you know, of course it doesn't match the image that you have when you open up a magazine in the UK and out flops the, an advert for MSF and you see images and you sort of imagine it's like that and of course it's not.[57]

Many of the sobering views expressed in the interview relate to two different issues. First, the insecurity about the overall effect of intervention in the Congo and, second, the personal problems with life in intervention and the nomadic lifestyle involved in it.

Reflections on intervention effects associated with humanitarian aid and peacekeeping fall into two camps: certain effects, and those which are uncertain, remain in doubt. Respondents are certain about some immediate positive results as well as possibly detrimental ones. Among humanitarians, there is absolute certainty that those patients treated in hospitals, health centres or in camps would not have been treated and saved without them. There is a feeling of security about this. A similar sense of certainty prevails among peacekeepers about the deterring effects of their military presence in villages and the success of heavily military operations like the Ituri-based 2004 Artémis mission.[58] Not surprisingly, the most material activities like fighting or giving medical treatment are generally seen as effective and beneficial.

There are a few certain effects, however, that are not necessarily seen as beneficial. The presence of international interveners is considered to have dubious effects on the local economy, is replacing the state in providing those services that the Congolese state is supposed to provide, and contributes to a brain-drain of well-educated Congolese.[59] The latter concerns both an internal brain-drain from the Congolese public sector to the international NGO and UN sector as well as, if they move up the hierarchy and become expatriates themselves in another 'crisis country', from the Congo to the international realm.

Harder to assess but fundamental for thinking about the overall effect of intervention are concerns about the long-term impact both humanitarian aid and peacekeeping have on a society, whether there is a tendency to over-estimate one's impact and whether the sum of little activities contributes to prolonging and fuelling conflict. These uncertainties cannot be taken too seriously because they would be paralyzing and have the potential to question the overall endeavour. They are openly discussed during operations however:

> I think that you could probably argue that the peacekeeping mission on the whole has been a good thing and reduced violence in a number of different ways. I am less convinced that the other parts of the peacekeeping mission, you know security sector reform rule of law bla bla bla, had any sort of impact. [...]
>
> Was it that [advocacy, KK] effort? Did that effort really have an impact [...]? And that I cannot be sure about despite how closely I was involved in it. That's why some of this stuff it is not surprising that you have to do things sometimes. No, you don't have to. You *decide* that on balance it's worth doing things. Only later can you calculate better if you were correct, maybe.[60]

Jean-Marie Guéhenno, former Under-Secretary General of the UN Department of Peacekeeping Operations and President of the International Crisis Group since 2014, openly stated in our interview that Napoleon's maxim 'on s'engage puis on voit' – 'We engage, then we see what happens' – could be used in peacekeeping and humanitarian aid too.[61] This was essentially how a mission proceeded. This means political judgment has it that something should be done, so a force or group of organizations is dispatched to a crisis zone. Actors deal with the consequences of their actions as they go along. What happens after they have gone home, in case they do go home, which is not self-evident in countries like the

Congo, remains uncertain and opaque. It also does not matter much. It matters to engage:

RESPONDENT: Because also another element which is tricky, which is not linked to the ethical dimension, although it is in a way, that in/I think it's Napoleon who said about strategy 'On s'engage'. You understand French a bit?

KK: Yeah.

RESPONDENT: 'On s'engage et puis on voit'. Which looked like a stupid statement from a very intelligent man. But it's actually a quite profound thing because the way I understand it having not been involved like Napoleon for the good or the bad but have been involved in action. You know, those people who tell you strategy is about thinking your moves a, b, c, d, e. That's nonsense.

KK: You can't anticipate.

RESPONDENT: Because I mean even a chess player with a limited set of rules and a limited chess board like this one [pointing to the chess board on the coffee table next to us, KK]. Even the great chess players they cannot anticipate much more than three or four strokes ahead and it's a limited set of rules and limited in a very well defined world. I mean I don't know how many, you know, it's simple, it's immensely more simple than the real world where the chess board is open-ended and where the number of pawns is unlimited and where there are no agreed rules. And so the notion that you can think several strokes ahead is absurd. What you need is, yes, you need to have a sense of where you want to go. That's where in a way philosophy, going back to first principles, helps. On s'engage and on voit, as you do something you change the picture. And then you/That allows you to get a sense of the actors that you would not have if you would not engage and that's/And strategy is that combination of throwing the dice and having a direction but not pretending that you can chart the course, the way ahead. I don't think that's realistic.

Another senior UN manager in New York who I asked about Jean-Marie Guéhenno's statement expresses this notion of acting without knowing the consequences clearly:

You know many of these things are unknowable. The unintended consequences of these things are essentially unknowable. [...] Similarly the engagement with ah or the interventions like Artemis and so on. We never know how they are going to work out. There is going to be some other sort of movement that happens because of that. Ahm, ah I think he's right you know that you try to do something and you see what happens. Ahm. [Long pause] Because I think you can do your best guess and you can do good analysis. But you are never going to be 100 per cent sure what is going to happen.[62]

This analysis applies to most decisions made by human beings. The future is not easily predicted. Foregrounding this insecurity of intended effects would, however, destabilize the self-evidence of intervention benefits that is ubiquitous on the public face of intervention. This operational reality of intervention comes to the fore under conditions of anonymity or expressed by somebody who has already had a great career and does not have to fear to be reprimanded.

Impact and lack of impact are sometimes hard to distinguish in intervention. Asked about successes and failures in her job as a UN peacekeeper, one senior staff member at UN DPKO New York told me about her contribution to a peace process in Sierra Leone. She first described the fact of getting the peace process started as an important success and an intervention that had an impact. In the next step, however, she recounts how the peace process fell apart and presents this as a failure. Taken together both episodes make it very hard to judge the impact of UN activities in this particular situation. However, the UN staff member clearly takes it as a success and instance of impact:

KK: And what would you consider as your main successes in a personal, where did you contribute the most you think?

RESPONDENT: I think I made a pretty good contribution I think to bringing the war to an end in Sierra Leone through the work I was doing there with the Special Envoy. Pretty proud of that. Pretty proud of the work I've done in Cambodia.

KK: Could you just say what did you do with this Envoy that contributed to?

RESPONDENT: We had to work with the rebel force, the Revolutionary United Front, to get them out of the bush and into negotiations with the government. And then produced a peace agreement in November 1996. And it was just myself and the Special Envoy that was working on that. In a peacemaking mission. I think the work that I did in support of the peace talks in Sun City when I was working in Kinshasa was very useful I think in terms of helping to facilitate and ensure. At one point we worked really hard to make sure that they stopped, they stopped for a certain reason. I was very closely involved in the missions that went around in the region to try to ensure that the peace talks got back on track. I think that was quite important.

KK: And were there any failures that you?

RESPONDENT: Oh, lots. No, I mean in Sierra Leone there was a coup after the peace agreement even though a part was adopted. So we had to leave and we then worked for the government in exile to try and get the rebels back out. And then eventually we put in a much larger peacekeeping operation. So that was a failure in its. For a variety of reasons the peace agreement didn't work.

KK: So was that the backside of?

RESPONDENT: Yes, we got a peace agreement in November 1996 but then there was not enough international support to really get it to move forward. And then the rebels came together with the army to push the government out. That was really bad. And there was a coup that we didn't see coming.[63]

Why this UN staffer considered the peace agreement a success in the first place is not quite clear. The cognitive dissonance at play in her remarks underlines how important the construction of impact is for maintaining belief in intervention's effects and legitimacy.[64]

Another interpretive lens that helps stabilize interveners' self-assessments is the tendency to over-estimate one's impact. In order to underline this tendency, a MSF staffer in Goma referred to an episode in Darfur, notorious among humanitarians. When in 2009 after being indicted by the International Criminal Court, Sudanese president Omar Bashir decided to withdraw the visas of a number of humanitarian organizations, among them the American NGO IRC and some of the MSF chapters, interveners were outraged. Thousands would die and be deprived of life-saving assistance, they argued. Mortality rates, however, did not surge:

> But the doom and gloom prophesies of the NGOs and the UN agencies never happened. So I think sometimes we over-inflate our importance about how necessary our assistance is. We forget that people have had coping mechanisms through a long time before we ever arrived.[65]

How people coped, how essential international NGOs are in some settings thus has to be assessed carefully. The impossible counterfactual analysis makes this hard, however. Intervention actors can count on this to keep operating.

Next to the insecurity of legitimate presence and impact, lifestyle problems are very prominent among interveners. As we have seen, living in Goma as a humanitarian or peacekeeper is seen as interesting and exciting by most but many feel uncomfortable about a number of aspects of their life there. The terminology used to describe this is quite strong at times ranging from 'crap' to 'bullshit'[66] to the more sophisticated expression of the 'aid game'[67] everybody involved is said to play.

Depending on seniority and the wealth of the employing organization, expats in Goma tend to live in beautiful mansions at the lakefront of Lac Kivu or in one of the hotels.[68] Junior staff often lives in shared flats which take turns in organizing parties which are open to most. Contractual benefits usually include rest and recreation, i.e. paid leave every six to eight weeks to be able to connect with friends and family back home, as well as either their own car or a car with driver at their disposal as means of transport in Goma. Public transport is considered too dangerous. The pay ranges from 1,000 dollars for very junior staff at one of the poorer NGOs to 20,000 dollars a month for senior UN positions. A humanitarian affairs officer at UNHCR, for example, with roughly three years of work experience and a master's degree earns about 11,000 dollars a month – and does not have to pay taxes.

This kind of lifestyle was described as excessive by a number of interview partners. The discrepancy between their lifestyle at home and the possibilities in Goma is too big.[69] In addition, there is an obvious gulf of wealth between most Congolese in Goma and the 'internationals'.

Most of these problems show to what extent interveners are caught up in constant negotiations with themselves about the decency and morality of what they

Figure 4.1 Mugunga IDP camp, Goma.

Figure 4.2 NGO residence, Goma.

are doing. Some things are fortunately seen as clearly beneficial but a wealth of aspects make expat work in these contexts psychologically challenging. A former field staffer who is glad to have finally made it back to an American city like New York expresses her relief like this:

> I think very high performing national staff gets to a certain level and say, 'ok now I want to be an expat'. I want to have school fees paid, I want to have rest and recreation and all that junk which comes with being an expat. Which I really don't miss. I'm so over expat lifestyle at this point as well. And part of that was I got out of my system and I'm so happy to be in New York not living that lifestyle anymore. The bank account has dwindled and unpaid bills now and sometimes I forget because I'm not used to pay bills but yeah I'm making my bed, I'm washing my own dishes, you get so cuddled living overseas as an international staff which I don't like at all. Driven. You know everything is done for you.[70]

Not only can the lifestyle in Goma become a nuisance, there is a severe price to pay in terms of family and relationships to people in interveners' country of origin or previous posts. A senior UN humanitarian manager in Goma told me:

> you're basically married to UNHCR. It's a little bit like going into combats I think. You really have to battle to have an outside life; you really must make a point. So it's a real everyday battle to have an outside life, to keep your personal life from your work life different and to have friends outside of UNHCR and to, yeah, to give priority also to them it's very very difficult. You know, in UNHCR you will hear it a lot from the families: 'do we have to become refugees for you to pay attention to us?'[71]

For some of the interveners it becomes hard to get back to their former lives at all, while others regard this as absolutely essential to stay healthy:

> RESPONDENT: So it's like you have the choice but you don't really because if you retract back to normal civilian life it is basically you lose who you are, I mean you lose, the stimulation is not there anymore. The purpose isn't there anymore. So it's not really a choice. It would be a failure to go back. [...] No but like if you ask somebody here, what are you gonna do next? You know, you get addicted to this lifestyle so to go back to a regular civilian life is almost impossible. There is no way I'm gonna go back there, ever, I'll never go back to Canada.[72]

> ---

> KK: And what are your plans for the future?
> RESPONDENT: Oh my god. [Both laughing]. Good question. It would be interesting to get your feedback on this. You see a lot of international staff here who are, excuse my French, psychopaths, brain-fucked, brain-dead. People who are somehow broken. There are quite a few who have been doing this

job for too long. They get into certain patterns, sometimes bordering the racist or a certain arrogance. Sometimes they are just burnt out and I do not blame them. It is a consequence of what you are doing here all the time. You have a lot of power as an expat, ok? In Germany, you are just a regular guy, walking around. Here, you can have every woman if you like, right? At this social level alone you can turn anybody into your friend because you have the money. And a lot of people want to profit from the money you have. The difference in power with which you come here is just extremely big.[73]

Conclusion

Intervention depends on people to be carried out. This chapter offered a broad panorama of motivations, moral considerations and sceptical reflections among individual interveners in Goma and New York to provide texture and a feel for the practice of intervention. Much of what individual interveners talk about will be quite surprising for readers who regularly donate money and believe in the straightforward morality of humanitarian aid and peacekeeping. Intervention is in fact often a much more mundane and messy practice.

What interveners told me indicates clearly how delicate the judgments are that make some of the interveners assess the overall impact of intervention[74] or the legitimacy they enjoy to go to the Congo at all.[75] Similarly to the way NGO publications advance contradictory positions on humanitarian principles, what counts as a success of intervention at one particular moment may turn into a failure a couple of months later as in the case of the UN's role in the Sierra Leone peace process.[76] Individual interveners negotiate these reflections constantly and arrive at different conclusions. They are insecure about their legitimate presence and their overall impact, but the structural possibility to do this job and its attractiveness ultimately prevail over these insecurities. Individuals stabilize intervention despite these insecurities because the structure of global inequalities opens up a job market that provides an ideal vessel for various professional and personal desires. Like jobs in the media or in PR these jobs are fast-paced, full of potential for experimentation and change but they exceed these jobs on a number of fronts: they offer more variety, more challenges, more satisfaction and sometimes a lot more money.[77]

In providing a panorama of individual concerns and reflections, I concentrated on two main issues. First, motivations and rewards prior to coming to the Congo and the gratifications during operational intervention. Second, I analysed various reflections that I prompted during the interview or that came up freely. These reflections concern the moral duty to intervene which was rejected almost by all. By contrast, interveners generally assume they have a right to work in the Congo. This right derives from the legal fact of a Security Council mandate or a work permit or from procedural legitimacy or the recognition by Congolese 'beneficiaries'. The scepticism voiced by interveners dealt with the question of

The interviewees in Goma have ended up in two kinds of positions since 2009. A number of them are still in Goma in the same or another job. Many of them have changed organizations, from MSF to Oxfam or from OCHA to UNHCR and work in London, Paris, Geneva or New York now. In a number of years, they will probably settle for the 'ideal' workload consisting of long phases at Western Headquarters, or as self-employed consultant, which allows them to do occasional short-term missions to the projects or countries they continue to care about.

The emerging literary genre of the humanitarian autobiography (Smirl, 2012; Alexander, 2013) confirms that the hardship and soul-searching that comes with the simultaneously highly gratifying work as a humanitarian or peacekeeper indicates a bifurcated field of intervention. At the individual level, it is highly unstable and transient because after roughly ten years a large majority of humanitarians and peacekeepers have stopped working in high-risk duty stations like the Congo, Iraq or South-Sudan. These ten years are like a 'rite of passage' (Smirl, 2012) towards a personal and professional life with less excitement and psychological duress. At the institutional level, however, the presence of international humanitarian NGOs and the UN is near constant and often growing. New cohorts of idealist humanitarians and peacekeepers flock to Goma, Kabul or Juba and perpetuate the practice of intervention. Only by taking the long view and keeping the historical legacies in mind, the practice of intervention can be understood as both in performative flux and continuously governed by a long-standing structure of inequality and lack of global democracy.

Notes

1 The 2009 UN OCHA 'Who What Where contact directory' for North Kivu allows for a sense of the most important actors in Goma because the list includes most of their personnel. MONUC: 119 staff (excluding military), UNHCR:29, UNICEF: 29, UN OCHA: 28, WFP: 17, ICRC: 29, Oxfam: 44, MSF: 35, Solidarités: 30, World Vision: 17, on file with author. Budgets: UNHCR (US$79 million) ICRC (US$52 million, calculated from Swiss Francs $60 million at April 2009 rate), MSF (France: US$9 million; Holland US$13 million); Oxfam, no data available. Calculated based on 2009 annual reports.
2 'saisir la réalité concrète du travail humanitaire' translation from the French, KK.
3 This stands for Medical Emergency Relief International, a London-based NGO.
4 This is a fictitious story, inspired by 'internationals' I met in Goma.
5 I did not feel comfortable asking everybody for their age. For this reason I have not included this information in the list of interviewees in the appendix on method.
6 NGO Goma 8, 30 September 2009.
7 NGO Goma 10, 9 October 2009.
8 NGO New York 1, 18 November 2011.
9 NGO Goma 3, 5 October 2009; MONUSCO Civilian Goma 4.
10 NGO Goma 18, 17 September 2009.
11 NGO Goma 17, 16 September 2009. Translated from the French, KK.

> Il y a la route, les gens qui se réinstallent il y a la société, les paysans qui recommencent à cultiver, les écoles qu'on a construites, pleins, donc c'est bon, c'est extrêmement motivant. On ne peut pas avoir ce genre de réalisation en Europe,

quand vous faites une école en Europe il y en a déjà cinquante ou cent dans la même ville donc c'est pas très motivant. Ici au Congo quand vous faites une école correcte suivant les standards qualitatifs et étatiques qui est propre etc. bon c'est l'unique sur toute la ville. Ca c'est extrêmement important, moi je trouve ca vraiment important.

12 MONUSCO Civilian Goma 4, 26 September 2009.
13 UN HQ New York 9, 9 December 2011.
14 MONUSCO Civilian Goma 2, 25 September 2009.
15 MONUSCO Civilian Goma 5, 2 October 2009.
16 NGO Goma 18, 17 September 2009.
17 MONUSCO Civilian Goma 4, 26 September 2009.
18 NGO Goma 10, 9 October 2009.
19 Field notes, Goma 2009.
20 UN Goma 1, 1 October 2009: Translation from the German, KK:

Ich mache meine Arbeit hier, weil das ein Job ist, für mich ist das ein Job, ein gut-bezahlter Job in Klammer auf, Klammer zu, den ich ungern aufgeben würde, für den ich bereit bin gewisse Risiken einzugehen, und Unbill in Kauf zu nehmen, zum Beispiel von der Familie getrennt zu sein und so weiter, das, kann ich alles mit mir abmachen innerlich, das kann ich verkraften, aber, dass ich jetzt sagen würde, ich hänge mit, mit, mit Herzblut an der leidenden Bevölkerung, das tut mir leid das sagen zu müssen, die werden auf Jahrzehnte noch weiter leiden.

21 UN HQ New York 2, 18 November 2011.
22 MONUSCO Civilian Goma 3, 25 September 2009.
23 MONUSCO Civilian Goma 4, 29 Septermber 2009.
24 MONUSCO Civilian Goma 2, 25 September 2009.
25 NGO Goma 2, 22 September 2009. Ttranslated from the German, KK:

Rettungssanitäter, rum fahren, Leute auflesen, zusammenflicken, oder irgendwie, Kanülen in sie reinstecken und sie ins Krankenhaus befördern, das habe ich gemacht, und das hat mir auch sehr viel Spaß gemacht, aber es war irgendwie intellektuell nicht herausfordernd genug. Das ist sehr mechanisch, und ich habe danach etwas gesucht, wo ich irgendwie das, dieses praktische, ehm, praktisch-sinnvolle mit irgendwie diesem eh, intellektuell her-, auch anspruchsvollen verbinden kann. Und das ist ja, das ist schon sehr stark gegeben in der human-itären Hilfe, ne? Also wie, wie du sagst, diese ganzen Widersprüche, diese ganzen Dilemmata, die findest du hier zuhauf. Wo du, wo du hin guckst. Aber gleichzeitig auch dieses praktisch erfüllende, dass du denkst, Mensch, jetzt, haben wir die Qualität von diesem Gesundheitszentrum schon, schon steigern können, ne? Das hat schon irgendwie, was weiß ich, diesen 20-Leuten, -tausend Leuten da drum herum hat das schon was gebracht. Das ist diese, diese Kombination die ich ziem-lich spannend finde.

26 NGO Goma 7, 16 September 2009.
27 NGO Goma 18, 17 September 2009. Translation from the French, KK.

Ici eh, c'est un fait de se remettre aussi en question beaucoup plus facilement. Tu penses que, bon, tu es dans un environnement très différent du tien dessus lequel tu es habitué depuis tu es un enfant. Tu remets en question beaucoup plus fac-ilement. Et de fait de te remettre en question te permet avancer beaucoup plus vite quoi. Donc voilà, c'est tout ça qui me, tout ça qui me plaît quoi.

28 NGO Goma 3, 5 October 2009. Translated from the German, KK.

Es erlaubt dir auch jeden Tag etwas zu lernen, das ist wichtig. Und auch vorwärts zu kommen, also gleichzeitig lernst du neue Kulturen und Länder kennen und,

und kannst gleichzeitig sehr viel von denen lernen, man bekommt sehr viel, viel Verantwortung. Ich find in, in den meisten humanitären Organisationen finden sich Leute, die wahrscheinlich, ja, die werden hingestellt und haben dann, [lacht], eh, Funktionen zu erfüllen die, die sehr viel verlangen, habe ich das Gefühl.

29 NGO Goma 17, 16 September 2009. Translated from the French, KK: 'moi je crois que ca vaut la peine de venir travailler ici parce-qu'il y a quand même une certaine liberté qu'on a pas en Europe'.
30 MONUSCO Civilian Goma 4, 29 September 2009.
31 UN HQ New York 6, 30 September 2011.
32 NGO Goma 4, 12 September 2009; NGO Goma 2, 22 September 2009; NGO Goma 3, 5 October 2009; MONUSCO Civilian Goma 3 25 September 2009; MONUSCO Civilian Goma 5, 2 October 2009; UN Humanitarian Goma 6, 20 September 2009.
33 UN Humanitarian Goma 6, 20 September 2009. 'Et je pense que les gens qui se le disent [that they do it for moral reasons, KK], je trouve que ça sonne faut quoi. Ca sonne très très faut. Parce que c'est toujours répondre a des intérêts personnel' Translation from the French, KK.
34 MONUSCO Civilian Goma 3, 25 September 2009.
35 NGO Goma 10, 9 October 2009; See also NGO Goma 4, 12 September 2009.
36 MONUSCO Civilian Goma 2, 25 September 2009; UN HQ New York 5, 23 September 2011.
37 UN Humanitarian Goma 1, 4 October 2009.
38 NGO New York 1, 18 November 2011.
39 MONUSCO Civilian Goma 4, 29 September 2009.
40 UN HQ New York 8, 16 November 2011.
41 NGO New York 1, 18 November 2011.
42 NGO Goma 20, 1 October 2009.

C'est la notion de devoirs-là ça pose … varie. Ca dépend de c'est derrière l'histoire aussi. Moi par exemple ici au Congo, morale oui parce que avant tout c'est des Africains comme moi. Des frères, hein. Du même continent etcetera, etcetera. Moi je regarde quand je regarde le Congo je regarde un frère. Ok, on est du même continent. On est tous Africains. On partage plus de choses que d'autres qui nous différencient […] Mais moi je peux leur dire ça et ils le prennent bien. L'autre il le dit oui c'est lui il a été colonialiste avant etcetera. Moi on ne peut pas dire ça avec moi. Non. Je suis colonialiste de quoi? Rien du tout. Raciste. Non je ne suis pas raciste. Raciste comment? Tu vois. Donc il y a cette facilité-là aussi de parler et quand l'occasion est là j'en profite pour dire.

Translated from the French, KK

43 UN Humanitarian Goma 1, 4 October 2009.
44 MONUSCO Civilian Goma 2, 25 October 2009.
45 UN HQ New York 8, 18 November 2009; MONUSCO Civilian Goma 4, 29 September 2009; MONUSCO Civilian Goma 6, 6 October 2009.
46 NGO Goma 6, 15 September 2009; UN Humanitarian Goma 6, 29 September 2009.
47 UN Humanitarian Goma 1, 4 October 2009; MONUSCO Civilian Goma 1, 2009.
48 NGO Goma 3, 5 October 2009.
49 MONUSCO Civilian Goma 3, 25 September 2009.
50 UN Humanitarian Goma 6, 20 September 2009. 'Il y a aucune législation internationale en tout cas qui m'en empêche'. Translation from the French, KK.
51 MONUSCO Civilian Goma 3, 25 September 2009.
52 NGO Goma 2, 22 September 2009.
53 NGO Goma 7, 16 September 2009.
54 MONUSCO Civilian Goma 9, 7 October 2009.
55 MONUSCO Civilian Goma 4, 29 September 2009.

56 UN HQ New York 8, 16 November 2011.
57 NGO Goma 10, 9 October 2009.
58 UN HQ New York 8, 16 November 2011; Jean-Marie Guéhenno, New York, 11 November 2011.
59 NGO New York 1, 18 November 2011; UN HQ New York 6, 30 September 2011; NGO Goma 2, 22 September 2009.
60 UN HQ New York 8, 16 November 2011.
61 Jean-Marie Guéhenno, New York, 11 November 2011.
62 UN HQ New York 8, 16 November 2011.
63 UN HQ New York 2, 18 November 2011.
64 See Marriage's take on the role of cognitive dissonance for 'international assistance' (2006).
65 NGO Goma 7, 16 September 2009.
66 NGO Goma 6, 15 September 2009; NGO Goma 10, 9 October 2009; NGO Goma 2, 22 September 2009; MONUSCO Civilian Goma 4, 29 September 2009.
67 NGO Goma 3, 5 September 2009; NGO Goma 7, 16 September 2009.
68 This is the residence I stayed in for the second half of my stay in Goma 2009. Picture taken by author.
69 These are IDP tents in one of the camps at the outskirts of Goma. Picture taken by author.
70 NGO New York 1, 18 November 2011.
71 UN Humanitarian 1 Goma, 5 October 2009.
72 MONUSCO Civilian Goma 3, 25 September 2009.
73 NGO Goma 2, 22 September 2009. Translated from the German:

> KK: Und ehm, was sind deine Pläne für die Zukunft? Respondent: ‚Ach, Gott oh Gott. [beide lachen] Ehm, gute Frage, also, [pause] wär spannend von dir da ein feedback zu erhalten, aber ehm, du siehst ja schon, ziemlich viele, vieles internationales Personal hier, die ziemlich, das ist jetzt viele, viele unschöne, ehm, Begriffe sind, Psychopathen, brain-fucked, brain-dead irgendwie also, Leute, die einfach irgendwie kaputt sind, gibt es hier schon einige, die das zu lange machen, oder, die auch irgendwie in bestimmte Verhaltensmuster fallen, das kann teilweise ganz rassistisch sein, teilweise kann es gewisse Arroganz sein, teilweise kann es einfach ausgebrannt sein, und das werfe ich ihnen gar nicht jetzt persönlich vor, sondern es ist einfach, denke ich auch eine Begleiterscheinung dessen was, wenn man das eine Zeit lang macht. Du hast hier viel, als expat hast du hier verdammt viel Macht, ja? Du bist in Deutschland, du bist dann irgendwie ein normaler Kerl, der rumhüpft, und hier kannst du irgendwie, wenn du willst, jede Frau haben, ne? Allein, also, allein auf dieser sozialen Ebene bist du einfach hier, und du, kannst dir jeden zum Freund machen, weil du einfach Geld hast und jeder, oder, viele Leute wollen profitieren von dem Geld was du hast. Dieses Machtgefälle ist einfach unheimlich groß, mit dem du hier herkommst.

74 Interview Jean-Marie Guéhenno, 11 November 2011, New York.
75 MONUSCO Civilian Goma 4, 29 September 2009.
76 UN HQ New York 2, 18 November 2011.
77 See above for a salary range of interveners in Goma.

Conclusion

During my research in Goma, I came across an unexpected political battle. In mid-2009, the provincial governor and the provincial parliament had announced to the humanitarian and peacekeeping organizations in the city that a new provincial regulation about their activities in the Congo was being drafted. This *édit* was to contain numerous provisions on Congolese oversight and control over these organizations and, most crucially, it introduced provincial taxes, which NGOs were to pay from then on.

The regulation stipulated that international support was welcome but that the relationship between the provincial government and international NGOs was a public-private one. Private companies had to pay taxes in the Congo and since the tax base of the province was meagre, 'private' international NGOs needed to pay taxes. What is more, the *édit* was also to introduce an oversight mechanism over all NGOs and UN activities in the area because the results of these organizations' work had proven 'imperceptible' to the provincial government (Provincial Government and Provincial Assembly North Kivu, 2009). It was high time Western support became more effective, the second draft of this regulation proclaimed.[1]

This intended governmental regulation led to an outcry among the UN and NGOs in Goma. Heads of office, managers of operations and staff members unequivocally condemned it as blatant and thinly-veiled corruption. They concurred that the only aim the provincial government had in mind with this was personal enrichment. An initiative that one could consider an honest attempt at executing government functions over the province of North Kivu was for interveners an attempt at preventing the UN and NGOs from doing their intervention work.

Despite the presumed absence of state and government in the east of the country (see Chapter 2), the reaction of the UN and NGOs in Goma was swift and forceful. They considered the *édit* as a serious threat and were determined to prevent the regulation from being promulgated. The UN Office for the Coordination of Humanitarian Affairs convoked all their NGO partners and sent a message of protest to the provincial governor and the planning minister.[2] Their strategy contained in the letter was two-fold. On the one hand, they played the card of distinction on the market of intervention. They did so in the letter by distinguishing themselves from development actors and appealed to the minister to be treated separately. Since humanitarians operated on universal humanitarian principles, they argued they could not be lumped together with more long-term and political development actors.[3] On the other hand, they asked the government to participate more actively in UN coordination forums like the cluster system, instead of imposing their own provincial coordination system on all the intervention actors in Goma.

After complex negotiations throughout 2009, the *édit* was finally passed by the provincial assembly on 18 May 2010. The UN and NGOs had failed in preventing government oversight – on paper – but they had managed to prevent the provincial government from levying taxes. In the course of these negotiations, two opposing views on international intervention were tangible. The provincial government asserted that intervention was a 'mess' and that interveners pursued their work randomly and not in line with government priorities. The provincial government thus judged intervention practice according to its operational face. Intervention actors, by contrast, claimed that a defunct and corrupt government wanted to stop them from doing their work effectively. This latter perspective was based on the public face of intervention. It implies that if interveners acted in line with government priorities, they would not be independent and impartial any longer and would not respond to the needs of the populations but to those of the government. When claiming to adhere to its public face, humanitarian aid is thus structurally hesitant to recognize and support political structures in their area of operations.

MONUSCO (MONUC at the time) was not part of this particular battle. Yet, the peacekeeping mission has faced the same dilemma enshrined in their contradictory mandate until the time of writing in 2015: protecting civilians and fighting alongside government forces that are sometimes the worst human rights violators in the area is a circle that cannot be squared. Both humanitarians and peacekeepers are thus constantly torn between working with or around the government which in public proclamations is made to be inexistent or malevolent.

Putting interveners into their place

The government official in charge of this *édit* was the provincial planning minister. Like many of the leading politicians in the Kivus and in Kinshasa, the planning minister hails from the Congolese diaspora. After studying in Tunisia he had moved to Belgium and had worked in youth reinsertion programmes where he advised youngsters on how to create their own private businesses to get back on their feet. He had also been active in the diaspora opposition against Mobutu and had returned to the Congo when the AFDL rebellion of 1997 had managed to end Mobutu's rule. The minister explained his rationale for devising this regulation to me as follows:[4]

> Ok. And now every organization has to announce itself when it arrives. Because at the time of which I told you I talked about jungle. [KK laughing]

An organization could come here which does not know which does not come see the authorities but it's like by chance when you are walking around that you realize that this particular organization has opened shop in that particular corner of the Province. When you ask for their papers, no, I have already arranged everything with Kinshasa. And us at the local level, the local authorities you don't know them. I told them that, still, you are coming to me, I do not want to be surprised finding someone in my living room without knowing how he managed to enter. You must knock first, that is the minimum. You announce yourself. Once you have announced yourself someone will say 'come in'. And someone will show you where to sit down. You cannot come in ignoring that this house has an owner. You will sit down in the living room, even worse, go straight to the bedroom. No, it doesn't work like that.

The self-confident and little coordinated way of going about the Congolese 'living room' is not an unusual charge. Coordination is an avowed challenge for intervention actors themselves. Even the public versions of external evaluations reveal that there is room for improvement (Global Public Policy Institute, 2010). The administrative structure of the cluster system and the role of UN OCHA which has grown continuously indicate that humanitarians themselves see the need to do something about coordination. The perception of the minister is thus not necessarily misplaced. In humanitarian hotspots like Goma, the flurry of organizations, projects and approaches may become overwhelming and an urge among provincial authorities might arise to do something about this.

During a UN meeting in Geneva I was part of in 2007, a former Mozambican minister recalled that when Western interveners arrived in Mozambique during the early 2000 flooding, national politicians and bureaucrats suddenly had to deal with all kinds of issues.[5] For example, when the interveners needed electricity, their plugs did not fit and the Mozambicans were expected to do something about that quickly so the interveners could get to work. When Mozambique was flooded again in 2006, they denied many organizations operating permits and even sent full cargo planes with aid goods back. The Mozambican government thought it wise to deal with the challenges they faced on their own terms without many of the NGOs which assumed the government would have to work in line with their approaches – including their industrial plug norms – instead of the other way around.

Back in Goma, the administrative process of getting the provincial *édit* passed was not an authoritarian measure, as might have been expected from a government that is assumed to be either broken or malevolent. The minister had provided the internationals with the first draft but, according to him, they had failed to react to it. Only when the interveners realized that the minister was serious, they started to think about it and then reacted forcefully and tried to stop the entire regulation. The planning minister had his own theory on why they did not react at first:

Ok. They didn't read it because, I finally understood their preoccupations. They thought that they were in a jungle. So when you impose order nobody believes you. Going into a forest where nothing exists and you want to say ok, now we start building some roads here.[6]

From the perspective of the provincial minister, Western intervention actors had failed to take the provincial government seriously because they assumed they were working in a jungle. They did not expect government structures and Congolese interference in the jungle. They thus had to be made aware that North Kivu was no jungle and that they were in somebody's 'living room' here (see interview excerpt above). Whatever the other administrative or financial rationales behind this regulation were, the minister clearly saw the regulation as a tool of relationship management. Interveners did not seem respectful enough of the country they decided to operate in.

The *édit* was not only about intervention, however. As it was a provincial initiative, it also touched on the difficult constitutional conflicts between the federal state in Kinshasa and the prerogatives of the provinces. The constitution passed in 2006 contains provincial and federal prerogatives as well as mixed ones. It also stipulates that 40 per cent of the federal tax revenues should be sent to the provinces (Liégeois, 2009). This constitutional requirement has hardly been implemented. The relationship between Kinshasa and the provinces is conflicted. As a consequence, the provinces fend for themselves and refrain from sending their tax revenues to Kinshasa and thereby violate the constitution in turn. Interveners have to navigate this complex constitutional situation.

The provincial minister deemed it insufficient that organizations active in his 'living room' claim to have received their operating permits in Kinshasa already. According to him, this was not enough because Kinshasa often does not communicate with the provinces on issues like these. In order to overcome this lack of communication, the provincial government thus wanted to be in charge of registering, welcoming, taxing and overseeing intervention in North Kivu. This conundrum can obviously create headaches for the UN and NGOs. The labyrinth of Congolese administrative and legal structures does not make life easy for them. The way they deal with this challenge, however, indicates to what extent they want to be left to their own devices instead of engaging with the Congolese government.

The aim of bringing the provincial government into intervention's coordination system illustrates clearly that the UN and NGOs in Goma do not pay much attention to crucial government prerogatives like oversight over actors active on their territory. North Kivu governor Julien Paluku is not known to be particularly corrupt. If state weakness was really an issue interveners wanted the Congo to help overcome, why did the UN and NGOs actively boycott attempts at increasing state authority? Increasing oversight is of course a matter of state authority. The answer to this, which I have elaborated in detail throughout this book, is straightforward: western intervention is broadly self-referential and quite content about this. The Congo and the Congolese government do not matter much as long as the organizations can do their work in the way they see fit.

These episodes of intense negotiations between Western intervention and political actors rarely make it into one of the Congo articles in the *New York Times*, *Le Soir* or the German *Tageszeitung*. These political battles, instances of intense lobbying, negotiations and their settlement by way of provincial regulation jar with the dominant ways of pathologizing the Congo in intervention. As this book has shown, paying more attention to the operational reality of intervention practice allows for a more nuanced picture of both intervention and the Congo.

The value and limits of practice theory

The analysis of humanitarian intervention practice in this book highlights through its practice approach numerous aspects of intervention that are rarely in focus in International Relations. Most particularly, they almost never are thought of in conjunction. First, the single-case study design and the choice of the Congo point to the need to situate the contemporary practice of intervention in history and the political economy of rule. The Congo case allows making this point effectively. Interveners' reflections and approaches to the Congo and their work reveal longstanding colonial legacies which would be invisible without this sensitivity to history. At the same time, the strategies of rule used by Mobutu in the past and by Joseph Kabila today have always played an important role for the way intervention is allowed to work in the country. Without sustained attention to their strategies of rule, the study of international intervention practice remains detached from its operating environment in much the same way intervention itself insulates itself from the Congo.

Second, the 'performative understanding of the world' (Büger and Gadinger, 2014: 13) that comes with practice theory allows for a meticulous look at how intervention actors and their practices constantly relate to the Congo and intervention work. This performance shapes and reproduces intervention. Intervention is situated in history and the political economy of rule in the Congo but it is also a relation in the moment. 'To be is to be related' (Mol, 2002: 53) and this book has discussed three important pillars of contemporary ways of relating to intervention and the Congo: intervention actors including think tanks constantly bring up a particular Congo image making it ripe for intervention (Chapter 2), they cater to the public through PR in order to succeed on the project market (Chapter 3), and intervention personnel carry out intervention practice because of particular rewards this job offers and leave it because much of it becomes too hard to bear after a few years (Chapter 4).

Approaching humanitarian intervention as a practice thus has the benefit of depth and detail with regards to how exactly individual interveners think and experience intervention, and how think tanks, the UN and NGO operate publicly to gain funding but compromise and negotiate on the ground. At the same time, a meticulous look at the relations in intervention also calls for a broader perspective that situates these practices in history and political economy. Entering practices on the ground makes this broader perspective inevitable. Congolese interviewees constantly bring up the history of colonialism, and political battles such as the one presented above force readers and analysts to take history seriously because it matters for contemporary relations. What is more, the Kabila government and its allies and contenders at the provincial level play an important role for how intervention practice plays out on the ground. Planning and health ministries have their own priorities and speeches given by Kabila in Goma almost always mean that the IDP situation changes or relations to Rwanda improve or worsen. The larger geopolitics and global political economy of the Congo also come in sight when European donors are played off against China in negotiations, or when the government decides to launch large agro-industrial parks to limit Congolese dependence on food imports.

The meticulous and ethnographic approach of a practice theory analysis thus comes with the benefit of depth and detail and an awareness of its own limits. In a sense, practice theory lays the groundwork for its own critique because entering a research problematic like 'how does intervention work and how does it manage to perpetuate itself' through practices and relations on the ground eventually comes up against the larger forces of history and global political economy. This book kept this challenge present but chose to deal with this conundrum by focusing on the values of practice theory and by only alluding to its limits.

Even from a practice theory perspective, however, a number of aspects are missing in this analysis of Congo intervention. This book has remained mostly in the human realm. To grasp the practices of stabilizing intervention more comprehensively, the non-human aspect of it would have to be brought into the picture. The black box of intervention can be opened further. Relief objects, attack helicopters, training workshops, relaxation parties, hiring procedures, the life in the 'cubicle' and many other things and practices were beyond the scope of this book.[7] The role of compounds and security companies might have explained how intervention practice in Goma is materially set to work.[8] This book has remained an anthropocentric piece of work.

A serious political economy of intervention, then, which is still largely absent in intervention scholarship, would have investigated further the interconnected nature of the Congolese government, their Western and Eastern supporters as well as the global-local economy of Goma and its surroundings.[9] This kind of research could show how much profit for important business elites interveners create through their consumption in bars and by renting expensive lakefront villas in Goma. It would also investigate to what extent aid goods and peacekeeping deployments impact on the livelihood and political strategies of the various constituencies affected by intervention. Most importantly, this perspective could also shed light on the structural change of international solidarity. Why has the NGO form become so prominent and how does this relate to the nature of contemporary capitalism?

Sceptical readers might say that this book has mainly articulated the inherent dilemma of politics: politics is always messier than it claims. In politics, as Max Weber wrote, the 'ethics of conviction' or the 'ethics of responsibility' clash and are ever irreconcilable (1919: 441–450). Some refer to pure convictions and laudable goals others focus on the practical results of their work. In politics, one or the other principle is necessarily violated. When humanitarians speak about the purity of their principles, these sceptics might argue, they are expressing their genuine ethics of conviction. When peacekeepers claim to protect civilians or to fight alongside the Congolese army and do not manage to do this in practice, this is just the inherent difficulty and unpredictability of politics. The pragmatic and contradictory practices taking place in Goma are the necessary implication of the messiness of politics.

Yet, the self-referential practices think tanks, humanitarian NGO and UN peacekeeping and many of the individual interveners engage in are not simply pure expressions of an ethics of conviction which does not anticipate its consequences. These practices and reflections instead have serious biases with important implications: they dispense with the Congolese, their government and their self-determined way of bringing the Congo back on its feet. This is a longstanding trait of intervention in the Congo. More than a shift in tone will be required to move towards less condescending forms of international solidarity.

Notes

1 Numerous versions of this regulation including the final one are on file with author.
2 Letter on file with author.
3 See Chapter 3 for more on the operational reality of these claims.
4 Provincial Government Goma 1, 9 October 2009.

> Bon voila. Et maintenant chaque organisation quand elle va arriver il faut d'abord qu'elle s'annonce. Parce que à l'époque comme cela j'ai parlé de jungle [KK. Laughing] une organisation pouvait arriver ici qui ne sait qui ne voit même pas les autorités mais c'est comme par hasard dans l'itinérance on va se rendre compte que tel organisation se trouve dans tel coin de la Provence. Quand vous demandez ses papiers non j'ai déjà tout arrangé avec Kinshasa. Et nous au niveau eh local, les autorités locales ne vous connaissez pas mais je leur avais dit j'ai dit mais quand même vous entrez chez moi, je ne peux pas être surpris de trouver quelqu'un maintenant dans mon salon et je ne sais pas comment il est entré. D'abord il faut toquer c'est la moindre des choses. Vous vous annoncez. Une fois vous vous annoncez on va dire entrez! Et on vous montre où vous installer. Ce ne pas que vous venez et que vous ignorez que cette maison a un propriétaire. Vous allez vous mettre au salon encore pire même aller dans la chambre à coucher. Ah non non ça ne va pas.
>
> Translation from the French, KK

5 Fieldnotes Geneva, 12 February 2007.
6 Provincial Government Goma 1, 9 October 2009.

> Bon, ils ne l'avaient pas lu parce que j'ai compris aussi finalement leurs préoccupations. Pour eux ils pensaient qu'il se trouvait dans une jungle donc quand vous mettez de l'ordre personne ne peut vous croire. Allez dans une fôret où il n'y a rien et vous voulez dire voilà, maintenant on commence à construire des rues ici.
>
> Translation from the French, KK

7 See Nikolas Kosmatopoulos' excellent ethnography on *Pacifying Lebanon* (2012) for an analysis along these lines.

8 The focus on aid compounds was pioneered by Mark Duffield (2010a). Peer Schouten and I have provided an analysis building on this (Koddenbrock and Schouten, 2014).
9 Adam Branch's work on human rights intervention in Northern Uganda (2011) is the most comprehensive political economy of intervention. See also Bliesemann de Guevara and Kühn (2013) and Stylianos Moshonas (2013).

Appendix
Interview guidelines

Goma 2009

Personal background

1 Could you tell me something about your biography? What did you do before you came here?

Congo

2 What is the Congo for you?
3 What part of Congolese history do you find particularly interesting or important?
4 What do you think about the current political situation?
5 Do you remember how your Congo image was before you came here?
6 What has changed?

Concepts

7 What is humanitarian aid for you?
8 What is development for you?
9 What are state-and peacebuilding for you?
10 What idea is behind these concepts?

Role and motivation

11 What is your role in the Congo?
12 Since when are you here?
13 Why do you do this work?
14 Do you feel you have a moral duty to do this kind of work?
15 Do you think you have the right to do this work?
16 What have been personal successes during your time here?
17 What have been failures?
18 What kind of preparation did you have before you came here?

19   What books have you read?
20   What sources of information do you use?
21   What are your plans for the future?

Organization

22   What is particular about your organization?
23   Which projects are difficult?
24   Which projects work particularly well?
25   How are decisions taken in your organization?
26   How many Congolese colleagues do you have?
27   What are their tasks and positions?
28   How do you see the challenges around the neutrality of staff?
29   How much do they earn?
30   How do you see the interaction between the three groups among your organization – Western expats, Southern expats and nationals?
31   How is your image of the Congolese?
32   How does your organization recruit people?
33   How do you see the contact with the population of Goma?

Mars question

34   Imagine you are on Mars and you see the world and next to you E.T. sitting there, you see the world, you see the Congo, you see the links between the world and the Congo and you see the different people engaged in the Congo. How would you describe that situation to a very smart E.T. sitting next to you?

New York 2011

Person and work

1   Could you tell me something about your biography? Education and work and family background
2   What did you do before you came here?
3   How does a typical workday look?

Congo

4   What is the Congo for you?

Role and motivation

5   Why do you do this work?
6   Do you feel you have a moral duty to do this kind of work?

7   Do you think you have the right to do this work?
8   What have been personal successes during your time here?
9   What have been failures?
10 What books do you read for work?
11 What are your most regular and trustworthy think tank or policy papers?
12 What sources of information do you use?
13 What are your plans for the future?

Organization

14 What is particular about your organization?
15 Which projects are difficult?
16 Which projects work particularly well?
17 How are decisions taken in your organization?
18 What are their tasks and positions?
19 How do you see the interaction between the three groups among your organization – Western expats, Southern expats and nationals?
20 How does your organization recruit people?

Mars question

21 Imagine you are on Mars and you see the world and next to you E.T. sitting there, you see the world, you see the Congo, you see the links between the world and the Congo and you see the different people engaged in the Congo. How would you describe that situation to a very smart E.T. sitting next to you?

List of interviewees

Based on three research stays:

Goma from 30 August to 15 October 2008 and from 25 August to 20 October 2009

New York from 30 August 2011 to 17 December 2011

Table A1.1 Research interviews carried out, 2009–2011

Number	Alias	Date	Nationality
Goma			
1	Donor Goma 1	5 October 2009	British
2	Donor Goma 2	9 October 2009	US
3	Donor Goma 3	12 September 2009	Belgian
4	Donor Goma 4	26 September 2009	Belgian
5	Donor Goma 5	26 September 2009	German
6	Donor Military Goma 1	30 September 2009	Belgian
7	Citizen Goma 1	29 September 2009	Congolese
8	Citizen Goma 2	29 September 2009	Congolese
9	Citizen Goma 3	5 October 2009	Congolese
10	MONUC Military Goma 1	14 September 2009	French
11	MONUC Military Goma 2	5 October 2009	Indian
12	MONUSCO Civilian Goma 1	25 September 2009	German
13	MONUSCO Civilian Goma 2	25 September 2009	Canadian
14	MONUSCO Civilian Goma 3	25 September 2009	British
15	MONUSCO Civilian Goma 4	29 September 2009	Belgian
16	MONUSCO Civilian Goma 5	2 October 2009	Belgian
17	MONUSCO Civilian Goma 6	6 October 2009	Ethiopian
18	MONUSCO Civilian Goma 7	24 September 2009	Mauritanian
19	MONUSCO Civilian Goma 8	24 September 2009	Dutch
20	MONUSCO Civilian Goma 9	7 October 2009	Austrian
21	NGO Goma 1	8 September 2009	German
22	NGO Goma 2	22 September 2009	German
23	NGO Goma 3	5 October 2009	Swiss
24	NGO Goma 4	12 September 2009	US
25	NGO Goma 5	14 September 2009	Italian
26	NGO Goma 6	15 September 2009	Canadian
27	NGO Goma 7	16 September 2009	British
28	NGO Goma 8	30 September 2009	Australian
29	NGO Goma 9	14 September	Australian
30	NGO Goma 10	9 October 2009	British
31	NGO Goma 11	10 September 2009	Congolese
32	NGO Goma 12	10 September 2009	Chilean
33	NGO Goma 13	11 September 2009	French
34	NGO Goma 14	14 September 2009	French
35	NGO Goma 15	15 September 2009	Italian
36	NGO Goma 16	15 September 2009	Congolese
37	NGO Goma 17	16 September 2009	Belgian
38	NGO Goma 18	17 September 2009	French
39	NGO Goma 19	18 September 2009	French
40	NGO Goma 20	1 October 2009	Senegalese
41	NGO Goma 21	17 September 2009	US
42	NGO Goma 22	26 September 2009	Spanish
43	UN Humanitarian Goma 1	4 October 2009	US
44	UN Humanitarian Goma 2	6 October 2009	Spanish
45	UN Humanitarian Goma 3	9 October 2009	Belgian
46	UN Humanitarian Goma 4	11 September 2009	Congolese
47	UN Humanitarian Goma 5	15 September 2009	French
48	UN Humanitarian Goma 6	20 September 2009	Belgian
49	UN Goma 1	1 October 2009	German

Table A1.1 Continued

Number	Alias	Date	Nationality
50	Provinical Government Goma 1	9 October 2009	Congolese
51	Provinical Government Goma 2	9 October 2009	Congolese
New York			
52	Jean-Marie Guéhenno	11 November 2011	French
53	UN HQ New York 1	23 September 2011	Belgian
54	UN HQ New York 2	18 November 2011	British
55	UN HQ New York 3	9 December 2011	US
56	UN HQ New York 4	2 December 2011	Irish
57	UN HQ New York 5	23 September 2011	Danish
58	UN HQ New York 6	30 September 2011	Swedish
59	UN HQ New York 7	12 October 2011	US
60	UN HQ New York 8	16 November 2011	Canadian
61	UN HQ New York 9	9 December 2011	Irish
62	UN HQ New York 10	20 October 2011	French
63	UN HQ New York 11	11 November 2011	Congolese
64	NGO New York 1	18 November 2011	US
65	NGO New York 2	14 December 2011	Canadian
Berlin			
66	NGO Berlin 1	29 July 2009	Luxembourgian

Bibliography

Abrahamsen, R. and Williams, M. (2011) Privatization in practice: power and capital in the field of global security. In: Adler, E. and Pouliot, V. (eds) *International Practices*. Cambridge University Press, Cambridge.

Abrams, P. (1988) Notes on the Difficulty of Studying the State. *Journal of Historical Sociology* 1 (1), 58–89.

Acuto, M. (ed.) (2014) *Negotiating Relief: The Politics of Humanitarian Space*. Oxford University Press, New York.

Acuto, M. and Curtis, S. (eds) (2013) *Reassembling International Theory: Assemblage Thinking and International Relations*. Palgrave, Houndmills.

Adler, E. and Pouliot, V. (2011a) International Practices: Introduction and Framework. In: Adler, E. and Pouliot, V. (eds) *International Practices*. Cambridge University Press, Cambridge, 3–35.

Adler, E. and Pouliot, V. (2011b) International Practices. *International Theory* 3 (1), 1–36.

Adler, E. and Pouliot, V. (eds) (2011c) *International Practices*. Cambridge University Press, Cambridge.

AfriMAP (2010) *République Démocratique du Congo: Démocratie et participation à la vie politique: une évaulation des premiers pas dans la IIIième République*. Johannesburg.

Agamben, G. (1998) *Homo sacer: Sovereign power and bare life*. Stanford University Press, Stanford.

Agamben, G. (2005) *State of exception*. University of Chicago Press, Chicago.

Agathangelou, A. M. and Ling, L. H. M. (2009) *Transforming world politics: From empire to multiple worlds*. Routledge, London, New York.

Agier, M. (2002) *Aux bords du monde, les refugiés*. Flammarion, Paris.

Agier, M. (2008) *Gérer les indésirables: Des camps de réfugiés au gouvernement humanitaire*. Flammarion, Paris.

Agier, M. (2010) Humanity as an Identity and Its Political Effects (A Note on Camps and Humanitarian Government). *Humanity: An International Journal of Human Rights, Humanitarianism and Development* 1 (1), 29–45.

Aihwa Ong and Collier, S. (eds) (2005) *Global Assemblages*. Blackwell Publishing, Malden.

Alberti, K. P., Grellety, E. and Lin, Y. C. *et al.* (2010) Violence against civilians and access to health care in North Kivu, Democratic Republic of Congo: three cross-sectional surveys. *Conflict and Health* 4 (1), 17.

Alexander, J. (2013) *Chasing chaos: My decade in and out of humanitarian aid*. Broadway Books, New York.

Allen, L. (2009) Martyr bodies in the media: Human rights, aesthetics, and the politics of immediation in the Palestinian intifada. *American Ethnologist* 36 (1), 161–180.

ALNAP (2003) *Participation by Crisis-Affected Populations in Humanitarian Action.* London.

Amnesty International (2009) *No end to war on women and children: North Kivu, Democratic Republic of Congo.* London.

Andersen, M. S. (2012) Legitimacy in State-Building: A Review of the IR Literature. *International Political Sociology* 6 (2), 205–219.

Andersen, M. S. and Neumann, I. B. (2012) Practices as Models: A Methodology with an Illustration Concerning Wampum Diplomacy. *Millennium – Journal of International Studies* 40 (3), 457–481.

Anderson, K. (2005) *Do global trade distortions still harm developing country farmers?* Centre for Economic Policy Research, London.

Anderson, M. B. (1999) *Do no harm: How aid can support peace or war.* Lynne Rienner Publishers, Boulder, London.

Anghie, A. (2004) *Imperialism, Sovereignty and the making of International Law.* Cambridge University Press, New York.

Anievas, A., Manchanda, N. and Shilliam, R. (2014) *Race and racism in international relations: Confronting the global colour line.* Routledge, London.

Aradau, C. and Huysmans, J. (2013) Critical Methods in International Relations: the politics of techniques, devices and acts. *European Journal of International Relations.* Available online first 28 June 2013.

Ashley, R. K. (1988) Untying the Sovereign State: A Double Reading of the Anarchy Problematique. *Millennium – Journal of International Studies* 17 (2), 227–262.

Atlani-Duault, L. (2005) *Au bonheur des autres: Anthropologie de l'aide humanitaire.* Publications de la Société d'ethnologie, Nanterre.

Austin, J. (1962) *How to do Things with Words.* Clarendon Press, Oxford.

Autesserre, S. (2008) The Trouble With Congo: How Local Disputes Fuel Regional Conflict. *Foreign Affairs* 87 (3), 94–110.

Autesserre, S. (2009) Hobbes and the Congo: Frames, Frames, Local Violence, and International Intervention. *International Organization* 63, 249–280.

Autesserre, S. (2010) *The trouble with the Congo: Local violence and the failure of international peacebuilding.* Cambridge University Press, New York.

Autesserre, S. (2012) Dangerous Tales: Dominant Narratives on the Congo and their unintended Consequences. *African Affairs* 111 (443), 202–222.

Autesserre, S. (2014) *Peaceland: Conflict Resolution and the Everyday Politics of International Intervention.* Cambridge University Press, New York.

Baaz, M. E. (2005) *The paternalism of partnership: A postcolonial reading of identity in development aid.* Zed Books, London.

Baaz, M. E. and Olsson, O. (2011) Feeding the Horse: Unofficial Economic Activities within the Police Force in the Democratic Republic of the Congo. *African Security* 4 (4), 223–241.

Baaz, M. E. and Stern, M. (2008) Making sense of violence: voices of soldiers in the Congo (DRC). *The Journal of Modern African Studies* 46 (1), 57–86.

Baaz, M. E. and Stern, M. (2009) Why do soldiers rape? *International Studies Quarterly* 53, 499–518.

Baaz, M. E. and Stern, M. (2010) *The Complexity of Violence: A critical analysis of sexual violence in the Democratic Republic of Congo (DRC).* The Nordic Africa Institute, Uppsala.

Baaz, M. E. and Stern, M. (2011) Whores, men, and other misfits: Undoing 'feminiza-tion' in the armed forces in the DRC. *African Affairs* 110 (441), 563–585.

Baaz, M. E. and Stern M. (2013) Willing reform? An analysis of defence reform initi-atives in the DRC. In: Bigsten A (ed.) *Globalization and development: Rethinking interventions and governance.* London, Routledge, 193–212.

Baaz M. E. and Verweijen, J. (2013) The volatility of a half-cooked bouillabaisse: Rebel–military integration and conflict dynamics in the eastern DRC. *African Affairs* 112 (449): 563–582.

Bachmann, J. (2012) Governmentality and Counterterrorism: Appropriating International Security Projects in Kenya. *Journal of Intervention and Statebuilding* 6 (1), 41–56.

Bachmann J., Bell, C., and Holmqvist, C. (2014) *War, police and assemblages of inter-vention.* Routledge, London.

Baku, F. (2009) L'agriculture congolaise à réinventer. *Défis Sud* 91, 9–11.

Balibar, É. (1991) Is there a neo-racism. In: Balibar, E. and Wallerstein, I. M. (eds) *Race, nation, class: Ambiguous identities.* Verso, London, New York, 17–28.

Balibar, É. and Wallerstein, I. M. (eds) (1991) *Race, nation, class: Ambiguous identities.* Verso, London, New York.

Barad, K. (2003) Posthumanist Performativity: Toward an Understanding of How Matter Comes to Matter. *Signs: Journal of Women in Culture and Society* 28 (3), 801–831.

Barad, K. (2007) *Meeting the Universe Halfway: Quantum Physics and the Entanglement of Matter and Meaning.* Duke University Press, Durham and London.

Barnett, M. (2008) Humanitarianism: A Brief History of the Present. In: Barnett, M. N. (ed.) *Humanitarianism in question: Politics, power, ethics.* Cornell University Press, Ithaca, NY, 1–48.

Barnett, M. (ed.) (2008) *Humanitarianism in question: Politics, power, ethics.* Cornell University Press, Ithaca, NY.

Barnett, M. (2009) Evolution without Progress: Humanitarianism in a World of Hurt. *International Organization* 63 (Fall), 621–663.

Barnett, M. (2010) *The international humanitarian order.* Routledge, London.

Barnett, M. (2011) *Empire of Humanity: A History of Humanitarianism.* Cornell Univer-sity Press, Ithaca, NY.

Barnett, M. (2012) International paternalism and humanitarian governance. *Global Con-stitutionalism* 1 (3), 485–521.

Barnett, M. and Finnemore, M. (2004) *Rules for the World: International Organizations in Global Politics.* Cornell University Press, Ithaca, NY.

Bartelson, J. (2001) *The Critique of the State.* Cambridge University Press, London.

Bass, G. (2008) *Freedom's Battle: The Origins of Humanitarian Intervention.* Knopf Publishing, New York.

Bayart, J.-F. (2005) Foucault au Congo. In: Granjon, M.-C. (ed.) *Penser avec Michel Foucault: Théorie critique et pratiques politiques.* Karthala, Paris.

Bayart, J.-F. (2006) *L'État en Afrique: La politique du ventre.* Fayard, Paris.

Bayart, J.-F. (2007) *Global subjects: A political critique of globalization.* Polity, Cam-bridge.

Bayart, J.-F. (2011) Postcolonial Studies: A Political Invention of Tradition? *Public Culture* 23 (1), 55–84.

Bayart, J.-F. and Bertrand, R. (2006) De quels 'Legs Colonial' parle-t-on? *Esprit* 12 (December), 134–160.

Bechtolsheimer, G. (2012) *Breakfast with Mobutu: Congo, the United States and the Cold War, 1964–1981.* PhD thesis, London.

Beckert, S. (2014) *Empire of cotton: A global history*. Knopf, New York.

Bellamy, A. (2004) The 'Next Stage' in Peace Operations Theory? *Security Dialogue* 11 (1), 17–38.

Bellamy, A. and Williams, P. (2010) *Understanding Peacekeeping*. Polity, Cambridge.

Bemba, L.-R. M. (2013) Après la visite des officiers supérieurs militaires africains au Nord Kivu. *L'Observateur Congo*, 18 March 2013.

Benner, T. (2011) Heart of Darkness. *Survival* 53 (5), 169–178.

Benner, T. and Rotmann, P. (2008) Learning to Learn? UN Peacebuilding and the Challenges of Building a Learning Organization. *Journal of Intervention and Statebuilding* 2 (1), 43–62.

Benner, T. and Rotmann, P. (2009) Heillos überfordert: UN-Friedenseinsätze und der Schutz von Zivilisten in Konfliktzonen. *Vereinte Nationen* (4), 147–152.

Benner, T. and Rotmann, P. (2010) Zehn Jahre Brahimi-Bericht: Die UN-Friedenssicherung steht weiterhin vor großen Herausforderungen. *Vereinte Nationen* (3), 115–119.

Benner, T., Mergenthaler, S. and Philip Rotmann (2012) *The New World of UN Peace Operations: Learning to Build Peace?* Oxford University Press, Oxford.

Berman, B. and Lonsdale, J. (2002) *Unhappy valley: Conflict in Kenya and Africa*, Currey, Oxford.

Beswick, D. (2009) The Challenge of Warlordism to Post-Conflict State-Building: The Case of Laurent Nkunda in Eastern Congo. *The Round Table* 98 (402), 333–346.

Bhabha, H. K. (2007) *The location of culture*. Reprinted. Routledge, London.

Bierschenk, T., Chauveau, J. P. and Olivier de Sardan, J. P. (eds) (1999) *Courtiers en développement. Les village africains en quete de projets*. Karthala, Paris.

Bilgin, P. and Morton, A. D. (2002) Historicising Representations of 'Failed States': Beyond the Cold-War Annexation of the Social Sciences? *Third World Quarterly* 23 (1), 55–80.

Binder, A., Koddenbrock, K. and Horváth, A. (2013) *Reflections on the inequity of humanitarian assistance: possible courses of action for Germany*. Global Public Policy Institute, Berlin. Available at: www.gppi.net/fileadmin/media/pub/2013/binder-et-al_2013_inequities-humanitarian-assistance.pdf.

Bliesemann de Guevara, B. (2009) *Staatlichkeit in Zeiten des Statebuilding: Intervention und Herrschaft in Bosnien und Herzegowina*. Lang, Frankfurt am Main.

Bliesemann de Guevara, B. (ed.) (2012) *Statebuilding and State-Formation: The political sociology of intervention*. Routledge, London.

Bliesemann de Guevara, B. (2014) Studying the International Crisis Group. *Third World Quarterly* 35 (4), 545–562.

Bliesemann de Guevara, B. and Kühn, F. P. (2011) 'The International Community Needs to Act': Loose Use and Empty Signalling of a Hackneyed Concept. *International Peacekeeping* 18 (2), 135–151.

Bliesemann de Guevara, B. and Kühn, F. (2013) The Political Economy of Statebuilding: Rents, Taxes and Perpetual Dependency. In: Chandler D and Timothy Sisk (eds) *The Routledge Handbook of International Statebuilding*. London, Routledge, 219–230.

Blore, S. and Smillie, I. (2010) *An ICGLR-based Tracking and Certification System for Minerals from the Great Lakes Region of Central Africa*, Partnership Africa Canada, Ontario.

Bøås, M. and Jennings, K. (2006) Insecurity and Development: The Rhetoric of the 'Failed State'. *The European Journal of Development Research* 17 (3), 385–395.

Böhm, A. (1994) Grounded Theory – Wie aus Texten Modelle und Theorien gemacht werden. In: Boehm, A., Mengel, A. and Muhr, T. (eds) *Texte verstehen Konzepte, Methoden, Werkzeuge*. Konstanz: University-Verl., Konstanz, 121–140.

Boltanski, L. and Chiapello, E. (1999) *Le nouvel esprit du capitalisme*. Gallimard, Paris.

Bonacker, T., Daxner, M., Free, J. H. and Zürcher, C. (eds) (2010) *Interventionskultur: Zur Soziologie von Interventionsgesellschaften*. VS Verlag für Sozialwissenschaften, Wiesbaden.

Bonwick, A. (2006) Who really protects civilians? *Development in Practice* 16 (3–4), 270–277.

Bornstein, E. and Redfield, P. (eds) (2010) *Forces of Compassion: Humanitarianism between Ethics and Politics*. School for Advanced Research Press, Santa Fe.

Bourdieu, P. (1977) *Outline of a Theory of Practice*. Cambridge University Press, New York.

Bourdieu, P. (2000) Making the Economic Habitus: Algerian Workers Revisited. *Ethnography* 1, 17–41.

Boyce, J. and Ndikumana, L. (2001) Is Africa a Net Creditor? New Estimates of Capital Flight from Severely Indebted Sub-Saharan African Countries, 1970–96. *Journal of Development Studies* 38 (2), 27–56.

Bradol, J.-H. and Jean-Hervé Jézéquel (2010) *Child Undernutrition: advantages and limits of a humanitarian medical approach*. MSF-Crash, Paris.

Bradol, J.-H. and Vidal, C. (1997) Les attitudes humanitaires dans la région des Grands Lacs. *Politique Africaine* (68), 69–77.

Braeckman, C. (2003) *Les nouveaux prédateurs: Politique des puissances en Afrique centrale*. Fayard, Paris.

Branch, A. (2011) *Displacing Human Rights: War and Intervention in Northern Uganda*. Oxford University Press, Oxford.

Bräutigam, D. (2009) *Rogue donors? The real story of Chinese aid and engagement in Africa*. Oxford University Press, Oxford.

Breakey, H. and Dekker, S. (2014) Weak Links in the Chain of Authority: The Challenges of Intervention Decisions to Protect Civilians. *International Peacekeeping* 21 (3), 307–323.

Breton-Le Goff, G. (2010) Ending Sexual Violence in the Democratic Republic of the Congo. *The Fletcher Forum for World Affairs* 24 (1), 13–40.

Breuer, F. (2009) *Reflexive Grounded Theory*. VS Verlag für Sozialwissenschaften, Wiesbaden.

Brigg, M. (2009) The Developer's Self: A non-deterministic Foucauldian Frame. *Third World Quarterly* 30 (8), 1411–1426.

Bryant, A. and Charmaz, K. (eds) (2007) *The SAGE handbook of grounded theory*. SAGE, Los Angeles.

Büger, C. and Bethke, F. (2014) Actor-networking the 'failed state'. *Journal of International Relations and Development* 17(1), 30–60.

Büger, C. and Gadinger, F. (2008) Praktisch Gedacht. *Zeitschrift für Internationale Beziehungen* 15 (2), 273–302.

Büger, C. and Gadinger, F. (2014) *International practice theory: New perspectives*. Palgrave Macmillan, Houndmills.

Büschel, H. and Speich, D. (2009) *Entwicklungswelten: Globalgeschichte der Entwicklungszusammenarbeit*. Campus-Verl., Frankfurt am Main.

Büscher, K. (2010) Humanitarian presence and urban development: new opportunities and contrasts in Goma, DRC. *Disasters* 34 (2), 256–273.

Büscher, K. and Vlassenroot, K. (2010) Humanitarian presence and urban development: new opportunities and contrasts in Goma, DRC. *Disasters* 34 (1), 256–273.

Butler, J. (1990) *Gender Trouble: Feminism and the Subversion of Identity*. Routledge, New York.

Cain K., Postlewait, H. and Thomson, A. (2006) *Emergency sex (and other desperate measures)*. Ebury, London.

Calhoun, C. (2004) A World of Emergencies: Fear, Intervention, and the Limits of Cosmopolitan Order: The 2004 Sorokin Lecture. *Canadian Journal of Sociology and Anthropology* 41, 373–395.

Calhoun, C. (2010) The Idea of Emergency: Humanitarian Action and Global (Dis)Order. In: Fassin, D. and Pandolfi, M. (eds) *Contemporary states of emergency: The politics of military and humanitarian interventions*. Zone Books, Brooklyn, NY, 29–58.

Call, C. T. (2011) Beyond the 'failed state': Toward conceptual alternatives. *European Journal of International Relations* 17 (2), 303–326.

Callaghy, T. M. (1984) *The state-society struggle: Zaire in comparative perspective*. Columbia University Press, New York.

Callaghy, T. M. (2001) *Intervention and transnationalism in Africa: Global-local networks of power*. Cambridge University Press, Cambridge.

Callon, M. (ed.) (1998) *The Laws of the Markets*. Blackwell Publishers, Oxford.

Callon, M. (2006) What Does it Mean to Say that Economics is Performative? Available at: http://halshs.archives-ouvertes.fr/docs/00/09/15/96/PDF/WP_CSI_005.pdf.

Campbell, D. (1998) *National Deconstruction: Violence, Identity and Justice in Bosnia*. University of Minnesota Press, Minneapolis.

Caplan, R. (2007) From collapsing states to neo-trusteeship: the limits to solving the problem of 'precarious statehood' in the 21st century. *Third World Quarterly* 28 (2), 231–244.

Carayannis, T. (2009) *The challenge of building sustainable peace in the DRC*. Center for Humanitarian Dialogue Background Paper, Geneva.

Carnahan, M., Gilmore And, S. and Durch, W. (2007) New Data on the Economic Impact of UN Peacekeeping. *International Peacekeeping* 14 (3), 384–402.

The Carter Center (2007) *Review of DRC Mining Review – Update and Recommendations*. Available at: www.cartercenter.org/documents/drc_mining_contracts_113007.pdf.

Castro Varela, M. d. M. and Dhawan, N. (2005) *Postkoloniale Theorie: Eine kritische Einführung*. Transcript-Verl., Bielefeld.

Center on International Cooperation (2012) *Annual Review of Global Peace Operations*. New York.

Chabal P. and Daloz J. (1999) *Africa works: Disorder as political instrument*. Zed Books, Bloomington.

Chandler, D. (1999) *Bosnia Faking Democracy After Dayton*. Pluto Press, London.

Chandler, D. (2002) *From Kosovo to Kabul and Beyond: Human Rights and International Intervention*. Pluto Press, London.

Chandler, D. (2006a) Back to the future? The limits of neo-Wilsonian ideals of exporting democracy. *Review of International Studies* 32, 475–494.

Chandler, D. (2006b) *Empire in denial: The politics of state-building*. Pluto Press, London.

Chandler, D. (2008) Review Essay: Human Security: The Dog That Didn't Bark. *Security Dialogue* 39 (4), 427–438.

Chandler, D. (2009a) *Hollow hegemony: Rethinking global politics, power and resistance*. Pluto Press, London.

Chandler, D. (2009b) Critiquing Liberal Cosmopolitanism – The Limits of the biopolitical approach. *International Political Sociology* 3, 53–70.

Chandler, D. (2010) *International Statebuilding: The Rise of Post-Liberal Governance*. Routledge, London.

Chandler, D. (2012) Resilience and human security: The post-interventionist paradigm. *Security Dialogue* 43 (3), 213–229.

Chandler, D. (2013) The World of Attachment? The Post-Humanist Challenge to Freedom and Necessity. *Millennium – Journal of International Studies* 51 (3), 516–534.

Chandler, D. and Timothy Sisk (eds) (2013) *A Routledge Handbook on Statebuilding*. Routledge, London.

Charmaz, K. (2009) *Constructing grounded theory: A practical guide through qualitative analysis*. Reprinted. SAGE, Los Angeles.

Chatterjee, P. (1993) *The nation and its fragments: Colonial and postcolonial histories*. Princeton University Press, Princeton, N.J.

Chatterjee, P. (1997) Beyond the Nation? Or Within? *Economic and Political Weekly* 32 (1–2), 30–34.

Cheah, P. (2007) Biopower and the New International Division of Reproductive Labour. *boundary 2* 34 (1), 79–113.

Cheah, P. (2008) Crises of Money. *Positions: East Asia Cultures Critique* 16 (1), 189–219.

Cheah, P. and Robbins, B. (eds) (1998) *Cosmopolitics: Thinking and feeling beyond the nation*. University of Minnesota Press, Minneapolis.

Checkel, J. T. (2004) Social constructivisms in global and European politics: a review essay. *Review of International Studies* 30 (2).

Chesterman, S. (2005) Great Expectations: UN Reform and the Role of the Secretary-General. *Security Dialogue* 36 (3), 375–377.

Chesterman, S. (2006a) *You, the people: The United Nations, transitional administration, and state-building*. Reprinted. Oxford University Press, Oxford.

Chesterman, S. (2006b) Does the UN have intelligence? *Survival* 48 (3), 149–164.

Chesterman, S. (2007) Ownership in Theory and in Practice: Transfer of Authority in UN Statebuilding Operations. *Journal of Intervention and Statebuilding* 1 (1), 3–26.

Chesterman, S., Ignatieff, M. and Thakur, R. C. (2005) *Making states work: State failure and the crisis of governance*. United Nations University Press, Tokyo.

Cho, J. (2006) Validity in qualitative research revisited. *Qualitative Research* 6 (3), 319–340.

Chojnacki, S. and Namberger, V. (2011) Frieden – oder: Vom Elend ein konstitutiver Begriff zu sein. *Leviathan* 39 (3), 333–359.

Chopra, J. and Weiss, T. G. (1992) Sovereignty Is No Longer Sacrosanct: Codifying Humanitarian Intervention. *Ethics and International Affairs* 6 (1), 95–117.

Chrétien, J.-P. (2003a) *L'Afrique des grands lacs. Deux mille ans d'histoire*. Flammarion, Paris.

Chrétien, J.-P. (2003b) *The great lakes of Africa: Two thousand years of history*. Zone Books, New York, NY.

Clarke, A. and Friese, C. (2007) Grounded Theorizing Using Situational Analysis. In: Bryant, A. and Charmaz, K. (eds) *The SAGE handbook of grounded theory*. SAGE, Los Angeles, 363–397.

Clegg, S. (1994) Weber and Foucault: Social Theory for the Study of Organizations. *Organization* 1 (1), 149–178.

Clifford, J. (1986) Introduction. In: Clifford, J. and George Marcus (eds) *Writing Culture: The Poetics and Politics of Ethnography*. University of California Press, Berkeley and Los Angeles, California, 1–26.

Clifford, J. and George Marcus (eds) (1986) *Writing Culture: The Poetics and Politics of Ethnography*. University of California Press, Berkeley and Los Angeles, California.

Coates, A. (1987) *The Commerce in Rubber – The first 250 Years*. Oxford University Press, Singapore.

Collier, P. (2007) *The bottom billion: Why the poorest countries are failing and what can be done about it*. Oxford University Press, Oxford, New York.

Collier, S. J. (2009) Topologies of Power: Foucault's Analysis of Political Government beyond 'Governmentality'. *Theory, Culture and Society* 26 (6), 78–108.

Comaroff, J. (2007) Beyond Bare Life: AIDS, (Bio)Politics, and the Neoliberal Order. *Public Culture* 19 (1), 197–219.

CASM – Communities and Artisanal and Small-Scale Mining Initiative (2008) *Walikale: Artisanal Cassiterite Mining and Trade in North Kivu Implications for Poverty Reduction and Security*. World Bank, Washington DC.

Conrad, J. (1995) *Heart of darkness: With the Congo diary*. Penguin Books, London.

Conrad, S. (2002) *Jenseits des Eurozentrismus: Postkoloniale Perspektiven in den Geschichts- und Kulturwissenschaften*. Campus-Verl., Frankfurt/Main.

Contessi, N. P. (2010) Multilateralism, Intervention and Norm Contestation: China's Stance on Darfur in the UN Security Council. *Security Dialogue* 41 (3), 323–344.

Cooley, A. and Ron, J. (2002) The NGO Scramble: Organizational Insecurity and the Political Economy of Transnational Action: International Security. *International Security* 27 (1), 5–39.

Cooper, F. (2009) *Colonialism in question: Theory, knowledge, history*. University of California Press, Berkeley.

Cooper, F. and Packard, R. M. (eds) (1997) *International development and the social sciences: Essays on the history and politics of knowledge*. University of California Press, Berkeley.

Cooper, F. and Stoler, A. L. (eds) (1997) *Tensions of empire: Colonial cultures in a bourgeois*. University of California Press, Berkeley.

Cornwall, A. (2007) Buzzwords and fuzzwords: deconstructing development discourse. *Development in Practice* 17 (4–5), 471–484.

Cornwall, A. and Brock, K. (2005) What Do Buzzwords Do for Development Policy? A Critical Look at 'Participation', 'Empowerment' and 'Poverty Reduction'. *Third World Quarterly* 26 (7), 1043–1060.

Cotton, J. (2007) Timor-Leste and the discourse of state failure. *Australian Journal of International Affairs* 61 (4), 455–470.

Cowen, M. P. and Shenton, R. W. (2004) *Doctrines of development*. Reprinted. Routledge, London.

Cox, R. W. (1997) *The new realism: Perspectives on multilateralism and world order*. United Nations University Press, Tokyo.

Cramer, C. (2006) *Civil war is not a stupid thing: Accounting for violence in developing countries*. Hurst, London.

Crawford, G. (2003) Partnership or power? Deconstructing the 'Partnership for Governance Reform' in Indonesia. *Third World Quarterly* 24 (1), 139–159.

Crewe, E. and Harrison, E. (1998) *Whose development? An ethnography of aid*. Zed Books, London.

Crombé, X. (2006) *Independence and Security*. CRASH, Paris.

Crombé, X. (2008) *Independence and Innovation, Looking Beyond the Magic of Words*. CRASH, Paris.

Crush, J. S. (1995) *Power of development*. Routledge, London.

Csete, J. (2002) *The war within the war: Sexual violence against women and girls in Eastern Congo*. Human Rights Watch, New York.

Cunliffe, P. (2012) Still the Spectre at the Feast: Comparisons between Peacekeeping and Imperialism in Peacekeeping Studies Today. *International Peacekeeping* 19 (4), 426–442.

Cusset, F. (2003) *French Theory: Foucault, Derrida, Deleuze and Cie et les mutations de la vie intellectuelle aux États-Unis*. La Découverte/Poche, Paris.

Darby, P. (2009) Rolling Back the Frontiers of Empire: Practising the Postcolonial. *International Peacekeeping* 16 (5), 699–716.

Darcy, J. and Hofmann, C.-A. (2003) *According to Need?: Needs assessment and decision-making in the humanitarian sector*. Overseas Development Institute, London.

Dauvin, P. and Siméant, J. (2002) *Le travail humanitaire: Les acteurs des ONG du siège au terrain*. Presses de Sciences Po, Paris.

Daxner, M. (2010) Das Konzept von Interventionskultur. In: Bonacker, T., Daxner, M., Free, J. H. and Zürcher, C. (eds) *Interventionskultur: Zur Soziologie von Interventionsgesellschaften*, VS Verlag für Sozialwissenschaften., Wiesbaden, 75–100.

Daxner, M., Free, Jan, Schüßler, M. and Thiele, U. (2007) Staatsgründungskrieg und Heimatdiskurs: Afghanistan-und die Grundlagen und Probleme humanitärer Interventionen. *Kommune. Forum für Politik, Ökonomie, Kultur* 25 (6), 62–81.

Day, C. and Reno, W. (2014) In Harm's Way: African Counter-Insurgency and Patronage Politics. *Civil Wars* 16 (2), 105–126.

Debrix, F. (1999a) Deterritorialised territories, borderless borders: the new geography of international medical assistance. *Third World Quarterly* 19 (5), 827–846.

Debrix, F. (1999b) *Re-envisioning peacekeeping: The United Nations and the mobilization of ideology*. University of Minnesota Press, Minneapolis.

Debrix, F. (2003) *Language, agency, and politics in a constructed world*. Sharpe, Armonk, NY.

Debrix, F. (2009) Nothing to Fear but Fear: Governmentality and the Biopolitical Production of Terror. *International Political Sociology* 3, 398–413.

Denskus, T. (2012) *How Peacebuilding has become a ritualised space: An aidnography from Germany and Nepal*. PhD Thesis, Brighton.

Denzin, N. K. (2001) The reflexive interview and a performative social science. *Qualitative Research* 1 (1), 23–46.

Depelchin, J. (1981) The Transformations of the Petty Bourgeoisie and the State in Post-Colonial Zaire. *Review of African Political Economy* 22 (20–41).

Der Derian, J. and Shapiro, M. J. (1989) *International/intertextual relations: Postmodern readings of world politics*. Lexington Books, Lexington.

Derrida, J. (1972) *Limited Inc.* Northwestern University Press, Evanston.

Derrida, J. (1976) *Of Grammatology*. Johns Hopkins University Press, Baltimore.

Derrida, J. (1986) Declarations of independence. *New Political Science* 7 (1), 7–15.

Development Initiatives (2014) *Global Humanitarian Assistance Report*. London.

Devisch, R. (1998) Colonial State Building in the Congo, and its Dismantling. *Journal of Legal Pluralism* 30 (42), 221–244.

Dillon, M. and Lobo-Guerrero, L. (2008) Biopolitics of security in the 21st century: an introduction. *Review of International Studies* 34 (2), 265–292.

Dillon, M. and Reid, J. (2000) Global Governance, Liberal Peace, and Complex Emergency. *Alternatives: Global, Local, Political* 25 (1), 117–143.

Dillon, M. and Reid, J. (2009) *The liberal way of war: Killing to make life live*. Routledge, London.

Distler, W. (2014) *Intervention als soziale Praxis: Interaktionserfahrungen im Alltag des Statebuilding am Beispiel der Internationalen Polizeimission im Kosovo*. Springer VS, Wiesbaden.

Donini, A. (2010) The far side: the meta functions of humanitarianism in a globalised world. *Disasters* 34 (2), 220–237.

Doss, A. (2008) Eyewitness: Crisis, Contention and Coherence – Reflections from the Field. *International Peacekeeping* 15 (4), 570–581.

Dossa, S. (2007) Slicing up 'Development': colonialism, political theory, ethics. *Third World Quarterly* 28 (5), 887–899.

Doty, R. L. (1996) *Imperial encounters: The politics of representation in North–South relations*. University of Minnesota Press, Minneapolis.

Doty, R. L. (1997) Aporia: A Critical Exploration of the Agent-Structure Problematique in International Relations Theory. *European Journal of International Relations* 3 (3), 365–392.

Douzinas, C. (2003) Humanity, military humanism and the new moral order. *Economy and Society* 32 (2), 159–184.

Doyle, M. (1983a) Kant, Liberal Legacies and Foreign Affairs part 1. *Philosophy and Public Affairs* (3), 205–235.

Doyle, M. (1983b) Kant, Liberal Legacies and Foreign Affairs part 2. *Philosophy and Public Affairs* 12 (4), 323–353.

Doyle, M. (2005) Three Pillars of the Liberal Peace. *American Political Science Review* 99 (3), 563–567.

Doyle, M. and Sambanis, N. (2000) International Peacebuilding: A Theoretical and Quantitative Analysis. *American Political Science Review* 94 (4), 779–801.

Doyle, M. and Sambanis, N. (2006) *Making war and building peace: United Nations peace operations*. Princeton University Press, Princeton, NJ.

Dreyfus, H. L., Rabinow, P. and Foucault, M. (eds) (1982) *Michel Foucault: beyond structuralism and hermeneutics*. Harvester Press, Brighton.

Duffield, M. (2002) Social Reconstruction and the Radicalization of Development: Aid as a Relation of Global Liberal Governance. *Development and Change* 33 (5), 1049–1071.

Duffield, M. (2006a) *Global governance and the new wars: The merging of development and security*. 4th imprint. Zed Books, London.

Duffield, M. (2006b) Racism, migration and development: The foundations of planetary order. *Progress in Development Studies* 6 (1), 68–79.

Duffield, M. (2008a) *Development, security and unending war: Governing the world of peoples*. Reprinted. Polity Press, Cambridge.

Duffield, M. (2008b) Global Civil War: The Non-Insured, International Containment and Post-Interventionary Society. *Journal of Refugee Studies* 21 (2), 145–165.

Duffield, M. (2010a) Risk-Management and the Fortified Aid Compound: Everyday Life in Post-Interventionary Society. *Journal of Intervention and Statebuilding* 4 (4), 453–474.

Duffield, M. (2010b) The Liberal Way of Development and the Development–Security Impasse: Exploring the Global Life-Chance Divide. *Security Dialogue* 51 (1), 53–76.

Duffield M (2012) Challenging environments: Danger, resilience and the aid industry. *Security Dialogue* 43 (5): 475–492.

Dunn, K. (2003) *Imagining the Congo: The international relations of identity*. Palgrave Macmillan, New York, NY.

Dunn, K. (2009a) Contested State Spaces: African National Parks and the State. *European Journal of International Relations* 15 (3), 423–446.

Dunn, K. (2009b) Afrikas zwiespältiges Verhältnis zu Empire und Empire. In: Randeria, S. and Eckert, A. (eds) *Vom Imperialismus zum Empire: Nicht-westliche Perspektiven auf Globalisierung*, Suhrkamp, Frankfurt am Main.

Dunne, T., Kurki, M. and Smith, S. (eds) (2007) *International relations theories: Discipline and diversity*. Oxford University Press, Oxford.

Dunning, T. (2005) Resource Dependence, Economic Performance, and Political Stability. *Journal of Conflict Resolution* 49 (4), 451–482.

Duroch, F. (2004) Le Viol, Arme de Guerre: L'humanitaire en désarroi. *Les Temps Modernes* 59 (627), 138–147.

Duroch, F., McRae, M. and Grais, R. F. (2011) Description and consequences of sexual violence in Ituri province, Democratic Republic of Congo. *BMC International Health and Human Rights* 11 (1), 5.

Duvall, R. and Arjun Chowdhury (2011) Practices of Theory. In: Adler, E. and Pouliot, V. (eds) *International Practices*. Cambridge University Press, Cambridge, 335–354.

Ecumenical Network Central Africa (2011) *Uranium Mining in the DR Congo: A radiant Business for European Nuclear Companies?* Berlin.

Edkins, J. (1996) Legality with a Vengeance: Famines and Humanitarian Relief in 'Complex Emergencies'. *Millennium – Journal of International Studies* 25 (3), 547–575.

Edkins, J. (1999) *Poststructuralism and international relations: Bringing the political back in*. Lynne Rienner Publishers, Boulder.

Edkins, J. (2000) *Whose Hunger?: Concepts of Famine, Practices of Aid*. University of Minnesota Press, Minneapolis.

Edkins, J. (2008) Biopolitics, communication and global governance. *Review of International Studies* 34, 211–232.

Ekeh, P. (1975) Colonialism and The Two Publics in Africa. *Comparative Studies in Society and History* 17 (1), 91–112.

Emirbayer, M. (1997) Manifesto for a Relational Sociology. *The American Journal of Sociology* 103 (2), 281–317.

Engelkamp, S., Glaab, K. and Graf, A. (eds) (2015) *Kritische. Normenforschung als Metatheorie und politische Praxis. Neue Wege in den Internationalen Beziehungen*. Nomos, Baden-Baden.

Englebert, P. (2003) Why Congo Persists: Sovereignty, Globalization and the Violent Reproduction of a Weak State, *QEH Working Paper Series*.

Englebert, P. (2009) *Africa: Unity, Sovereignty and Sorrow*. Lynne Rienner, Boulder.

Englebert, P. and Tull, D. (2008) Postconflict Reconstruction in Africa Flawed Ideas about Failed States. *International Security* 32 (4), 106–139.

Englund, H. (2010) The Anthropologist and his Poor. In: Bornstein, E. and Peter Redfield (eds) *Forces of Compassion: Humanitarianism between Ethics and Politics*. School for Advanced Research Press, Santa Fe, 71–94.

Enough Project (2009) *A Comprehensive Approach to Congo's Minerals*. Washington DC.

Enough Project (2010) *Congo's Enough Moment*. Washington DC.

Enough Project (2011) *Certification: The Path to Conflict-Free Minerals from Congo*. Washington DC.

Ensler, E. (2007) Women Left for Dead – and the Man Who's Saving Them. *Glamour Magazine*, August 2007.

Epstein, C. (2010) Who speaks? Discourse, the subject and the study of identity in international politics. *European Journal of International Relations* 17 (2), 327–350.

Eriksen, S. (2005) The Congo war and the prospects for state formation: Rwanda and Uganda compared. *Third World Quarterly* 26 (7), 1097–1113.

Eriksen, S. (2009) The Liberal Peace Is Neither: Peacebuilding, State building and the Reproduction of Conflict in the Democratic Republic of Congo. *International Peacekeeping* 16 (5), 652–666.

Escobar, A. (1995) *Encountering Development: The Making and Unmaking of the Third World*. Princeton University Press, Princeton.

Esteves, P. (2010) Peace Operations and the Government of Humanitarian Spaces. *International Peacekeeping* 17 (5), 613–628.

European Commission (2008) *EU Consensus on Humanitarian Aid*. Brussels.

European Union (2003) *A Secure Europe in a better world*. Brussels.

Exenberger, A. and Hartmann, S. (2011) *Extractive Institutions in the Congo: A Long History Told in Brief*. Available at: http://vkc.library.uu.nl/vkc/seh/research/Lists/Events/Attachments/12/CH3.Exenberger-Hartmann.Introduction%20Congo.pdf.

Fairhead, J. (1992) Paths of Authority: Roads, the State and the Market in Eastern Zaire. *The European Journal of Development Research* 4 (2), 17–35.

Fanon, F. (1981) *Die Verdammten dieser Erde*. Suhrkamp, Frankfurt am Main.

Fanon, F. (2008) *Black skin, white masks*. Grove Press, New York.

FAO (2010) *The State of Food Security in the World*. Rome.

Fassin, D. (2006) La biopolitique n'est pas une politique de la vie. *Sociologies et sociétés* 38, 35–48.

Fassin, D. (2007) Humanitariansim as politics of life. *Public Culture* 19 (3), 499–520.

Fassin, D. (2009) Another Politics of Life is Possible. *Theory, Culture and Society* 26 (5), 44–60.

Fassin, D. (2010) Heart of Humaneness: The Moral Economy of Humanitarian Intervention. In: Fassin, D. and Pandolfi, M. (eds) *Contemporary states of emergency: The politics of military and humanitarian interventions*. Zone Books, Brooklyn, NY, 269–293.

Fassin, D. (2012) *Humanitarian Reason: A Moral History of the Present*. University of California Press, Berkeley.

Fassin, D. and Pandolfi, M. (eds) (2010) *Contemporary states of emergency: The politics of military and humanitarian interventions*. Zone Books, Brooklyn, NY.

Fatal Transactions (2006) *The State vs. the People: Governance, mining and the transitional regime in the Democratic Republic of Congo*. Amsterdam.

Fearon, J. (2008) The Rise of Emergency Relief Aid. In: Barnett, M. N. (ed.) *Humanitarianism in question: Politics, power, ethics*. Cornell University Press, Ithaca, NY, 49–72.

Feldman, G. (2011) If ethnography is more than participant observation, then relations are more than connections: The case for non-local ethnography in a world of apparatuses. *Anthropological Theory* 11 (4), 375–395.

Ferguson, J. (2007) *Global shadows: Africa in the neoliberal world order*. Duke University Press, Durham.

Ferguson, J. (2007 [1990]) *The anti-politics machine: 'development', depoliticization, and bureaucratic power in Lesotho*. University of Minnesota Press, Minneapolis.

Ferguson, J. and Akhil Gutpa (1997) Discipline and Practice: 'The Field' as Site, Method and Location in Anthropology. In: Ferguson, J. and Akhil Gutpa (eds) *Anthropological Locations*. University of California Press, Berkeley, 1–47.

Ferguson, J. and Akhil Gutpa (eds) (1997) *Anthropological Locations*. University of California Press, Berkeley.

Feyerabend, P. K. (2008) *Against method*. Verso, London.

Finnemore, M. and Sikkink, K. (1998) International Norm Dynamics and Political Change. *International Organization* 52 (4), 887–917.

Fisher, M. (2013) Why did infamous war criminal Bosco Ntaganda just surrender at a U.S. embassy? *Washington Post Blog*, 18 March 2013.

Fisher, W. (1997) Doing good? The Politics and Antipolitics of NGO Practices. *Annual Review of Anthropology* 26, 439–464.

Foucault, M. (2001a) Méthodologie pour la connaissance du monde: Comment se débarrasser du Marxisme. In: Foucault, M. (2001) *Dits et Écrits II. 1976–1988.* Gallimard, Paris, 595–618.

Foucault, M. (2001b) Naissance de la biopolitique. In: Foucault, M. (2001) *Dits et Écrits II. 1976–1988.* Gallimard, Paris, 818–825.

Foucault, M. (2001c) Qu'est-ce qu'est les Lumières. In: Foucault, M. (2001) *Dits et Écrits II. 1976–1988.* Gallimard, Paris, 1381–1397.

Foucault, M. (1970) *The Order of Things. An archaeology of the human sciences.* Tavistock Publications, London.

Foucault, M. (1972) *The Archaeology of Knowledge.* Tavistock Publications, London.

Foucault, M. (1980) *The History of Sexuality: The Will to Knowledge.* Vintage Books, New York.

Foucault, M. (1982) The Subject and Power. In: Dreyfus, H. L., Rabinow, P. and Foucault, M. (eds) *Michel Foucault: beyond structuralism and hermeneutics.* Harvester Press, Brighton.

Foucault, M. (1991) Politics and the study of discourse. In: Burchell, G., Gordon, C. and Miller, P. M. (eds) *The Foucault effect: Studies in governmental nationality; with two lectures by and an interview with Michel Foucault.* Harvester Wheatsheaf, London, 53–72.

Foucault, M. (1995) *Discipline and punish: The birth of the prison.* 2nd Vintage Books edition. Vintage Books, New York.

Foucault, M. (2001) *Dits et Écrits II. 1976–1988.* Gallimard, Paris.

Foucault, M.(2003) *Society must be defended: Lectures at the Collège de France, 1975–76.* 1st edition. Picador, New York.

Foucault, M. (2007) *The politics of truth.* Semiotext(e), Los Angeles, CA.

Foucault, M. (2008a) *The birth of biopolitics: Lectures at the Collège de France, 1978–79.* Palgrave Macmillan, Basingstoke, England, New York.

Foucault, M. (2008b) *Analytik der Macht.* Orig.-Ausg., 3. Aufl., [Nachdr.]. Suhrkamp, Frankfurt am Main.

Foucault, M. (2009) *Security, territory, population: Lectures at the Collège de France 1977–78.* Palgrave Macmillan, Basingstoke.

Franke, U. and Roos, U. (2010) Actor, structure, process: transcending the state personhood debate by means of a pragmatist ontological model for International Relations theory. *Review of International Studies* 36 (4), 1057–1077.

Friedrichs, J. and Kratochwil, F. (2009) On Acting and Knowing: How Pragmatism Can Advance International Relations Research and Methodology. *International Organization* 63, 701–731.

Friis, K. (2010) Peacekeeping and Counter-insurgency – Two of a Kind?: International Peacekeeping. *International Peacekeeping* 17 (1), 49–66.

Fukuyama, F. (2004) *State-building: Governance and world order in the 21st century.* Cornell University Press, Ithaca, NY.

Gambino, A. (2008) *Congo – Securing Peace, Sustaining Progress.* Washington DC.

Garfinkel, H. (1967) *Studies in Ethnomethodology.* Prentice-Hall International Inc., London.

Garrett, N., Sergiou, S. and Vlassenroot, K. (2009) Negotiated peace for extortion: the case of Walikale territory in eastern DR Congo. *Journal of Eastern African Studies* 3 (1), 1–21.

Geenen, S. and Claessens, K. (2013) Disputed access to the gold sites in Luhwindja, eastern Democratic Republic of Congo. *The Journal of Modern African Studies* 51 (1), 85–108.

Gegout, C. (2009) The West, Realism and Intervention in the Democratic Republic of Congo (1996–2006). *International Peacekeeping* 16 (2), 231–244.

George, A. L. and Bennett, A. (2005) *Case studies and theory development in the social sciences.* MIT Press, Cambridge.

German Development Institute (2009) *User's Guide on Measuring Fragility.* Bonn.

Gettleman, J. (2007) Rape Epidemic Raises Trauma of Congo War. *New York Times*, October 2007.

Ghani, A. and Clare Lockhart (2008) *Fixing Failed States: A Framework for Rebuilding a Fractured World.* Oxford University Press, Oxford.

Ghosh, A. (1994) The Global Reservation: Notes toward an Ethnography of International Peacekeeping. *Cultural Anthropology* 9 (3), 412–422.

Gibson, B. (2007) Accomodating Critical Theory. In: Bryant, A. and Charmaz, K. (eds) *The SAGE handbook of grounded theory.* SAGE, Los Angeles, 436–453.

Ginifer, J. (2002) Eyewitness: Peacebuilding in the Congo: Mission Impossible? *International Peacekeeping* 9 (3), 121–128.

Givoni, M. (2011a) Humanitarian Governance and Ethical Cultivation: Medecins sans Frontieres and the Advent of the Expert-Witness. *Millennium – Journal of International Studies* 40 (1), 43–63.

Givoni, M. (2011b) Beyond the Humanitarian/Political Divide: Witnessing and the Making of Humanitarian Ethics. *Journal of Human Rights* 10 (1), 55–75.

Glaser, B. G. and Strauss, A. L. (2009 [1967]) *The discovery of grounded theory: Strategies for qualitative research*, 4. paperback printing. Aldine, New Brunswick.

Global Public Policy Institute (2010) *Cluster Approach Evaluation 2 Synthesis Report.* Berlin.

Global Witness (2009) *Faced with a Gun, What Can you Do?: War and the Militarization of Mining in Eastern Congo.* London.

Global Witness (2010a) *The hill belongs to them: The need for international action on Congo's conflict minerals trade.* London.

Global Witness (2010b) *Do No Harm: Excluding Minerals from the Supply Chain.* London.

Global Witness (2011a) *Congo's Minerals Trade in the Balance: Opportunities and Obstacles to Militarization.* London.

Global Witness (2011b) *China and Congo: Friends in Need.* London.

Goetze, C. and Bliesemann Guevara, B. de (2012) The 'statebuilding habitus': UN staff and the cultural dimension of liberal intervention in Kosovo. In: Bliesemann Guevara, B. de (ed.) *Statebuilding and State-Formation: The political sociology of intervention.* Routledge, London, 198–213.

Government of the DR Congo (2011) *Tableau Récapitluatif des Recettes Extérieures 2011.* Kinshasa.

Government of the DR Congo (2009) *Programme de Stabilisation de Reconstruction des Zones sortant des conflits armés STAREC.* Kinshasa.

Grais, R. F., Luquero, F. J., Grellety, E., Pham, H., Coghlan, B. and Salignon, P. (2009) Learning lessons from field surveys in humanitarian contexts: a case study of field surveys conducted in North Kivu, DRC 2006–2008. *Conflict and Health* 3 (1), 8.

Granjon, M.-C. (ed.) (2005) *Penser avec Michel Foucault: Théorie critique et pratiques politiques*. Karthala, Paris.

Grillo, R. D. and Stirrat, R. (eds) (1997) *Discourses of development: Anthropological perspectives*. Berg, Oxford, New York.

Grovogui, S. N. (2002) Regimes of Sovereignty: International Morality and the African Condition. *European Journal of International Relations* 8 (3), 315–338.

Guilhot, N. (2005) *The democracy makers: Human rights and international order*. Columbia University Press, New York.

Guilhot, N. (2012) The Anthropologist as Witness: Humanitarianism between Ethnography and Critique. *Humanity: An International Journal of Human Rights, Humanitarianism and Development* 3 (1), 81–101.

Gupta, A. and Ferguson, J. (1997) *Anthropological Locations: Boundaries and Grounds of a Field Science*. University of California Press, Berkeley.

Gupta, A. and Sharma, A. (eds) (2006) *Anthropology of the State*. Blackwell Publishers Ltd, Malden, Oxford, Victoria.

Hacking, I. (2004) Between Michel Foucault and Erving Goffman: between discourse in the abstract and face-to-face interaction. *Economy and Society* 33 (3), 277–302.

Hall, S. (1996) Who needs Identity? In: Hall, S. and Du Gay, P. (eds) *Questions of cultural identity*. SAGE, London, 1–17.

Hall, S. and Du Gay, P. (eds) (1996) *Questions of cultural identity*. SAGE, London.

Hannerz, U. (2004) *Foreign News: Exploring the World of Foreign Correspondents*. The University of Chicago Press, London.

Hansen, L. (2006) *Security as practice: Discourse analysis and the Bosnian war*. Routledge, New York.

Hansen, L. (2011) Performing Practices: A Poststructuralist Analysis of the Muhammad Cartoon Crisis. In: Adler, E. and Pouliot, V. (eds) *International Practices*. Cambridge University Press, Cambridge, 280–309.

Hansen, T. B. and Stepputat, F. (2001a) Introduction. In: Hansen, T. B. and Stepputat, F. (eds) *States of Imagination*. Duke University Press, Durham.

Hansen, T. B. and Stepputat, F. (eds) (2001b) *States of Imagination*. Duke University Press, Durham.

Harmer, A. (2008) Integrated Missions: A Threat to Humanitarian Security? *International Peacekeeping* 15 (4), 528–539.

Harper, R. H. R. (1998) *Inside the IMF: An Ethnography of Documents, Technology and Organizational Action*. Academic Press, San Diego.

Harrel-Bond, B. (1986) *Imposing Aid: Emergency Assistance to Refugees*. London: Oxford University Press.

Harvard Humanitarian Initiative (2010) *'Now the world is without me': An Investigation of Sexual Violence in Eastern Democratic Republic of Congo*.

Haskell, T. (1985) Capitalism and the Origins of the Humanitarian Sensibility, part 1. *American Historical Review* 90 (2), 339–361.

Haskell, T. (1985) Capitalism and the Origins of the Humanitarian Sensibility, part 2. *American Historical Review* 90 (3), 547–566.

Haver, K. (2008) *Out of Site: Building better responses to displacement in the Democratic Republic of the Congo by helping host families*. London.

Heathershaw, J. (2007) Peacebuilding as Practice: Discourses from Post-conflict Tajikistan. *International Peacekeeping* 14 (2), 219–236.

Heathershaw, J. (2008) Seeing like the International Community: How Peacebuilding Failed (and Survived) in Tajikistan. *Journal of Intervention and Statebuilding* 2 (3), 329–351.

Heathershaw, J. (2012) Conclusions – neither built nor formed – the transformation of post-conflict states and international intervention. In: Bliesemann Guevara, B. de (ed.) *Statebuilding and State-Formation: The political sociology of intervention.* Routledge, London, 246–259.

Heathershaw, J. (2013) Towards better theories of peacebuilding: beyond the liberal peace debate. *Peacebuilding* 1 (2): 275–282.

Hedges, C. (2003) *War is a force that gives us meaning.* Reprinted. Anchor Books, New York.

Hehir, A. and Robinson, N. (eds) (2007) *State-building: Theory and practice.* Routledge, London.

Helman, G. and Ratner, S. (1992) Saving Failed States. *Foreign Policy* 89, 3–20.

Herbst, J. I. (2000) *States and power in Africa: Comparative lessons in authority and control.* Princeton University Press, Princeton, NJ.

Herbst, J. and Greg Mills (2009) There is no Congo. *Foreign Policy,* available at: http://foreignpolicy.com/2009/03/18/there-is-no-congo/, last accessed 24 May 2015.

Higate, P. and Henry, M. (2009) *Insecure Spaces: Peacekeeping, power and performance in Haiti, Kosovo and Liberia.* Zed Books, London.

Hill, J. (2005) Beyond the Other? A postcolonial critique of the failed state thesis. *African Identities* 3 (2), 139–154.

Hobsbawm, E. J. and Ranger, T. O. (1983) *The Invention of Tradition.* Cambridge University Press, Cambridge.

Hobson, J. (2007) Is critical theory always for the white West and for Western imperialism? Beyond Westphalian towards a post-racist critical IR. *Review of International Studies* 33 (1), 91–116.

Hobson, J. M. (2012) *The Eurocentric conception of world politics: Western international theory, 1760–2010.* Cambridge University Press, New York.

Hobson, J. and Hall, M. (2010) Liberal International Theory: Eurocentric but not always Imperialist? *International Theory* 2 (2), 210–245.

Hochschild, A. (1998) *King Leopold's ghost: A story of greed, terror, and heroism in Colonial Africa.* Houghton Mifflin, Boston.

Holt, V. and Taylor, G. (2009) *Protecting Civilians in the Context of UN Peacekeeping Operations Successes, Setbacks and Remaining Challenges.* New York.

Honig, B. (2009) *Emergency Politics: Paradox, Law, Democracy.* Princeton University Press, Princeton.

Hoppe, K. (2014) *Chasing misery: An anthology of essays by women in humanitarian responses.* CreateSpace Independent Publishing Platform.

Hudson, A. (2012) *Democratic Republic of Congo: Taking a Stand on Security Sector Reform.* Available at: www.oenz.de/fileadmin/users/oenz/PDF/DRC_SSR-Report_2012.pdf.

Hughes, C. and Pupavac, V. (2005) Framing Post-Conflict Societies: International Pathologisation of Cambodia and the Post-Yugoslav States. *Third World Quarterly* 26 (6), 873–889.

Human Rights Watch (2002) *The War within the War: Sexual Violence Against Women and Girls in Eastern Congo.* New York.

Human Rights Watch (2009) *Soldiers who Rape, Commanders who Condone.* New York.

Human Rights Watch (2010) *Always on the Run: The Vicious Cycle of Displacement in Eastern Congo.* New York.

Human Security Report Project (2009) *Human Security Report: The Shrinking Costs of War.* New York.

Humphreys, M., Sachs, J. and Stiglitz, J. E. (eds) (2007) *Escaping the resource curse*. Columbia University Press, New York.

Hüsken, T. (2006) *Der Stamm der Experten: Rhetorik und Praxis des Interkulturellen Managements in der deutschen staatlichen Entwicklungszusammenarbeit*, Transcript, Bielefeld.

Huysmans, J. (2011) What's in an act? On security speech acts and little security nothings. *Security Dialogue* 42 (4–5), 371–383.

Inayatullah, N. and Blaney, D. L. (2004) *International relations and the problem of difference*. Routledge, New York.

Institut Français des Relations Internationales (2008) *Candide au Congo L'échec annoncé de la réforme du secteur de sécurité*. Paris.

Institut Français des Relations Internationales (2009) *How to reform peacemaking in the Democratic Republic of Congo: When peace processes become international 'systems of organized action'*. Paris.

Institute for Security Studies (2008) *Assessing Security Sector Reform and its Impact on the Kivu Provinces*. Pretoria.

Inter-Agency Standing Committee (2011) *Operational Guidance for Coordinated Assessments in Humanitarian Crises*. New York.

Inter-Agency Standing Committee (2012) *Multi-Cluster/Sector Initial Rapid Assessment (MIRA)*. New York.

International Alert (2010a) *The Complexity of Resource Governance in a Context of State Fragility: The Case of Eastern DRC*. London.

International Alert (2010b) *The Role of the Exploitation of Natural Resources in Fuelling and Prolonging Crises in Eastern DRC*. London.

International Alert (2010c) *The Complexity of Resource Governance in a Context of State Fragility: An Analysis of the Mining Sector in the Kivu Hinterlands*. London.

International Alert (2010d) *War is not yet over*. London.

International Alert (2010e) *Land, power and identity: Roots of violent conflict in Eastern DRC*. London.

International Alert (2010f) *Refugees in Eastern DRC: A discussion document*. London.

International Committee of the Red Cross (1996) *The Fundamental Principles of the Red Cross and Red Crescent Societies*. Geneva.

International Committee of the Red Cross (2008a) *The ICRC: Its Mission and Work*. Geneva.

International Committee of the Red Cross (2008b) *Enhancing Protection for Civilians in Armed Conflict and other Situations of Violence*. Geneva.

International Committee of the Red Cross (2009) *Annual Report*. Geneva.

International Committee of the Red Cross (2010) *ICRC Prevention Policy*. Geneva.

International Committee of the Red Cross (2011a) *ICRC Strategy 2011–2014: Achieving Significant Results for People in Need*. Geneva.

International Committee of the Red Cross (2011b) *Assistance: Assistance Offered for People Affected by Armed Conflict and other Situations of Violence*. Geneva.

International Committee of the Red Cross (2012) *2011 Financial and Funding Information Overview*. Available at: www.icrc.org/eng/assets/files/annual-report/current/icrc-annual-report-financial-overview.pdf.

International Crisis Group (1998) *North Kivu – Into the Quagmire? An Overview of the Current Crisis in North Kivu*. Geneva.

International Crisis Group (2003) *The Kivus: The Forgotten Crucible of the Congo Conflict*. Brussels.

International Crisis Group (2005) *The Congo's Transition is Failing: Crisis in the Kivus.* Brussels.

International Crisis Group (2006) *Security Sector Reform in the Congo.* Brussels.

International Crisis Group (2007) *Congo: Bringing Peace to North Kivu.* Brussels.

International Crisis Group (2009) *Congo: Five Priorities for a Peacebuilding Strategy.* Brussels.

International Crisis Group (2010a) *Congo: A Stalled Democratic Agenda.* Brussels.

International Crisis Group (2010b) *Congo: No Stability in Kivu despite Rapprochement with Rwanda.* Brussels.

International Peace Information Service (2008) *Mapping Conflict Motives: Eastern DRC.* Brussels.

International Peace Information Service (2009a) *Militarized Mining Areas in the Kivus.* Brussels.

International Peace Information Service (2009b) *Africa's Natural Resources in a Global Context.* Brussels.

International Peace Information Service (2010) *The Complexity of Resource Governance in a Context of State Fragility: The Case of Eastern DRC.* Brussels.

International Peace Institute (2011) *Renewing MONUSCO's Mandate: What Role Beyond the Elections?* New York.

International Rescue Committee (2007) *Mortality in the Congo: An Ongoing Crisis.* New York.

Ivison, D. (2002) *Postcolonial liberalism.* Cambridge University Press, Cambridge, UK.

Jackson, P. T. (2008) Can Ethnographic Techniques Tell Us Distinctive Things About World Politics? *International Political Sociology* 2 (1), 91–93.

Jackson, P. T. and Nexon, D. H. (1999) Relations Before States: Substance, Process and the Study of World Politics. *European Journal of International Relations* 5 (3), 291–332.

Jackson, R. H. and Rosberg, C. G. (1982) Why Africa's Weak States Persist: The Empirical and the Juridical in Statehood. *World Politics* 35 (1), 1–24.

Jaeger, H.-M. (2010) UN Reform, Biopolitics, and Global Governmentality. *International Theory* 2 (1), 50–86.

Jahn, B. (2007a) The Tragedy of Liberal Diplomacy: Democratization, Intervention, Statebuilding (Part 1). *Journal of Intervention and Statebuilding* 1 (1), 87–106.

Jahn, B. (2007b) The Tragedy of Liberal Diplomacy: Democratization, Intervention, Statebuilding (Part 2). *Journal of Intervention and Statebuilding* 1 (2), 211–229.

Jahn, B. (2009) Liberal internationalism: from ideology to empirical theory – and back again. *International Theory* 1 (3), 409–438.

Jahn, B. (2010) Universal languages?: A reply to Moravcsik. *International Theory* 2 (1), 140–156.

Jennings, R. C. (2011) Sovereignty and political modernity: A genealogy of Agamben's critique of sovereignty. *Anthropological Theory* 11 (1), 23–61.

Jewsiewicki, B. (1972) Notes sur l'histoire socio-économique du Congo (1880–1960). *Etudes d'Histoire Africaine* (3), 209–241.

Jones, B. G. (2005) Africa and the Poverty of International Relations. *Third World Quarterly* 26 (6), 987–1003.

Jones, B. G. (2008) The global political economy of social crisis: Towards a critique of the 'failed state' ideology. *Review of International Political Economy* 15 (2), 180–205.

Joseph, J. (2010a) The limits of governmentality: Social theory and the international. *European Journal of International Relations* 16 (2), 223–246.

Joseph, J. (2010b) What can Governmentality do for IR? *International Political Sociology* 4 (2), 202–204.

Jung, D. (1998) Weltgesellschaft als theoretisches Konzept der Internationalen Beziehungen. *Zeitschrift für Internationale Beziehungen* 5 (2), 241–271.

Kabamba, P. (2012) External Economic Exploitation in the DRC: 1990–2005. *African Studies Review* 55 (1), 123–130.

Kalthoff, H., Hirschauer, S. and Lindemann, G. (eds) (2008) *Theoretische Empirie: Zur Relevanz qualitativer Forschung*, Orig.-Ausg., 1. Aufl. Suhrkamp, Frankfurt am Main.

Kalyvas, S. N. and Balcells, L. (2010) International System and Technologies of Rebellion: How the End of the Cold War Shaped Internal Conflict. *American Political Science Review* 104 (03), 415–429.

Kapoor, I. (2008) *The postcolonial politics of development*. Routledge, London.

Keller, R. (2004) *Diskursforschung: Eine Einführung für SozialwissenschaftlerInnen*. Leske + Budrich, Opladen.

Keller, R. (ed.) (2006) *Handbuch sozialwissenschaftliche Diskursanalyse*, VS Verlag für Sozialwissenschaften., Wiesbaden.

Keller, R. (ed.) (2012) *Macht-Diskurs-Subjekt*. Suhrkamp, Frankfurt am Main.

Kennes, E. (2005) The Mining Sector in Congo: The Victim or the Orphan of Globalization? In: Marysse, S. and Reyntjens, F. (eds) *The political economy of the Great Lakes Region in Africa: The pitfalls of enforced democracy and globalization*. Palgrave Macmillan, Houndmills, Basingstoke, Hampshire, New York, 152–189.

Kenyatta, J. (1978 [1938]) *Facing Mount Kenya: The tribal life of the Gikuyu*. Kenway Publications, Nairobi.

Kerner, I. (2008) *Differenzen und Macht: Zur Anatomie von Rassismus und Sexismus*. Campus, Frankfurt am Main.

Kessler, O. (2009) Toward a Sociology of the International? International Relations between Anarchy and World Society. *International Political Sociology* 3, 87–108.

KfW Entwicklungsbank and Bundesamt für Geowissenschaften und Rohstoffe (2007) *Les ressources naturelles en République démocratique du Congo – Un potentiel de développement*. Frankfurt am Main.

Koddenbrock, K. (2008) *Smart-Sanctions against Failed States: Strengthening the State through UN Smart Sanctions in Angola and the DR Congo*. VDM Verlag Dr. Müller, Wiesbaden.

Koddenbrock, K. (2009a) *European Commission and United States Approaches to Linking Relief, Rehabilitation and Development*. Johns Hopkins University Press, Washington DC.

Koddenbrock, K. (2009b) *European Commission and United States Approaches to Linking Relief, Rehabilitation and Development in the DR Congo*. Johns Hopkins University Press, Washington.

Koddenbrock, K. (2012a) The International Self and the Humanitarianization of Politics: A Case Study of Goma, DR Congo. In: Bliesemann de Guevara, B. de (ed.) *Statebuilding and State-Formation: The political sociology of intervention*. Routledge, London, 214–229.

Koddenbrock, K. (2012b) Recipes for Intervention – Western policy papers imagine the Congo. *International Peacekeeping* 19 (5), 1–16.

Koddenbrock, K. (2013a) The Failed-State Effect: Statebuilding and State Stories from the Congo. In: Chandler, D. and Timothy Sisk (eds) *A Routledge Handbook on Statebuilding*. Routledge, London.

Koddenbrock K. (2013b) Strategic essentialism and the possibilities of critique in peacebuilding. *Global Dialogue Series* 2, Center for Global Cooperation.

Koddenbrock K. (2014a) Malevolent politics: The government as blind spot in the International Crisis Group's analysis of the Democratic Republic of Congo. *Third World Quarterly*, 35 (4), 669–685.

Koddenbrock K. (2014b) Strategies of critique in IR: From Foucault and Latour towards Marx. *European Journal of International Relations*. Available online first 26 August 2014.

Koddenbrock K. and Schouten P. (2014) Intervention as Ontological Politics: security, pathologization, and the failed state effect in Goma. In: Bachmann, Jan; Colleen Bell, Caroline Holmqvist, *The New Interventionism – Perspectives on war: police assemblages*. Routledge, London, 183–204.

Koskenniemi, M. (1995) Police in the Temple. *European Journal of International Law* 6 (1), 325–348.

Koseknniemi, M. (2005) *From Apology to Utopia: The Structure of International Legal Argument*. Cambridge University Press, Cambridge.

Kosmatopoulos, N. (2011) Toward an Anthropology of State Failure: Lebanon's Leviathan and Peace Expertise. *Social Analysis* 55 (3), 115–142.

Kosmatopoulos, N. (2012) *Pacifying Lebanon: Violence, Power and Expertise in the Middle East*. PhD thesis, Zürich.

Krasner, S. (2004) Sharing Sovereignty: New Institutions for Collapsed and Failing States. *International Security* 29 (2), 85–120.

Kratochwill, F. (2011) Making sense of 'international practices'. In: Adler, E. and Pouliot, V. (eds) *International Practices*. Cambridge University Press, Cambridge.

Krause, M. (2014) *The Good Project: Humanitarian Relief NGOs and the Fragmentation of Reason*. Chicago University Press, Chicago.

Laclau, E. and Mouffe, C. (1985) *Hegemony and Socialist Strategy: Towards a Radical Democratic Politics*. Verso, London.

Laïdi, Z. (1998) L'urgence ou la dévalorisation culturelle de l'avenir. *Esprit* 240, 8–20.

Laïdi, Z. (2000) *Le sacre du présent*. Flammarion, Paris.

Laïdi, Z. (2006) *Un monde privé de sense*. Hachette, Paris.

Larémont, R. R. (ed.) (2004) *Borders, Nationalism and the African State*. Lynne Rienner Publishers, Boulder.

Latour, B. (1988) *The Pasteurization of France*. Harvard University Press, Cambridge.

Latour, B. (1993) *We have never been Modern*. Harvard University Press, Cambridge.

Latour, B. (2000) When Things Strike Back: possible contribution of 'science studies' to the social sciences. *British Journal of Sociology* 51 (1), 107–123.

Latour, B. (2005a) *Nous n'avons jamais été moderne*. La Découverte/Poche, Paris.

Latour, B. (2005b) *Reassembling the Social: An Introduction to Actor-Network-Theory (Clarendon Lectures in Management Studies)*. Oxford University Press, New York.

Laudati, A. (2013) Beyond Minerals: Evidence for a Broadened 'Ecologies of Violence' in Eastern Democratic Republic of Congo. *Review of African Political Economy* 40 (135), 32–50.

Law, J. (2004) *After Method: Mess in Social Science Research*. Routledge, London.

Law, J. (2009) Seeing Like a Survey. *Cultural Sociology* 3 (2), 239–256.

Law, J. and Urry, J. (2004) Enacting the social. *Economy and Society* 33 (3), 390–410.

Le Billon, P. and Nicholls, E. (2007) Ending 'Resource Wars': Revenue Sharing, Economic Sanction or Military Intervention? *International Peacekeeping* 14 (5), 613–632.

Leibfried, S. and Zürn, M. (2005) *Transformations of the state?* Cambridge University Press, Cambridge.

Lemarchand, R. (1964) *Political awakening in the Belgian Congo*. Greenwood Press, Westport, Connecticut.

Lemarchand, R. (1997) Patterns of State Collapse and Reconstruction in Central Africa: Reflections on the Crisis in the Great Lakes Region. *Africa Spectrum* 32 (2), 173–193.

Lemarchand, R. (2007) Patterns of State Collapse and Reconstruction in Central Africa: Reflections on the Crisis in the Great Lakes. Available at: www.africa.ufl.edu/asq/v1/3/2.htm.

Lemke, T. (2005) 'A Zone of Indistinction' – A Critique of Giorgio Agamben's Concept of Biopolitics. *Outlines* 7 (1), 3–13.

Lemke, T. (2008) Eine Analytik der Biopolitik. Überlegungen zu Geschichte und Gegenwart eines umstrittenen Begriffs. *Behemoth. A Journal on Civilization* 1 (1), 72–89.

Lemke, T. (2011) Beyond Foucault: From Biopolitics to the Government of Life. In: Bröckling, U., Krasmann, S. and Lemke, T. (eds) *Governmentality: Current Issues and Future Challenges*. Routledge, London, 165–184.

Lewis, D. (1973) Anthropology and Colonialism. *Current Anthropology* 14 (5), 581–602.

Lewis, D. and Mosse, D. (2006a) Encountering Order and Disjuncture: Contemporary Anthropological Perspectives on the Organization of Development. *Oxford Development Studies* 34 (1), 1–13.

Lewis, D. and Mosse, D. (2006b) *Development brokers and translators: The ethnography of aid and agencies*. Kumarian Press, Bloomfield, CT.

Li, T. M. (2007) *The will to improve: Governmentality, development, and the practice of politics*. Duke University Press, Durham, NC.

Liégeois, M. (2009) Acteurs et Enjeux du Processus de Décentralisation. In: Trefon, T. (ed.) *Réforme au Congo (RDC): Attentes et désillusions*. L'Haramattan, Paris, 67–85.

Lumumba-Kasongo, T. (1992) Zaire's Ties to Belgium: Persistence and Future Prospects in Political Economy. *Africa Today* 39 (3), 23–48.

Lynch, M. (2001) Ethnomethodology and the Logic of Practice. In: Schatzki, T., Karin Knorr-Cetina and Eike von Savigny (eds) *The Practice Turn in Contemporary Theory*. Routledge, London, 131–149.

Macfarlane, J. (2007) Sovereignty and Standby: The 1964 Conference on UN Peacekeeping Forces. *International Peacekeeping* 14 (5), 599–612.

MacGaffey, J. (1983) How to Survive and Become Rich amongst Devastation: The Second Economy in Zaire. *African Affairs* 82 (328), 351–366.

MacGinty, R. and Richmond, O.P. (2013) The Local Turn in Peace Building: a critical agenda for peace. *Third World Quarterly* 34 (5), 763–783.

MacKenzie, D. A., Muniesa, F. and Siu, L. (eds) (2007) *Do economists make markets?: On the performativity of economics*. Princeton University Press, Princeton.

Malkki, L. (1995) Refugees and Exile: From 'Refugee Studies' to the National Order of Things. *Annual Review of Anthropology* 24, 495–523.

Malkki, L. (1996) Speechless Emissaries: Refugees, Humanitarianism, and Dehistoricization. *Cultural Anthropology* 11 (3), 377–404.

Mamdani, M. (1996) *Citizen and subject: Contemporary Africa and the legacy of late colonialism*. Princeton University Press, Princeton.

Mamdani, M. (2002) *When victims become killers: Colonialism, nativism, and the genocide in Rwanda*. Princeton University Press, Princeton.

Mamdani, M. (2009) *Saviors and survivors: Darfur, politics, and the War on terror*. 1st edition. Pantheon Books, New York.

Mararo, S. B. (2005) Kivu and Ituri in the Congo War: The Roots and Nature of a Linkage. In: Marysse, S. and Reyntjens, F. (eds) *The political economy of the Great Lakes Region in Africa: The pitfalls of enforced democracy and globalization*. Palgrave Macmillan, New York, 190–222.

Marchal, J. (1996) *L'Etat Libre du Congo: Paradis Perdu – L'Histoire du Congo 1876–1900, Volume 1*. Borgloon, Bruxelles.

Marcus, G. (2010) Experts, Reporters, Witnesses: The Making of Anthropologists in States of Emergency. In: Fassin, D. and Pandolfi, M. (eds) *Contemporary states of emergency: The politics of military and humanitarian interventions*. Zone Books, Brooklyn.

Marriage, Z. (2006) *Not breaking the rules, not playing the game: International assistance to countries at war*. Hurst, London.

Marriage, Z. (2010) Congo Co: Aid and Security. *Conflict, Security and Development* 10 (3), 353–377.

Martineau, P. (2003) *La Route Commerciale du Coltan*. Faculté de Science Politique et de Droit, Montréal.

Marysse, S. and Reyntjens, F. (eds) (2005) *The political economy of the Great Lakes Region in Africa: The pitfalls of enforced democracy and globalization*. Palgrave Macmillan, New York.

Mathieu, P. and Tsongo, M. A. (1998) Guerres paysannes au Nord-Kivu (République Démocratique du Congo), 1937–1994. *Cahiers d'Études Africaines* 38 (150/152), 385–416.

Mayer M (2012) Chaotic Climate Change and Security. *International Political Sociology* 6 (2), 165–185.

Mbembe, A. (2001) *On the postcolony*. University of California Press, Berkeley.

Mbembe, A. (2011) Provincializing France? *Public Culture* 23 (1), 85–119.

McEwan, C. (2009) *Postcolonialism and development*. Routledge, London, New York.

McFalls, L. (2010) Benevolent Dictatorship: The Formal Logic of Humanitarian Government. In: Fassin, D. and Pandolfi, M. (eds) *Contemporary states of emergency: The politics of military and humanitarian interventions*. Zone Books, Brooklyn, NY, 317–333.

Médecins Sans Frontières (2006) *Rapid health assessment*. Available at: www.refbooks.msf.org/MSF_Docs/En/Rapid_health/RAPID_HEALTH_en.pdf. Last accessed 22 March 2013.

Médecins Sans Frontières (2010a) *Rapport moral du Dr Marie-Pierre Allié*. Paris.

Médecins Sans Frontières (2010b) *Rapport Annuel 2009/2010*. Paris.

Médecins Sans Frontières (2011) *Humanitarian Negotiations Revealed*. Paris.

Médecins Sans Frontières (2012a) In *the Eyes of Others: How People in Crises Perceive Humanitarian Aid*. Paris.

Médecins sans Frontières (2012b) *International Financial Report 2011*. Available at: www.msf.org/msf/articles/2012/06/msf-financial-report-2011.cfm?CFID=76f1cfd4-0386-4196-8238-9e1d73351922andCFTOKEN=0.

Medick, H. (1984) Missionare im Ruderboot: Ethnologische Erkenntnisweisen an die Herausforderungen der Sozialgeschichte. *Geschichte und Gesellschaft: Zeitschrift für Historische Sozialwissenschaft* 10 (3), 295–320.

Mehta, U. (1990) Liberal Strategies of Exclusion. *Politics and Society* 18, 427–454.

Meister, R. (2011) *After evil: A politics of human rights*. Columbia University Press, New York.

Melmoth, S. (2007) République démocratique du Congo: décentralisation et sortie de conflit. *Afrique contemporaine* 221 (1), 75.

Miall, H. (2007) The EU and the Peacebuilding Commission. *Cambridge Review of International Affairs* 20 (1), 29–45.

Migdal, J. and Schlichte, Klaus (2005) Rethinking the State. In: Schlichte, K. (ed.) *The dynamics of states: The formation and crises of state domination*. Ashgate, Aldershot, Hants, 1–40.

Milliken, J. (1999) The Study of Discourse in International Relations. *European Journal of International Relations* 5 (2), 225–254.

Mitchell, T. (1991) The Limits of the State: Beyond Statist Approaches and Their Critics. *American Political Science Review* 85 (1), 77–96.

Mitchell, T. (2002) *Rule of Experts: Egypt, Techno-Politics, Modernity*. University of California Press, Berkeley and Los Angeles, California.

Mitchell, T. (2006) Society, Economy and the State-Effect. In: Gupta, A. and Sharma, A. (eds) *Anthropology of the State*. Blackwell Publishers Ltd, Malden, Oxford, Victoria.

Mitchell, T. (2008) Rethinking economy. *Geoforum* 39 (3), 1116–1121.

Mitchell, T. (2009) Carbon democracy. *Economy and Society* 38 (3), 399–432.

Mol, A. (1999) Ontological politics. A word and some questions. *The Sociological Review* 46, 74–89.

Mol, A. (2002) *The Body Multiple: Ontology in Medical Practice*. Duke University Press, Durham and London.

Moore, D. (2001) Neoliberal globalisation and the triple crisis of 'modernisation' in Africa: Zimbabwe, the Democratic Republic of the Congo and South Africa. *Third World Quarterly* 22 (6), 909–929.

Moore, D. (2004) The Second Age of the Third World: from primitive accumulation to global public goods? *Third World Quarterly* 25 (1), 87–109.

Moravcsik, A. (2010a) 'Wahn,Wahn, Überall Wahn': A reply to Jahn's critique of liberal internationalism. *International Theory* 2 (1), 113–139.

Moravcsik, A. (2010b) Tilting at windmills: a final reply to Jahn. *International Theory* 2 (1), 157–173.

Moshonas, S. (2013) Looking beyond reform failure in the Democratic Republic of Congo. *Review of African Political Economy* 40 (135): 132–140.

Mosse, D. (2004) Is good policy unimplementable? Reflections on the ethnography of aid policy and practice. *Development and Change* 35 (4), 639–671.

Mosse, D. (2006) Anti-social anthropology? Objectivity, objection, and the ethnography of public policy and professional communities. *Journal of the Royal Anthropological Institute* 12, 935–956.

Mosse, D. (2011) *Adventures in Aidland: The anthropology of professionals in international development*. Berghahn Books, New York.

Mosse, D. and Lewis, D. (2005) *The aid effect: Giving and governing in international development*. Pluto, London.

Moyn, S. (2010) *The last utopia: Human rights in history*. Belknap Press of Harvard University Press, Cambridge, Massachusetts.

Mudimbe, V. Y. (1994) *The idea of Africa*. Indiana University Press, Bloomington.

Mudimbe, V. Y. (1999) *The invention of Africa: Gnosis, philosophy, and the order of knowledge*. Indiana University Press Bloomington.

Nasu, H. (2011) Operationalizing the Responsibility to Protect in the Context of Civilian Protection by UN Peacekeepers. *International Peacekeeping* 18 (4), 364–378.

Ndaywel è Nziem, I. (1998a) *Histoire générale du Congo: De l'héritage ancien à la république démocratique*. Duculot, De Boeck and Larsier, Bruxelles.

Ndaywel è Nziem, I. (1998b) Du Congo des rébellions au Zaïre des pillages. *Cahiers d'Études Africaines* 38 (150), 417–439.

Ndaywel è Nziem, I. (2012) *Nouvelle Histoire du Congo: Des origines à la République Démocratique*. Le Cri Editions, Bruxelles.

Ndikumana, L. and Boyce, J. (1998) Congo's Odious Debts: External Borrowing and Capital Flight in Zaire. *Development and Change* 29 (2), 195–217.

Nelson, C. (ed.) (1988) *Marxism and the interpretation of culture*. University of Illinois Press, Urbana.

Neocleous, M. (2000) *The fabrication of social order: A critical theory of police power*. Pluto Press, Sterling.

Nest, M. (2006) *The Democratic Republic of Congo: Economic Dimensions of War and Peace*. Lynne Rienner, Boulder.

Netherlands Institute of International Relations Clingendael (2010) *Supporting SSR in the DRC: Between a Rock and a Hard Place*. The Hague.

Netherlands Institute of International Relations Clingendael (2011) *Increasing Security in the DR Congo: Gender-Responsive Strategies for Combating Sexual Violence*. The Hague.

Netherlands Institute of International Relations Clingendael (2012) *The Political Economy of State-building in Situations of Fragility and Conflict*. The Hague.

Neumann, I. B. (1996) Self and Other in International Relations. *European Journal of International Relations* 2 (2), 139–174.

Neumann, I. B. (2002) Returning Practice to the Linguistic Turn: The Case of Diplomacy. *Millennium – Journal of International Studies* 31 (3), 627–651.

Neumann, I. B. (2007) 'A Speech That the Entire Ministry May Stand for,' or: Why Diplomats Never Produce Anything New. *International Political Sociology* 1 (1), 183–200.

Newbury, D. (2012) The Continuing Process of Decolonization in the Congo: Fifty Years Later. *African Studies Review* 55 (1), 131–141.

Nietzsche, F. (1993) *Zur Genealogie der Moral: Eine Streitschrift*. Reclam, Stuttgart.

Nzongola-Ntalaja, G. (2002) *The Congo from Leopold to Kabila: A People's History*. Zed Books, London.

O'Callaghan, S. and Gilbride, K. (2008) *From the Grass-Roots to the Security Council: Oxfam's Humanitarian Advocacy in Darfur, the Democratic Republic of Congo and Uganda*. London.

O'Callaghan, S. and Pantuliano, S. (2007) *Protective action: Incorporating civilian protection into humanitarian response*. Overseas Development Institute, London.

Odom, T. (1978) *Shaba II: The French and Belgian Intervention in Zaire in 1978*. Combat Studies Institute, Fort Leavenworth, Kansas.

OECD (2011) *Supporting Statebuilding in Situations of Conflict and Stability*. Paris.

Olivier Sardan, J.-P. de (2005) *Anthropology and Development*. Zed Books, London.

Onana, R. and Taylor, H. (2008) MONUC and SSR in the Democratic Republic of Congo. *International Peacekeeping* 15 (4), 501–516.

Orchard, P. (2010) The Perils of Humanitarianism: Refugee and IDP Protection in Situations of Regime-Induced Displacement. *Refugee Survey Quarterly* 29 (1), 38–60.

Orford, A. (2011) *International authority and the responsibility to protect*. Cambridge University Press, Cambridge, New York.

Orford, A. (2012) In Praise of Description. *Leiden Journal of International Law* 25, 609–625.

Oxfam (2006) *Promises to Keep: Evaluation of the Implementation of Oxfam's Strategic Plan 2001–2006 Synthesis Report*. London.

Oxfam (2007) *Strategic Plan 2007–2012*. London.

Oxfam (2008) *For a Safer Tomorrow: Protecting Civilians in a Multipolar World*. London.

Oxfam (2011a) *Protection of Civilians in 2010: Facts, figures, and the UN Security Council's Response*. London.

Oxfam (2011b) *Whose Aid is it Anyway? Politicizing Aid in Conflicts and Crises.* London.

Oxfam (2012) *Crises in a New World Order: Challenging the Humanitarian Project.* London.

Oxley, M. (2001) *Measuring humanitarian need.* London.

Paddon, E. and Lacaille, Guillaume (2011) *Stabilising the Congo.* Policy Briefing 8, Refugee Studies Center, University of Oxford, Oxford.

Pandolfi, M. (2003) Contract of mutual (in)difference: Governance and the humanitarian apparatus in contemporary Albania and Kosovo. *Indiana Journal of Global Legal Studies* 10 (1), 369–381.

Pandolfi, M. (2008) Laboratory of Intervention: The Humanitarian Governance of the Postcommunist Balkan Territories. In: Good, M.-J. D. (ed.) *Postcolonial disorders.* University of California Press, Berkeley.

Paris, R. (2002a) Human Security: Paradigm Shift or Hot Air. *International Security* 26 (2), 87–102.

Paris, R. (2002b) International peacebuilding and the 'mission civilatrice'. *Review of International Studies* 28 (4), 637–656.

Paris, R. (2004) *At war's end: Building peace after civil conflict.* Cambridge University Press, Cambridge.

Paris, R. (2010) Saving Liberal Peacebuilding. *Review of International Studies* 36, 337–265.

Paris, R. (2011) Ordering the World: Academic Research and Policymaking on Fragile States. *International Studies Review* 13 (1), 58–71.

Paris, R. (2014) The 'Responsibility to Protect' and the Structural Problems of Preventive Humanitarian Intervention. *International Peacekeeping* 21 (5): 569–603.

Paris, R. and Sisk, T. (2009) *The dilemmas of statebuilding: Confronting the contradictions of postwar peace operations.* Routledge, London, New York.

Passoth, J.-H. and Rowland, N. J. (2010) Actor-Network State. *International Sociology* 25 (6), 818–841.

Peemans, J. (1975) The Social and Economic Development of Zaire since Independence: An Historical Outline. *African Affairs* 174 (295), 148–179.

Peyer, C. (2011) *Contrats, droits humains et fiscalité: comment une entreprise dépouille un pays. Le cas de Glencore en République Démocratique du Congo.* Geneva.

Pickering, A. (1994) After Representation: Science Studies in the Performative Idiom. *PSA: Proceedings of the Biennial Meeting of the Philosophy of Science Association,* 413–419.

Pictet, J. (1979) *Les Principes fondamentaux de la Croix-Rouge : commentaire.* Available at: www.icrc.org/fre/resources/documents/misc/fundamental-principles-commentary-010179.htm. Last accessed 24 May 2015.

Pole Institute (2008) *La Guerre au Nord-Kivu: Au-Delà des Clichés.* Goma.

Pole Institute (2011) *The North Kivu mining sector: Report on the reopening of the mines.* Goma.

Pottier, J. (2010) Representations of Ethnicity in the Search for Peace: Ituri, Democratic Republic of Congo. *African Affairs* 109 (434), 23–50.

Pouligny, B. (2003) UN peace operations, INGOs, NGOs, and promoting the rule of law: exploring the intersection of international and local norms in different postwar contexts. *Journal of Human Rights* 2 (3), 359–377.

Pouligny, B. (2006) *Peace operations seen from below: UN missions and local people.* Kumarian Press, Bloomfield.

Pouligny, B. (2009) *Supporting Local Ownership in Humanitarian Action*. GPPi Policy Paper 1, Berlin.

Pouliot, V. (2008) The Logic of Practicality: A Theory of Practice of Security Communities. *International Organization* 62 (2), 257–288.

Provincial Government and Provincial Assembly North Kivu (2009) *Projet d'édit No ... portant modalité pratique de mise en oeuvre du partenariat avec les acteurs humanitaires et de développement fonctionnant sur l'étendue de la province du Nord-Kivu.* Goma.

Provincial Government and Provincial Assembly North Kivu (2010) *Dispositions génerales applicables aux institutions philantropiques oeuvrant dans les domaines humanitaires et du développement en province du Nord-Kivu.* Goma.

Prunier, G. (2009) *Africa's world war: Congo, the Rwandan genocide, and the making of a continental catastrophe.* Oxford University Press, New York.

Pugh, M. (2004) Peacekeeping and Critical Theory. *International Peacekeeping* 11 (1), 39–58.

Pupavac, V. (2001) Therapeutic Governance: Psycho-social Intervention and Trauma Risk Management. *Disasters* 25 (4), 358–372.

Pupavac, V. (2006) The politics of emergency and the demise of the developing state: Problems for humanitarian advocacy. *Development in Practice* 16 (3/4), 255–269.

Pupavac, V. (2008) Refugee Advocacy, Traumatic Representations and Political Disenchantment. *Government and Opposition* 43 (2), 270–292.

Pyyhtinen, O. and Sakari Tamminen (2011) We have never been only human: Foucault and Latour on the question anthropos. *Anthropological Theory* 11 (2), 135–152.

Rabinow, P. and Rose, N. (2006) Biopower Today. *BioSocieties* 1 (2), 195–217.

Radmann, W. (1978) The Nationalization of Zaire's Copper: From Union Minière to Gécamines. *Africa Today* 25 (4), 25–47.

Raeymakers, T. (2007) *The Power of Protection: Governance and Transborder Trade on the Congo-Ugandan Frontier.* Ghent University, Ghent.

Rancatore, J. (2010) It is Strange: A Reply to Vrasti. *Millennium – Journal of International Studies* 39 (1), 65–77.

Rancière, J. (1998) *Disagreement: Politics and Philosophy.* University of Minnesota Press, Minnesota.

Randeria, S. and Eckert, A. (eds) (2009) *Vom Imperialismus zum Empire: Nicht-westliche Perspektiven auf Globalisierung.* Suhrkamp, Frankfurt am Main.

Rapley, T. J. (2001) The art(fulness) of open-ended interviewing: some considerations on analysing interviews. *Qualitative Research* 1 (3), 303–323.

Ratner, S. and Helman, G. (1992) Anarchy Rules: Saving Failed States. *Foreign Policy* 89.

Razack, S. (2004) *Dark threats and white knights: The Somalia Affair, peacekeeping, and the new imperialism.* University of Toronto Press, Toronto, Buffalo.

Reckwitz, A. (2002) Toward a Theory of Social Practices A Development in Culturalist Theorizing. *European Journal of Social Theory* 5 (2), 243–263.

Reckwitz, A. (2003) Grundelemente einer Theorie sozialer Praktiken: Eine sozialheoretische Perspektive. *Zeitschrift für Soziologie* 32 (4), 282–301.

Reckwitz, A. (2006) *Das hybride Subjekt: Eine Theorie der Subjektkulturen von der bürgerlichen Moderne zur Postmoderne.* Velbrück Wissenschaft, Weilerswist.

Reckwitz, A. (2008a) Praktiken und Diskurse. Eine sozialtheoretische und methodologische. Relation. In: Kalthoff, H., Hirschauer, S. and Lindemann, G. (eds) *Theoretische Empirie: Zur Relevanz qualitativer Forschung.*

Reckwitz, A. (2008b) *Subjekt*. Transcript-Verl., Bielefeld.

Redfield, P. (2005) Doctors, Borders and Life in Crisis. *Cultural Anthropology* 20 (3), 328–361.

Redfield, P. (2006) A less modest witness: Collective advocacy and motivated truth in a medical humanitarian movement. *American Ethnologist* 33 (1), 3–26.

Redfield, P. (2012) The Unbearable Lightness of Expats: Double Binds of Humanitarian Mobility. *Cultural Anthropology* 27 (2), 358–382.

Redfield, P. (2013) *Life in crisis: The ethical journey of Doctors without Borders*. University of California Press, Berkeley.

Reid, J. (2005) The Biopolitics of the War on Terror: a critique of the 'return of imperialism' thesis in international relations. *Third World Quarterly* 26 (2), 237–252.

Reid, J. (2010) The Biopoliticization of Humanitarianism: From Saving Bare Life to Securing the Biohuman in Post-Interventionary Societies. *Journal of Intervention and Statebuilding* 4 (4), 391–411.

Reinhard, W. (2002) *Geschichte der Staatsgewalt: Eine vergleichende Verfassungsgeschichte Europas von den Anfängen bis zur Gegenwart*. Beck, München.

Reno, W. (1998) Mines, Money, and the Problem of State-Building in Congo. *Issue: A Journal of Opinion* 26 (1), 14–17.

Reno, W. (2006) Congo: From state collapse to 'absolutism' to state failure. *Third World Quarterly* 27 (1), 43–56.

Resource Consulting Services (2009) *Trading conflict for development: Utilising the trade in minerals from Eastern Congo for Development*, London.

Reuter, J. and Villa, P.-I. (eds) (2010) *Postkoloniale Soziologie: Empirische Befunde, theorethische Anschlüsse, politische Intervention*. Transcript, Bielefeld.

Reyntjens, F. (2009) *The Great African War: Congo and Regional Geopolitics, 1996–2006*. Cambridge University Press, New York.

Richmond, O. (2007) Critical Research Agendas for Peace: The Missing Link in the Study of International Relations. *Alternatives. Global, Local, Political* 32 (1), 247–274.

Richmond, O. (2009) A post-liberal peace: Eirenism and the everyday. *Review of International Studies* 35 (03), 557.

Richmond, O. (2010a) Between Peacebuilding and Statebuilding, Between Social Engineering and Post-Colonialism. *Civil Wars* 12 (1–2), 167–175.

Richmond, O. (2010b) Resistance and the Post-liberal Peace. *Millennium* 38 (3), 665–692.

Rift Valley Institute (2012) *North Kivu: The background to conflict in North Kivu province of eastern Congo*. Nairobi.

Risse, T. (2000) Let's argue: Communicative Action in World Politics. *International Organization* 54 (1), 1–39.

Rist, G. (2007) *Le développement: Histoire d'une croyance occidentale*. 3. éd. revue et augm. Presses de Sciences Po, Paris.

Rist, G. (2008) *The history of development: From Western origins to global faith*. 3rd edition. Zed Books, London.

Romkema, H. (2007) *Opportunities and Constraints for the Disarmament and Repatriation of Foreign Armed Groups in the Democratic Republic of Congo: The cases of the FDLR, FNL and ADF/NALU*. Consultant's report to the Multi-Country Demobilization and Reintegration Programme (MDPR).

Rose, N., O'Malley, P. and Valverde, M. (2006) Governmentality. *Annual Review of Law and Social Science* 2 (1), 83–104.

Rosenau, J. (1969) Intervention as Scientific Concept. *The Journal of Conflict Resolution* 13 (2), 149–171.

Rosenau, J. and Czempiel, E. O. (1992) *Governance without government: Order and change in world politics*. Cambridge University Press, Cambridge, New York.

Rosenberg, J. (2005) Globalization Theory: A Post Mortem. *International Politics* 42 (1), 2–74.

Rosenberg, J. (2006) Why is There No International Historical Sociology? *European Journal of International Relations* 12 (3), 307–340.

Rosenow, D. (2009) Decentring Global Power: The Merits of a Foucauldian Approach to International Relations. *Global Society* 23 (4), 497–517.

Rottenburg, R. (2009a) *Far-fetched facts: A parable of development aid*. MIT Press, Cambridge, Massachussets.

Rottenburg, R. (2009b) Social and public experiments and new figurations of science and politics in postcolonial Africa. *Postcolonial Studies* 12 (4), 423–440.

Rubenstein, J. C. (2008) The Distributive Commitments of International NGOs. In: Barnett, M. N. (ed.) *Humanitarianism in question: Politics, power, ethics*. Cornell University Press, Ithaca, NY, 215–234.

Rubinstein, R. A. (2005) Intervention and Culture: An Anthropological Approach to Peace Operations. *Security Dialogue* 36 (4), 527–544.

Rubinstein, R. A. (2008) *Peacekeeping under fire: Culture and intervention*. Paradigm Publishers, Boulder.

Rubinstein, R. and Keller, D. S. M. (2008) Culture and Interoperability in Integrated Missions. *International Peacekeeping* 15 (4), 540–555.

Rutazibwa, O. U. (2010) The Problematics of the EU's Ethical (Self) Image in Africa: The EU as an 'Ethical Intervener' and the 2007 Joint Africa–EU Strategy. *Journal of Contemporary European Studies* 18 (2), 209–228.

Rutazibwa, O. U. (2013) What If We Took Autonomous Recovery Seriously? A Democratic Critique of Contemporary Western Ethical Foreign Policy. *Ethical Perspectives* 20 (1), 81–108.

Sabaratnam, M. (2011) IR in Dialogue … but Can We Change the Subjects? A Typology of Decolonising Strategies for the Study of World Politics. *Millennium – Journal of International Studies* 39 (3), 781–803.

Sabaratnam, M. (2013) Avatars of Eurocentrism in the critique of the liberal peace. *Security Dialogue* 44 (3): 259–278.

Sachs, W. (ed.) (1992) *The Development Dictionary: The Guide to Knowledge as Power*. Zed Books, London.

Said, E. (1993) *Culture and Imperialism*. Vintage Books, New York.

Said, E. (2003 [1979]) *Orientalism*. 25th anniversary edition with a new preface by the author. Vintage Books, New York.

Salter, M. B. (ed.) (2013) *Research methods in critical security studies: An introduction*. Routledge, New York.

Salter, M. and Mutlu, C. (2013) *Research methods in critical security studies*. Routledge, London.

Schatzberg, M. (1988) *The Dialectics of Oppression in Zaire*. Indiana University Press, Bloomington.

Schatzberg, M. (1989) Military Intervention and the Myth of Collective Security: The Case of Zaire. *Journal of Modern African Studies* 27 (2), 315–340.

Schatzberg, M. (2012) The Structural Roots of the DRCs Current Disasters: Deep Dilemmas. *African Studies Review* 55 (1), 117–121.

Schatzki, T. R. (1996) *Social practices: A Wittgensteinian approach to human activity and the social*. Cambridge University Press, New York.

Schatzki, T. (2001) Introduction: Practice Theory. In: Schatzki, T., Karin Knorr-Cetina and Eike von Savigny (eds) *The Practice Turn in Contemporary Theory*. Routledge, London.

Schatzki, T., Knorr-Cetina, K. and von Savigny, E. (eds) (2001) *The Practice Turn in Contemporary Theory*. Routledge, London.

Schimmel, V. (2006) Humanitarianism and politics: the dangers of contrived separation. *Development in Practice* 16 (3–4), 303–315.

Schlag, G. (2012) Into the 'Heart of Darkness' – EU's civilising mission in the DR Congo. *Journal of International Relations and Development* 12, 321–344.

Schlichte, K. (1998) Postkolonialer Habitus und Klientelismus in der französischen Afrikapolitik. *Zeitschrift für Internationale Beziehungen* 5 (2), 309–343.

Schlichte, K. (2005a) *Der Staat in der Weltgesellschaft: Politische Herrschaft in Asien, Afrika und Lateinamerika*. Campus-Verl., Frankfurt/Main.

Schlichte, K. (ed.) (2005b) *The dynamics of states: The formation and crises of state domination*. Ashgate, Aldershot.

Schlichte, K. (2007) Administering Babylon – On the Crooked Ways of State Building and State Formation. *Politorbis* (42), 35–39.

Schlichte, K. (2008) Uganda, Or: The Internationalisation of Rule. *Civil Wars* 10 (4), 369–383.

Schlichte, K. (2012a) Der Streit der Legitimitäten: Der Konflikt als Grund einer historischen Soziologie des Politischen. *Zeitschrift für Friedens- und Konfliktforschung* 1 (1), 9–43.

Schlichte, K. (2012b) *Cubicle Land: On the Sociology of Internationalized Rule*. In IIs Arbeitspapier No. 38, Bremen.

Schlichte, K. and Veit, A. (2007) *Coupled Arenas: Why State-building is so Difficult*. Working Paper Micropolitics of Armed Groups, Berlin.

Schouten, P. (2013) The Materiality of State Failure: Social Contract Theory, Infrastructure and Governmental Power in Congo. *Millennium – Journal of International Studies* 41 (3), 553–574.

Scott, D. (2012) The Traditions of Historical Others. *Symposia on Gender, Race and Philosophy* 8 (1).

Scott, J. C. (1998) *Seeing like a state: How certain schemes to improve the human condition have failed*. Yale University Press, New Haven.

Sedra, M. (ed.) (2010) *The Future of Security Sector Reform*. The Centre for International Governance Innovation, Ontario.

Sending, O. J. (2010) *Professionalization of Peace Operations: Causes, Dynamics and Effects*. Oslo.

Sending, O. J. and Neumann, I. B. (2006) Governance to Governmentality: Analyzing NGOs, States, and Power. *International Studies Quarterly* 50 (3), 651–672.

Sending, O. J. and Neumann, I. B. (2011) Banking on power: how some practices in an international organization anchor others. In: Adler, E. and Pouliot, V. (eds) *International Practices*. Cambridge University Press, Cambridge, 231–253.

Sergiou, S. (2012) *Conflict Causes Revisited: Die Enstehungsgeschichte der Ostkongolesischen CNDP-Rebellion*, PhD Thesis, Bremen.

Sewell, W. (1992) A Theory of Structure: Duality, Agency and Transformation. *American Journal of Sociology* 98 (1), 1–29.

Shevchenko, O. and Fox, R. (2008) 'Nationals' and 'expatriates': Challenges of fulfilling 'sans frontières' ('without borders') ideals in international humanitarian action. *Health and Human Rights* 10 (1).

SIPRI (2010) *Controlling Conflict Resources in the Democratic Republic of the Congo.* Stockholm.

Slaughter, A.-M. (1995) International Law in a World of Liberal States. *European Journal of International Law* 6 (4), 503–538.

Slim, H. (2002) Not Philanthropy But Rights: The Proper Politicisation of Humanitarian Philosophy. *The International Journal of Human Rights* 6 (1), 1–22.

Smirl, L. (2012) The state we are(n't) in: Liminal subjectivity in aid worker auto-biographies. In: Bliesemann Guevara, B. de (ed.) *Statebuilding and State-Formation: The political sociology of intervention.* Routledge, London, 230–245.

Sontag, S. (1964) *Against Interpretation.* Available at: www.coldbacon.com/writing/sontag-againstinterpretation.html.

Soussan, J. (2008) *MSF and Protection: Pending or Closed?: Discourse and practice surrounding the 'protection of civilians'.* CRASH, Paris.

Spivak, G. C. (1976) Translator's Preface. In: Derrida, J. (ed.) *Of Grammatology.* Johns Hopkins University Press, Baltimore, 9–87.

Spivak, G. C. (1988a) Can the subaltern speak? In: Nelson, C. (ed.) *Marxism and the interpretation of culture.* University of Illinois Press, Urbana, 271–313.

Spivak, G. C. (1988b) *In other worlds: Essays in cultural politics.* Routledge, New York.

Spivak, G. C. (1993) *Outside in the teaching machine.* Routledge, New York.

Spivak, G. C. (2003) *A critique of postcolonial reason: Toward a history of the vanishing present.* 4th print. Harvard University Press, Cambridge.

Spivak, G. C. (2007) Religion, Politics, Theology: A Conversation with Achille Mbembe. *boundary 2* 34 (2), 149–170.

Spivak, G. C. and Landry, D. (1996) *The Spivak reader: Selected works of Gayatri Chakravorty Spivak.* Routledge, New York, NY.

Stearns, J. K. (2011a) *Dancing in the glory of monsters: The collapse of the Congo and the great war of Africa,* Public Affairs, New York.

Stearns, J. K. (2011b) Rediscovering Congo. *Foreign Policy* (May 12).

Stearns, J. K. (2012) *Countries at a Crossroads 2012: Democratic Republic of Congo.* Washington DC.

Stiftung Wissenschaft und Politik (2011) *Schwache Staaten, erfolgreiche Eliten: Außenpolitische Strategien afrikanischer Krisenländer.* Berlin.

Stirrat, R. (2008) Mercenaries, Missionaries and Misfits: Representations of Development Personnel. *Critique of Anthropology* 28 (4), 406–425.

Stirrat, R. and Henkel, H. (1997) The Development Gift: The Problem of Reciprocity in the NGO World. *The ANNALS of the American Academy of Political and Social Science* 554 (1), 66–80.

Stoler, A. L. and Cooper, F. (1997) Between Metropole and Colony: Rethinking a Research Agenda. In: Cooper, F. and Stoler, A. L. (eds) *Tensions of empire: Colonial cultures in a bourgeois world.* University of California Press, Berkeley, London, 1–56.

Strauss, A. L. (1987) *Qualitative analysis for social scientists.* Cambridge University Press, Cambridge, New York.

Strauss, A. L. and Corbin, J. (1998) *Basics of Qualitative Research Techniques and Procedures for Developing Grounded Theory.* SAGE, California, London.

Strübing, J. (2008) *Grounded Theory: Zur sozialtheoretischen und epistemologischen Fundierung des Verfahrens der empirisch begründeten Theoriebildung,* VS Verlag für Sozialwissenschaften, Wiesbaden.

Sylvester, C. (1999) Development Studies and Postcolonial Studies: Disparate Tales of the Third World. *Third World Quarterly* 20 (4), 703–721.

Sylvester, C. (2006) Bare life as a development/postcolonial problematic. *The Geographical Journal* 172 (1), 66–77.

Tegera, A. (2007) *RD Congo: Liens de Facade et Lieux de Fractures*. Goma.

Terry, F. (2002) *Condemned to repeat? The paradox of humanitarian action*. Cornell University Press, Ithaca, London.

Thant, M.-U. and Sellwood, E. (2000) *Knowledge and Multilateral Interventions: The UN's Experiences in Bosnia and Cambodia*. London.

Ticktin, M. (2011) *Casualties of care: Immigration and the politics of humanitarianism in France*. University of California Press, Berkeley.

Tilley, H. (2011) *Africa as a living laboratory: Empire, development, and the problem of scientific knowledge, 1870–1950*. University of Chicago Press, Chicago.

Titeca, K. and Herdt, T. de (2011) Real governance beyond the failed state: Negotiating education in the Democratic Republic of the Congo. *African Affairs* 110 (439), 213–231.

Trefon, T. (2004) *Reinventing order in the Congo: How people repond [i.e. respond] to state failure in Kinshasa*. Zed Books, London.

Trefon, T. (2009a) Public Service Provision in a Failed State: Looking Beyond Predation in the Democratic Republic of Congo. *Review of African Political Economy* (119), 9–21.

Trefon, T. (ed.) (2009b) *Réforme au Congo (RDC): Attentes et désillusions*. L'Haramattan, Paris.

Trefon, T. (2011) *Congo masquerade: The political culture of aid inefficiency and reform failure*. Zed Books, London.

Trotha, T. von (1994) *Koloniale Herrschaft: Zur soziologischen Theorie der Staatsentstehung am Beispiel des 'Schutzgebietes Togo'*. Mohr, Tübingen.

Tull, D. M. (2005) *The reconfiguration of political order in Africa: A case study of North Kivu (DR Congo)*. Inst. für Afrika-Kunde, Hamburg.

Tull, D. M. (2009) Peacekeeping in the Democratic Republic of Congo: Waging Peace and Fighting War: International Peacekeeping. *International Peacekeeping* 16 (2), 215–230.

Tull, D. M. (2010) Troubled state-building in the DR Congo: the challenge from the margins. *The Journal of Modern African Studies* 48 (04), 643–661.

Turner, T. (2007) *The Congo wars: Conflict, myth and reality*. Zed Books, London.

UNHCR (2008) *Global Needs Assessment Pilot Report*. Available at: www.unhcr. org/48ef09a62.pdf. Last accessed 22 March 2013.

United Nations (1945) *UN Charter*. Available at: www.un.org/en/documents/charter/. Last accessed 24 May 2015.

United Nations (1992) *An Agenda for Peace*. New York.

United Nations (2000) *Report of the Panel on United Nations Peace Operations*. New York.

United Nations (2002) *Final Report of the Panel of Experts on the Illegal Exploitation of Natural Resources and Other Forms of Wealth of the Democratic Republic of the Congo*. New York.

United Nations (2003) *Interim report of the Special Rapporteur on the situation of human rights in the Democratic Republic of the Congo*. New York.

United Nations (2005) *Final Report of the Group of Experts on the Democratic Republic of Congo*. New York.

United Nations (2008a) *Final Report of the Group of Experts on the Democratic Republic of Congo*. New York.

United Nations (2008b) *United Nations Peacekeeping Operations: Principles and Guidelines.* New York.

United Nations (2009a) *Secretary General Report on the Protection of Civilians in Armed Conflict.* New York.

United Nations (2009b) *Interim Report of the Group of Experts on the Democratic Republic of Congo.* New York.

United Nations (2009c) *Consolidated Report on Investigations conducted by the United Nations Joint Human Rights Office (UNJHRO) into grave Human Rights abuses committed in Kiwanja, North Kivu, in November 2008.* New York.

United Nations (2009d) *A New Partnership Agenda: Charting a New Horizon for UN Peacekeeping.* New York.

United Nations (2009e) OCHA *Protest note against 'édit'.* On file with author.

United Nations (2010a) *Final Report of the Group of Experts on the Democratic Republic of Congo.* New York.

United Nations (2010b) *Global Challenges and their Impact on International Humanitarian Action.* New York.

United Nations (2010c) *Monitoring Peace Consolidation: United Nations Practitioners' Guide to Benchmarking.* New York.

United Nations (2010d) *Democratic Republic of the Congo 1993–2003: Report of the mapping exercise documenting the most serious violations of human rights and international humanitarian law committed within the territory of the Democratic Republic of the Congo between March 1993 and June 2003.* New York.

United Nations (2011a) *Final report of the Group of Experts on the Democratic Republic of Congo.* New York.

United Nations (2011b) *To Stay and Deliver: Good Practice for Humanitarians in Complex Security Environments.* New York.

United Nations (2011c) *Civilian capacity in the aftermath of conflict: Independent* report of the Senior Advisory Group. New York.

United Nations (2011d) *Framework for Drafting Comprehensive Protection of Civilians (POC) Strategies in UN Peacekeeping Operations.* New York.

United Nations (2012a) *Interim report of the Group of Experts on the Democratic Republic of Congo.* New York

United Nations (2012b) *Final report of the Group of Experts on the Democratic Republic of Congo.* New York

United Nations (2013a) *Scale of assessments for the apportionment of the expenses of the United Nations.* New York.

United Nations (2013b) *World Humanitarian Data and Trends.* New York.

United Nations (2013c) *Security Council Resolution 2098.*

United Nations (2015) *WFP Enterprise Risk Management Policy.* Rome.

United States Government (2002) *The National Security Strategy.* Available at: http://georgewbush-whitehouse.archives.gov/nsc/nss/2002/. Last accessed 22 March 2013.

Utas, M. (2005) Victimcy, Girlfriending, Soldiering: Tactic Agency in a Young Woman's Social Navigation of the Liberian War Zone. *Anthropological Quarterly* 78 (2), 403–430.

van Reybrouck, D. (2012 [2010]) *Kongo – Eine Geschichte.* Suhrkamp, Berlin.

Vansina, J. (1964) *Le Royaume Kuba.* Musée Royale de l'Afrique Centrale, Tervuren.

Vansina, J. (2010) *Being Colonized: The Kuba Experience in Rural Congo, 1880–1960.* The University of Wisconsin Press, Madison.

Veit, A. (2010) *Intervention as Indirect Rule: The Politics of Civil War and State-building in Ituri.* Campus-Verl., Frankfurt.

Veit, A. (2012) International Intervention and the Congolese Army. In: Bliesemann Guevara, B. de (ed.) *Statebuilding and State-Formation: The Political Sociology of Intervention.* Routledge, London, 40–56.

Veit, A. and Klaus Schlichte (2012) Three Arenas: The Conflictive Logic of External Statebuilding. In: Bliesemann Guevara, B. de (ed.) *Statebuilding and State-Formation: The political sociology of intervention.* Routledge, London.

Von Billerbeck, G. (2012) *Congo: crisis in East deflects attention from need for reforms from Kinshasa.* Available at: http://africanarguments.org/2012/12/20/analysis-of-internal-workings-of-congos-kabila-regime-wins-african-argument-of-the-year/. Last accessed 24 May 2015.

Vrasti, W. (2008) The Strange Case of Ethnography and International Relations. *Millennium – Journal of International Studies* 37 (2), 279–301.

Vrasti, W. (2010) Dr. Strangelove, or How I Learned to Stop Worrying about Methodology and Love Writing. *Millennium – Journal of International Studies* 39 (1), 79–88.

Waal, A. de (1997) *Famine Crimes: Politics and The Disaster Relief Industry in Africa.* Indiana University Press.

Waldschmidt, A., Klein, A., Korte, M. T. and Dalman-Eken, S. (2009) *Das Wissen der Leute: Bioethik, Alltag und Macht im Internet.* VS Verlag für Sozialwissenschaften, Wiesbaden.

Walker, P. and Maxwell, D. G. (2009) *Shaping the humanitarian world.* Routledge, Milton Park, Abingdon, Oxon, New York.

Walters, W. (2011) Foucault and Frontiers: Notes on the Birth of the Humanitarian Frontier. In: Bröckling, U., Krasmann, S. and Lemke, T. (eds) *Governmentality: Current issues and future challenges.* 1st publication. Routledge, New York, 138–164.

Warner, D. (2013) Henry Dunant's Imagined Community: Humanitarianism and the Tragic. *Alternatives. Global, Local, Political* 38 (1), 3–28.

Wasserman, J. A., Clair, J. M. and Wilson, K. L. (2009) Problematics of grounded theory: innovations for developing an increasingly rigorous qualitative method. *Qualitative Research* 9 (3), 355–381.

Watson, S. (2011) The 'human' as referent object? Humanitarianism as securitization. *Security Dialogue* 42 (1), 3–20.

Weber, C. (1992) Reconsidering statehood: examining the sovereignty/intervention boundary. *Review of International Studies* 18 (03), 199–216.

Weber, C. (1998) Performative States. *Millennium – Journal of International Studies* 27 (1), 77–95.

Weber, M. (1919) *Politik als Beruf.* Available at: http://ebookbrowse.com/weber-politik-als-beruf-pdf-d120778266. Last accessed 2 March 2015.

Weber, M. and Roth, G. (1978) *Economy and society: An outline of interpretive sociology.* University of California Press, New York.

Weinstein, J. (2005) *Autonomous Recovery and International Intervention in Comparative Perspective.* Available at: www.cgdev.org/files/2731_file_WP57.pdf. Last accessed 22 March 2013.

Weiss, H. F. and Carayanis, T. (2004) The Enduring Idea of the Congo. In: Larémont, R. R. (ed.) *Borders, Nationalism and the African State.* Lynne Rienner Publishers, Boulder.

Weiss, T. G. and Hoffman, P. J. (2007) The Fog of Humanitarianism: Collective Action Problems and Learning-Challenged Organizations. *Journal of Intervention and Statebuilding* 1 (1), 47–65.

Weissman, F. (2010) 'Not In Our Name': Why Médecins Sans Frontières Does Not Support the 'Responsibility to Protect'. *Criminal Justice Ethics* 29 (2), 194–207.

Weldes, J. and Saco, D. (1996) Making State Action Possible: The United States and the Discursive Construction of 'The Cuban Problem', 1960–1994. *Millennium – Journal of International Studies* 25 (2), 361–395.

Wells, J. (2011) Coltan – a minefield in the Congo. *The Star*, 4 July 2011.

Wendt, A. (2004) The State as Person in International Theory. *Review of International Studies* 30, 289–316.

Weston, C. and Gandell, T. (2001) Analyzing Interview Data: The Development and Evolution of a Coding System. *Qualitative Sociology* 24 (3), 381–400.

White, S. (2014) *Now What? The International Response to Internal Displacement in the Democratic Republic of the Congo.* Brookings Institution, Washington DC.

Wight, C. (1999) MetaCampbell: the epistemological problematics of perspectivism. *Review of International Studies* 25 (2), 311–316.

Willame, J.-C. (1997) *Banyarwanda et Banyamulenge: Violences ethniques et gestion de l'identitaire au Kivu.* Institut africain-CEDAF, L'Harmattan, Bruxelles, Paris.

Wilson, R. and Brown, R. D. (eds) (2009) *Humanitarianism and suffering: The mobilization of empathy.* Cambridge University Press, Cambridge.

Witte, L. de (2002) *The assassination of Lumumba,* Verso, London, New York.

Woodward, S. L. (2007) Do the Root Causes of Civil War Matter? On Using Knowledge to Improve Peacebuilding Interventions. *Journal of Intervention and Statebuilding* 1 (2), 143–170.

World Bank (2008) *Democratic Republic of Congo Growth with Governance In the Mining Sector.* Washington DC.

World Bank (2011) *World Development Report 2011: Background case study Democratic Republic of Congo.* Washington DC.

World Bank (2012) *Resilience of an African Giant: Boosting Growth and Development in the Democratic Republic of Congo.* Washington DC. Available at: https://openknowledge.worldbank.org/handle/10986/2359.

Yamashita, H. (2008) 'Impartial' Use of Force in United Nations Peacekeeping: International Peacekeeping. *International Peacekeeping* 15 (5), 615–630.

Young, C. (1965) *Politics in the Congo: Decolonization and Independence.* Princeton University Press, Princeton.

Young, C. (1994) The Shattered Illusion of the Integral State. *Journal of Modern African Studies* 32 (2), 247–263.

Young, C. (2004) The end of the post-colonial state in Africa? Reflections on changing African political dynamics. *African Affairs* 103 (410), 23–49.

Young, C. and Turner, T. (1985) *The Rise and Decline of the Zairian State.* The University of Wisconsin Press, Madison.

Young, R. J. C. (2007) *Postcolonialism: An historical introduction,* Blackwell, Malden, MA.

Young, R. J. C. (2011) Bayart's Broken Kettle. *Public Culture* 23 (1), 167–175.

Zacharie, A. (2009) De la Dette au Développement: Un Chemin Semé d'Embauches. In: Trefon, T. (ed.) *Réforme au Congo (RDC): Attentes et désillusions.* L'Haramattan, Paris, 103–118.

Zanotti, L. (2010) UN Integrated Peacekeeping Operations and NGOs: Reflections on Governmental Rationalities and Contestation in the Age of Risk. *International Peacekeeping* 17 (1), 17–31.

Zartman, I. W. (1995) *Collapsed states: The disintegration and restoration of legitimate authority.* Lynne Rienner, Boulder.

Zehfuss, M. (2002) *Constructivism in international relations: The politics of reality.* Cambridge University Press, Cambridge, New York.

Ziai, A. (2006a) Post-Development: Ideologiekritik in der Entwicklungstheorie. *Politische Vierteljahresschrift* 47 (2), 193–218.

Ziai, A. (2006b) *Zwischen Global Governance und Post-Development*. Verlag Westfälisches Dampfboot, Münster.

Index

www.ingramcontent.com/pod-product-compliance
Lightning Source LLC
Chambersburg PA
CBHW050517280326
41932CB00014B/2353